THE SHAKESPEAREAN ENIGMA
AND
AN ELIZABETHAN MANIA

THE
SHAKESPEAREAN ENIGMA
AND
AN ELIZABETHAN MANIA

BY

JOHN F. FORBIS

AMS PRESS
NEW YORK

Reprinted from the edition of 1924, New York
First AMS EDITION published 1970
Manufactured in the United States of America
International Standard Book Number: 0–404–02458–0

29065

Library of Congress Number: 75–136375

AMS PRESS INC.
NEW YORK, N.Y.

CONTENTS

PART I

PART II

CONTENTS

THE SHAKESPEREAN ENIGMA

I

THE authentic facts relating to the life, habits and writings of Shakespeare are curiously vague and meager, if not altogether wanting. When it is considered that it is little more than three hundred years since he lived and wrote, and that many of his plays and all of his poetry were published during his lifetime, some of the plays and poems several times, and that seven years after his death all of his plays were carefully gathered and published in one volume, all this indicating a serious interest in his works, it is hardly conceivable that there should not have survived reliable knowledge touching the man in his relations with those with whom he lived. Aside from his works, thus printed, not a written or printed sentence has been found that is known to have emanated from his pen. And yet he lived at a time when correspondence was a common thing among intellectual people, and when contemporaneous writers wrote and published much concerning men of importance and note, descriptive of their habits, appearance and manner of living.

Had letters to or from Shakespeare ever existed, or had he been of sufficient interest or importance in his lifetime to have excited others to discuss him, we cannot bring ourselves to believe that destruction would have overwhelmed all these precious records, before the general interest in the man had become such as to have given all such things great value, and have insured their preservation. And yet nothing has been found, or in probability will ever be found, from which it might reasonably be concluded that there was any considerable interest in Shakespeare's personality in his lifetime.

After most diligent search, a few references in contemporaneous writings have been found to indicate that Shakespeare's writings while he lived had some recognition, for they were highly praised, in the few instances where they were mentioned at all. But there is nothing at all found commensurate with the intellectual interest that should have been excited by works that were then recognized for their beauty and high literary character, and which have constantly grown in esteem, until they have been by universal consent accorded the highest place in the literature of all times.

It is a further notable fact that Shakespeare personally excited little or no interest. He seems to have lived unnoticed and unattached. No proof has been adduced from which we may conclude that he had friends or close associates; that he lived with, or apart from, or that he ever visited, his family; or how, or where he lived; or that he ever revisited his old home, where his family is supposed to have continued to reside, after he departed therefrom for London, except the officially recorded facts that he purchased property in Stratford, and is buried there. While it is generally believed that he lived in London, there is but little, if any positive evidence of the fact; there is also a *tradition* that he was an actor, and yet the evidence as to this is extremely slight, and not conclusive.

Anything that would bring any enlightenment upon any of these subjects would be received with interest. The amount of research that has been expended to develop something along these lines, would surely have met with some success, were it not the fact that really nothing exists, and probably never did exist, of a written or lasting nature, that could gratify the longing for light upon these or any other matters, relating to him.

All of this has been said so often, and is so well understood, that it is needless to be repeated as a simple matter of information. The excuse for saying it over again is to emphasize the conditions, which are in themselves so extraordinary as to have a bearing, somewhat indirectly, upon what is to follow, for there must be a cause for conditions so unusual, and what is to follow may develop the cause, and thus conditions become a material witness in proof of the theory to be expounded.

Notwithstanding these puzzling conditions, it is a fact that Shakespeare lived, and wrote wonderfully and voluminously, and at this distance from the time of his living, and after the fruitless search of so many years, it is believed there remains but one field, and that not unexplored, where it may yet be hoped to find some long-buried treasure, that will reward the desire for information. That field is his written works. All other stores may be considered as exhausted, and as having yielded little, or nothing. The only source remaining is what Shakespeare said of himself—what he may have been willing to preserve of himself.

In the great mass of his writings there is nothing to indicate any hidden meaning—nothing obscure enough to lead us to conclude that there might be something concealed beneath a surface, which shows plainly its own precious contents. The very nature of his dramatic works is such, in their impersonal character, as to preclude the possibility of Shakespeare being seen in or through them. His characterizations are so vivid and so various, that in them all mankind may be viewed in panorama, but Shakespeare himself is always out of sight. In all of his wonderful portrayal of others in his plays, he has not left the slightest trace of Shakespeare himself.

There is one source however, though not altogether unexplored, which is still promising to the investigator, and that is *The Sonnets* and some of his poems. *The Sonnets* are so puzzling and enigmatical, that it is hard to believe that they mean what they pretend to say. No one can read them thoughtfully without feeling that there is something hidden in their depths, and that he is invited to find it if he can.

The history of the Sonnets is briefly this: there are 154 of them; two of these—138 and 144—in somewhat different form from what they are generally known, were published as a part of *The Passionate Pilgrim* in 1599. Otherwise none of the Sonnets, so far as is known, were published until 1609, when Shakespeare was 45 years old. In 1598, Meres in his *Palladis Tamia* mentioned several of Shakespeare's plays in a highly laudatory way, and also referred to the Sonnets as "his sugered Sonnets among private friends." They were published as a whole in 1609, nearly in the form in which they are now generally printed, and so far as known were not published again in Shakespeare's lifetime. He died seven years after this publication. The publication of 1609 is known as the quarto, and in it the Sonnets are numbered in consecutive order. They have been published several times, not in the order found in the quarto, but otherwise grouped, to suit the ideas of editors or publishers, who sought thereby to improve the order, and thus to assist in their better understanding. The consecutive order of the quarto is the one in which they will be treated, and with a few exceptions it is believed it is the order in which they were composed.

The following dedication was printed, preceding the Sonnets, in the 1609 quarto:

TO . THE . ONLY . BEGETTER . OF . THESE . INSUING . SONNETS . MR . W . H . ALL . HAPPINESSE . AND . THAT . ETERNITIE . PROMISED . BY . OUR . EVER-LIVING . POET . WISHETH . THE . WELL-WISHING . ADVENTURER . IN . SETTING . FORTH . T . T .

Shakespeare is not supposed to be the author of the dedication. There is no reason for believing that he had anything to do with it, and in itself it would not be considered of any importance or interest, except for the fact that "Mr. W. H." is mentioned. That has led many to imagine that "W. H." are the initials of the individual to whom the Sonnets were originally addressed. Much pains have been taken to identify the person represented by the initials, but nothing satisfactory has resulted. The dedication will be passed until the Sonnets have been treated.

Many students of the Sonnets have come to the conclusion that they are, to some extent, biographical, and it has been imagined that if they could be properly read or construed, they would divulge something concerning their author. Reading them according to their obvious meaning is extremely perplexing. A sonnet read by itself may impress the reader as very beautiful, and its meaning as evident. Another one may be found equally as beautiful, and its meaning also evident, but as between the two there is a confusion of subjects and ideas, if not a contradiction, and this lack of accordance continues on throughout, until taking them all together, there is much confusion of meaning, and it has been found impossible to construe all of them as addressed to any one of ordinary human qualities. It has generally been presumed that the first 126 sonnets are all written to the same person, a young man, but when all have been read, and each digested, there remains in the reader's mind a strange and unnatural incongruity, and a lack of consecutive thought and incident. The young recipient of the sonnets seems to be lauded at times beyond all human perfection, importing in the author the most perfect trust and love. The author is ever promising to immortalize the subject in his verse, and often attributes to the subject the power of inspiring the author in all that he does. And again, this same young man, is charged by the author with outrageous perfidy and falsity and betrayals, and then the poet instead of defying him in a manly way, submits with abject servility, and instead of condemnation and denouncement, heaps on him the most lavish praise and renews towards him his vows of confidence and love. The subject can do nothing, however damnifying, that Shakespeare does not forgive, and then often takes on himself the responsibility for the injury that has been inflicted by his devoted friend.

In the latter, or "Dark Woman," sonnets, the poet expresses in the same sonnet the most devoted fascination and love, and the blackest horror and hatred for his mistress. These "Dark Woman" sonnets are those following the 126th, and continuing to and including the 152nd. These are plainly addressed, generally, to a female character, and all who have studied the sonnets agree in putting them in a different group from the 126 preceding.

The last two sonnets—153 and 154—seem to be altogether disconnected from the other two groups. These two sonnets express identically the same ideas, in treating of the same subject. Their meaning becomes altogether plain, when the poet's illness, referred to in them, is identified, and the sonnets construed with reference to it.

No matter what might be the result of a complete analysis of the sonnets, if the key for their interpretation has been found, no disclosure of Shakespeare's moral character can be made, that would make him appear weaker or more pusillanimous than does the obvious and literal reading, which explorers have heretofore given them.

The solution of the sonnets will not develop a strong moral hero of the author, as every lover of his poetry would wish might be done. He will not be shown in all respects as an ideal man, but he will be raised infinitely above the morally weak, servile, prostituted and unnatural man that wears the outward dress in which the Sonnets have enrobed him, and it will be a relief to divest him of these debasing habiliments, though it be not possible to reinvest him in spotless robes.

This means, of course, that in the proposed solving of the problems of the Sonnets, that the outward or obvious readings are to be stripped off, and that there is to be found beneath, a new, reasonable, clear, and satisfactory reading, not at all in consonance with the interpretations which have been attempted through a literal reading It should not be necessary to warn the reader, that in the translation of the sonnets from their obvious or apparent, to the real or hidden meaning, there must be some—much—elasticity allowed in the construing or meaning of words. The author of the sonnets was a man of vast imagination. Very few objects or emotions impressed him simply by or with their names. It was in the quality of his mind to see and describe by analogy. His metaphors were endless, and he had the power of lucidity in the use of them, that make things and actions, thoughts and passions, appear plainer when presented by comparative methods, than when bluntly announced. He did not respect restrictions in the meanings of words, but used them daringly and recklessly whenever he found them pregnant with the power of suggestion.

In order to read the Sonnets and poems, and to extract their meaning, it is believed that it would be helpful to preface them with a brief statement of Shakespeare's habits and mental characteristics, as they are set out in these writings, by himself. Whatever shall be stated as to these will not be founded in imagination or impression, but upon the divulgements which these writings, themselves, make, and from which it is believed that the conclusions to be expressed can with certainty be drawn:

In his youth, as he was approaching manhood, Shakespeare, probably as did the most of the young men of his time, contracted the habit of using intoxicants, and at the same time was developing his poetic art. Undoubtedly he appreciated the dangers threatening him through the excessive use of intoxicants, and sought to restrain himself in the indulgement, and very likely began a course of absolute abstinence. It was a question with him, whether he was at his best, when free from stimulants, or when writing under the inspiration which he imagined he gained through them. However that may have been, he followed the dictates of his better senses, and restricted himself in the uses of wine, and while thus denying his appetite, he was endeavoring to continue his poetical course. Prior to and during this time of abstention he gained a reputation as a poet, and had won his own confidence in himself and in his artistic powers. He also believed, which was probably true, that he had won the admiration and approval of all, and was held in the highest esteem. While much of the foregoing may be deduced from The Sonnets, it is more specifically set forth in *The Lover's Complaint,* in its recitals.

After Shakespeare had proceeded for a way on his course of abstinence, he imagined that his powers as a poet were beginning to stale. Whether this came from the fact that he had become irrecoverably poisoned by his youthful indulgence, or, as he seems to have thought to be the case, that his only inspiration came through the use of wine, is not for us to determine. All that can be said is, that Shakespeare concluded, that without wine there would be an end to his art, and that he had accomplished his best, and that nothing worthy could follow. It would seem that he had determined to sacrifice all, rather than return to wine and its use, and that he had consented to bury his aspirations as a poet. It was in this state of mind that he wrote that most enigmatical poem, *The Phoenix and the Turtle,* wherein he resigns all hope, and celebrates the obsequies of the Phoenix—his Genius.

Although he would thus seem to have determined on an unending course of abstinence and temperance, at all cost, his strength of resolution was not sufficient to continue to restrain him. Either his appetite, or the appeal of his genius, which he believed could thrive only on wine, overcame his good intentions and sent him back to his stimulant. In The Sonnets he makes the latter his excuse, in order, as he declares, that he might live and perpetuate himself in his works. He returned to wine joyously, but with fear, caution and misgivings. He rejoiced because he thought it would be of real assistance, but he feared the enthralling effects. In all of the poems to be reviewed, he looks upon himself as of double nature—himself and his genius,—each attracting, and each repelling the other. His genius, or art, loved and demanded wine, while his moral nature despised and rejected it. The history of the conflict of the two is recorded in the first 18 sonnets. He was aware that beneath the tempting offer there lurked an ambush of danger and destruction. His better nature rebelled and refused to submit, to be debauched, and plead that reason might have her hearing. But his love, his passionate love—his art—urged and plead and showed that there was no other way; that without this inspiring, fertile help, there could be no increase and no son of his genius; without it he must die, and worms become his heirs, and that there could be no immortality in his lines. He chided himself for his waste in "niggarding," and for squandering his unused beauty, and plead for the prostitution of his better self, in order that the image of his youth might not become extinct. The offspring for which he plead was not his bodily heirs, but his immortal poetry, in which he might live when his body should be dead.

After the 18th sonnet it is recorded that Shakespeare surrendered to these importunities to admit wine—the betrayer—and his better-self is cast out, and in its place is enthroned the tempter, which becomes his only love and master, and this leads him, through his infatuation to the very brink of hell.

After Shakespeare had admitted, and become reconciled to the spoiler, he personified it as the spirit of his love. He then blessed and deified it, and felt that he owed it his undying gratitude and devotion; that he must sing its praises and give it every due, even to the limit of making it the author of his unparalleled verse. He promised to distil it and give it an immortality, because through it had his verse come into being, inspired by life, youth and beauty. His inspiring angel was to him perennial and youth-preserving, and through it his faculties were multiplied ten fold, and then by ten. He felt that without it there would be an end and doom of his inspiration wherein resided his youth and beauty, and he made it the master-mistress of his passion.

When Shakespeare began the Sonnets he looked forward to the age of 40 as the end of his fruitful labor. He felt that whatever was to be done by him, must be done in the period of his youth; that youth only is fair, tender, sweet, fresh, golden, beauteous, lovely, brave, true, glorious. In youth only could he bear fruit; his time was therefore opportune and short, and its waste an unthrift; only while his sun was ascending could he expect to hold the eye of the observer; the evening—the declining—sun is feeble age, that "reeleth from the sky," and all the eyes that had paid homage to the morning sun are now "turned another way." But, all this may be read in the tale of the Sonnets.

But, it will be asked: to whom were the Sonnets addressed? For the purpose of applying the proposed test it is not material to inquire. That the test may have a fair trial, the reader is asked to believe, tentatively, of course, that they were not addressed to anyone. Or, if they were addressed, or purported to be addressed, it was part of the disguise, by which their true meaning was concealed. If this proposal shall be accepted, it is confidently believed, that upon a full reading and a mature consideration, it must be conceded that further inquiry on the subject would be unnecessary. But, even should it after all be agreed that the given key fully unlocks the meaning of the Sonnets, there will still exist a very natural curiosity as to why they should have been written in this most perplexing form. This curiosity may never be satisfied. There is, however, a theory to be advanced, which at present cannot be developed, but must await a detailed examination of the Sonnets.

In asking the reader to conclude, for the time being, that the Sonnets were not addressed at all, it is the purpose to ask him to eliminate from his consideration all third parties, except in a few instances arising as the Sonnets are pursued, and which will be considered when such Sonnets as do refer to other parties, are under review. As the Sonnets progress, Shakespeare personifies Wine, and gives it a separate and distinct existence from his own, and makes it quite as real as if it were flesh and blood, possessing individual character, mentality and power, and this counterfeit is so true to life, that all who have attempted to construe the Sonnets have accepted it as real and substantial, and have thereby been confounded.

The greatest difficulty in reading the obscured meaning into the Sonnets will be encountered in the first 18. Superficially considered these sonnets would appear to be addressed to a young man, advising him to marriage and the begetting of children. The young man addressed is supposed to be a friend and associate of the writer, or perhaps a patron. All of this will be found to be illusory, for there was no such purpose in mind. The whole figure is deceptive, and the deception consists in the use, or rather misuse, of words, and in the fact that it is written in the third person, when it should have been in the first throughout, had there been no purpose to disguise the meaning.

The solution proposed is: The person addressed is none other than Shakespeare, himself; the marriage advised is the espousal of, surrender to, Wine, and the progeny to be begotten are not children of the body, but the products of the mind,— poetry. By the use of these substitutions the obscurities of these 18 sonnets will be found to dissolve, and their meaning will become clear and consistent. There are also other instances in these sonnets where words of well known meaning have been applied in an unusual manner, and with unauthorized meanings, and yet, keeping in view the key as given, and Shakespeare's plan to use words in an analogous, rather than in a direct, sense, in order to continue the illusion, the meaning which he proposed the words should have at once becomes evident. This will appear as the sonnets are read and discussed.

This same solution will not be found applicable after the first 18 sonnets. Thereafter the disguise becomes less complete, and the plan of the sonnets changed, and the meaning will be more easily arrived at, and the difficulties of less moment.

Though perhaps not always necessary, suggestive readings will be appended to each sonnet, showing how it should be read and interpreted in order to bear out the proposed construction. These suggestions, of course, are not an attempt to improve either the sense or beauty of the Sonnets. On the contrary, the effort will be rather to destroy their beauty, which in a large measure is the disguise under which their meaning is concealed. To many of the sonnets suggestions are not necessary, but it is felt that it would be better to err on the side of excessive elucidation, rather than let it be suspected that something might be passed which is not capable of adaptation to the proposed theory.

In the construction of the first 18 sonnets, consider Shakespeare in soliloquy, addressing himself in the third person, which, with men, is not an unusual habit. In the suggestions to these sonnets, in order to bring out the meaning clearly, first person pronouns and verbs to correspond, will be substituted for those of the third person.

SONNET 1.

From fairest creatures we desire increase,
That thereby beauty's rose might never die,
But as the riper should by time decease,
His tender heir might bear his memory;
But thou, contracted to thine own bright eyes,
Feed'st thy light's flame with self-substantial fuel,
Making a famine where abundance lies,
Thyself thy foe, to thy sweet self too cruel.
Thou that art now the world's fresh ornament
And only herald to the gaudy spring,
Within thine own bud buriest thy content
And, tender churl, mak'st waste in niggarding.
    Pity the world, or else this glutton be,
    To eat the world's due, by the grave and thee.

Suggestions: From fairest creatures (inspired minds) we desire increase (product), that thereby beauty's rose (genius) might never die, but as the riper (better matured) should by time decease (decay) his tender heir (poetry) might bear his memory;

But I contracted to my own bright eyes (natural and unassisted qualities) feed my light's flame (mind) with self-substantial fuel (my own uninspired thoughts) making a famine (lack of product) where abundance (possible inspiration) lies, myself my foe to my sweet self (genius) too cruel.

I that am now the world's fresh ornament (new idol) and only herald to the gaudy spring (only poet of nature) within my bud bury my content (for lack of inspiration bury my possibilities), and, tender churl, make waste niggarding (waste my opportunities by abstinence from stimulants).

Pity the world, (impoverished by my silence) or else this glutton be, (get inspiration through the use of wine) to eat the world's due, (drink wine that the world may have its due) by the grave and me. (After death and while I live.)

SONNET 2.

When forty winters shall besiege thy brow
And dig deep trenches in thy beauty's field,
Thy youth's proud livery, so gazed on now,
Will be a tatter'd weed, of small worth held:
Then being ask'd where all thy beauty lies,
Where all the treasure of thy lusty days,
To say, within thine own deep-sunken eyes,
Were an ill-eating shame and thriftless praise.
How much more praise deserved thy beauty's use,
If thou couldst answer 'This fair child of mine
Shall sum my count and make my old excuse,'
Proving his beauty by succession thine!
    This were to be new made when thou art old,
    And see thy blood warm when thou feel'st it cold.

Suggestions: When forty winters shall besiege my brow, and dig deep trenches in my beauty's field, (my work shall show decline) my youth's proud livery (present fame) so gazed on now, will be a tattered weed (dress) of small worth held;

Then being asked where all my beauty (fame) lies, where all the treasure (works) of my lusty days, to say within my own deep-sunken eyes, (old age without work to show) were an all-eating shame and thriftless praise. (Shameful and unimproved.)

How much more praise deserved, my beauty's youth (the genius of my youth) if I could answer 'This fair child of mine (completed work) shall sum my count and make my old excuse, proving his beauty (poetry) by succession mine.'

This were to be new made when I am old, and see my blood warm when I feel it cold.

SONNET 3.

Look in thy glass, and tell the face thou viewest
Now is the time that face should form another;
Whose fresh repair if now thou not renewest,
Thou dost beguile the world, unbless some mother.
For where is she so fair whose unear'd womb
Disdains the tillage of thy husbandry;
Or who is he so fond will be the tomb
Of his self-love, to stop posterity?
Thou art thy mother's glass, and she in thee
Calls back the lovely April of her prime:
So thou through windows of thine age shalt see,
Despite of wrinkles, this thy golden time.
    But if thou live, remember'd not to be,
    Die single, and thine image dies with thee.

Suggestions: Look in my glass, and tell the face I view, now is the time that face should form another; (produce its works) whose fresh repair if now I not renew, (if I do not continue and improve) I do beguile (cheat) the world, unbless some mother. (Opportunity.)

For where is she so fair whose uneared womb (opportunity) disdains the tillage of my husbandry? (That will not yield to my genius?) Or who is he so fond will be the tomb of his self love to stop posterity? (Who so self respecting, that he will not seize the inspiration that will accomplish his work?)

I am my mother's (youth's) glass, and she in me calls back the lovely April of her prime; so I through windows of my age shall see, despite of wrinkles, this my golden time. (As I now see the beauty of my youth, so shall I in my old age see that this is my golden time.)

But if I live, remembered not to be (if I do not produce works worthy of remembrance), die single (as I am without inspiration), and my image dies with me.

In interpreting these first three of the sonnets, the text has been followed literally, except in changing the pronouns and their verbs from the second to the first person, to emphasize the fact that Shakespeare is speaking to himself and not to another. Suggestions have also been inserted in parentheses, showing the meaning of the text, as the writer would have it construed, in order to bear out the construction which is being contended for, and which it is believed is the construction intended by the poet. These parenthetical insertions are sometimes confusing, but it was felt that in the construction of a few of the sonnets, the exact text and the interpretation contended for, should be put side by side to show the manner of interpreting from one set of words, intended to be obscure, to another set which attempts to make the meaning plain, and to strip off the obscurity.

Hereafter in the suggestions, the entire text will not be given, but condensations will be used instead, and very often paraphrases will be employed. The Suggestions however will be divided into four paragraphs. The first paragraph will represent the proposed readings of the first four lines of the sonnet; the second paragraph of the second four lines; the third of the third four lines, and the fourth paragraph of the last two lines. It will thus be an easy matter to compare the paraphrased reading with the text of the sonnet, and it is believed that much confusion will be avoided.

SONNET 4.

Unthrifty loveliness, why dost thou spend
Upon thyself thy beauty's legacy?
Nature's bequest gives nothing, but doth lend,
And being frank, she lends to those are free.
Then, beauteous niggard, why dost thou abuse
The bounteous largess given thee to give?
Profitless usurer, why dost thou use
So great a sum of sums, yet canst not live?
For having traffic with thyself alone,
Thou of thyself thy sweet self dost deceive.
Then how, when nature calls thee to be gone,
What acceptable audit canst thou leave?
    Thy unused beauty must be tomb'd with thee,
    Which, used, lives th' executor to be.

Unthrifty loveliness (unused ability) why spend upon myself my beauty's legacy? (The talents that have been bestowed upon me.) Nature does not give, but lends to those who are free. (Adventurous.)

Beauteous niggard (talents starved) why not use the ability that has been given to you? Profitless usurer, why exhaust your stores, and yet you cannot live? (You cannot produce worthy work.)

For living within myself alone, (uninspired by wine) I cheat myself of sweet fame. When I come to die what account of my talents can I leave?

My unused talents must be tombed with me, which if used would live as my executor. (Successor.)

SONNET 5.

Those hours that with gentle work did frame
The lovely gaze where every eye doth dwell,
Will play the tyrants to the very same
And that unfair which fairly doth excel:
For never-resting time leads summer on
To hideous winter and confounds him there;
Sap check'd with frost and lusty leaves quite gone,
Beauty o'ersnow'd and bareness every where:
Then, were not summer's distillation left,
A liquid prisoner pent in walls of glass,
Beauty's effect with beauty were bereft,
Nor it, nor no remembrance what it was:
 But flowers distill'd, though they with winter meet,
 Leese but their show; their substance still lives sweet.

Time in which I have accomplished lovely work, that every eye admires, will deal harshly with what I have done, and will make that unfair, which is only fairly good.

For never-resting time leads summer into winter; sap is checked with frost, leaves quite gone, beauty snowed under, and barrenness everywhere.

Then if the work of my genius is not done, and preserved in walls of glass, (secure from time's decay) beauty's effects (what work has been accomplished) will die with my talents, and will leave no remembrance of what my talent was.

But flowers distilled (accomplished work) though they meet with winter, lose but their show; their substance still lives.

SONNET 6.

Then let not winter's ragged hand deface
In thee thy summer, ere thou be distill'd:
Make sweet some vial; treasure thou some place
With beauty's treasure, ere it be self-kill'd.
That use is not forbidden usury,
Which happies those that pay the willing loan;
That's for thyself to breed another thee.
Or ten times happier, be it ten for one;
Ten times thyself were happier than thou art,
If ten of thine ten times refigured thee:
Then what could death do, if thou shouldst depart,
Leaving thee living in posterity?
    Be not self-will'd, for thou art much too fair
    To be death's conquest and make worms thine heir.

Then let not winter's (old age's) hand deface in me my summer (lusty age) ere I be distilled: Make sweet some vial; enrich some place with the product of my genius, ere my genius be self-killed. (By refusing the inspiration of wine.)

It is not forbidden to use that which would make the user happy, if he be willing to pay the price; (referring to the use of wine and the consequences) that is if I breed another self (fame), or I would be ten times happier if I could breed ten instead of one;

Ten times myself (product) were happier than I am, but if ten of myself could each ten times refigure me: then what could death do, if I should die leaving my works living in posterity?

Be not self-willed (stubborn) for I am much too fair to be death's conquest, and make worms my heir.

Shakespeare reasons with himself, that without stimulants he would die without a lasting fame, but with stimulants he would be multiplied ten times ten in his capacity for production, and would achieve a wonderful fame. He is therefore trying to reason himself into the adoption of that which would make him happier and more productive.

SONNET 7.

Lo, in the orient when the gracious light
Lifts up his burning head, each under eye
Doth homage to his new-appearing sight,
Serving with looks his sacred majesty;
And having climb'd the steep-up heavenly hill,
Resembling strong youth in his middle age,
Yet mortal looks adore his beauty still,
Attending on his golden pilgrimage;
But when from highmost pitch, with weary car,
Like feeble age, he reeleth from the day,
The eyes, 'fore duteous, now converted are
From his low tract, and look another way:
    So thou, thyself out-going in thy noon,
    Unlook'd on diest, unless thou get a son.

In the orient when the sun rises, those under it do it homage, worshipping it as sacred;

But having reached the meridian, as youth in its middle age, the worshippers continue to adore it, attending on its golden pilgrimage; (noon, its golden time)

But when from noon, with weary car, the sun declines, (reeleth from the day) the eyes which have been duteous, are then diverted, and look another way.

So I, out-going in my noon, unlooked on die, unless I get a son. (Fame.)

SONNET 8.

Music to hear, why hear'st thou music sadly?
Sweets with sweets war not, joy delights in joy.
Why lovest thou that which thou receivest not gladly,
Or else receivest with pleasure thine annoy?
If the true concord of well tuned sounds,
By unions married, do offend thine ear,
They do but sweetly chide thee, who confounds
In singleness the parts that thou shouldst bear.
Mark how one string, sweet husband to another,
Strikes each in each by mutual ordering;
Resembling sire and child and happy mother,
Who, all in one, one pleasing note do sing:
    Whose speechless song, being many, seeming one,
    Sings this to thee: 'Thou single wilt prove none.'

Music to hear, why do I hear it sadly? (Whilst Wine charms me, why do I accept it sadly?) Why do I love that which I receive not gladly, or am annoyed when I find I receive it with pleasure? (Here is conflict between enjoyment and the fear of consequences—between appetite and conscience.)

If the true concord of sounds by unions married, (produced by wine) offend my ear (cause me fear), they do but chide me who in singleness (by abstinence) confounds the parts that I should hear (sober, am not in accord with the harmony that wine produces).

Mark how one string, husband to another strikes in mutual ordering, resembling sire and child and happy mother (the trinity of Shakespeare, poetry and wine), who, all in one, one pleasing note do sing:

Who being many, but seeming one, sing this to me, 'Thou single will prove none.' (In yourself, without wine, you will accomplish nothing.)

SONNET 9.

Is it for fear to wet a widow's eye
That thou consumest thyself in single life?
Ah! if thou issueless shalt hap to die,
The world will wail thee, like a makeless wife;
The world will be thy widow, and still weep
That thou no form of thee hast left behind,
When every private widow well may keep
By children's eyes her husband's shape in mind.
Look, what an unthrift in the world doth spend
Shifts but his place, for still the world enjoys it;
But beauty's waste hath in the world an end,
And kept unused, the user so destroys it.
   No love toward others in that bosom sits
   That on himself such murderous shame commits.

Is it for fear to wet a widow's eye, that you waste yourself in single life? (Refuse wine.) If I issueless (without product) shall die, the world will wail me like a makeless (unproductive) wife;

The world will be my widow, and weep that I have left behind no works, when the widow with children may keep her husband's shape in mind.

What the unthrift spends in the world he leaves, when he is gone, and the world continues to enjoy it; but what genius wastes is lost, and if he does not cultivate his talents he destroys them

There is no love (consideration) for others in him, who shamefully destroys his own beauty and fame.

(In the first two lines Shakespeare asks himself, if he is afraid to indulge in, or wed, wine, lest he should die and leave it a widow. The point is not made as to the effect upon the widow, wine, although it is so expressed, so much as it is as to himself. The question really is, 'Are you afraid that indulgence will shorten your life?' Then he proceeds, to say, 'If you should not indulge you will die issueless, and the world will be your widow, and weep that you have left no children,—no poetry.')

SONNET 10.

For shame! deny that thou bear'st love to any,
Who for thyself art so unprovident.
Grant, if thou wilt, thou art beloved of many,
But that thou none lovest is most evident;
For thou art so possess'd with murderous hate
That 'gainst thyself thou stick'st not to conspire,
Seeking that beauteous roof to ruinate
Which to repair should be thy chief desire.
O, change thy thought, that I may change my mind!
Shall hate be fairer lodged than gentle love?
Be, as thy presence is, gracious and kind,
Or to thyself at least kind-hearted prove:
 Make thee another self, for love of me,
 That beauty still may live in thine or thee.

For shame! I should deny that I bear love to any, when I am for myself so improvident. (So reluctant to use my advantage.) Granted I am beloved by many, but that I love none is evident;

For I am so possessed with hate (of the cup) that against my own self I conspire, seeking to ruin that beauteous roof (genius) which it should be my chief desire to repair. (Improve.)

I must change my thoughts, (hate) that I may change my mind. (Judgment.) Shall hate be cherished more than love? I should be as my presence is, gracious and kind, or at least kind-hearted to myself.

I should make me another self, for my love's sake, that beauty (accomplishments) still may live in mine and me.

SONNET 11.

As fast as thou shalt wane, so fast thou grow'st
In one of thine, from that which thou departest;
And that fresh blood which youngly thou bestow'st
Thou mayst call thine when thou from youth convertest.
Herein lives wisdom, beauty and increase;
Without this, folly, age and cold decay:
If all were minded so, the times should cease
And threescore year would make the world away.
Let those whom Nature hath not made for store,
Harsh, featureless and rude, barrenly perish:
Look, whom she best endow'd she gave the more;
Which bounteous gift thou shouldst in bounty cherish:
   She carved thee for her her seal, and meant thereby
   Thou shouldst print more, not let that copy die.

As I shall wane, (grow older) so fast shall I grow in one of mine
(my works) from that which I depart; (my youth) (As I leave my
youth I shall wane in age but increase in fame) and that fresh blood
(wine) which I bestow in youth I may call mine, when my youth has
departed.

Herein lives wisdom, beauty and increase; without (wine) folly, age,
and cold decay: if all were minded so (so bent on abstinence in matters
of increase) the world would be depopulated in three score years.

Let those whom Nature has not made for store, (to perpetuate their
talents) the harsh, featureless and rude, barrenly perish, but to the best
endowed Nature gave the more, having which bounteous gift I should
cherish it.

She carved me for her seal, (distinction) and meant that I should
print more (perpetuate the beauty of my mind) nor let it die.

SONNET 12.

When I do count the clock that tells the time,
And see the brave day sunk in hideous night;
When I behold the violet past prime,
And sable curls all silver'd o'er with white;
When lofty trees I see barren of leaves,
Which erst from heat did canopy the herd,
And summer's green all girded up in sheaves,
Borne on the bier with white and bristly beard,
Then of thy beauty do I question make,
That thou among the wastes of time must go,
Since sweets and beauties do themselves forsake
And die as fast as they see others grow;
    And nothing 'gainst Time's scythe can make defence
    Save breed, to brave him when he takes thee hence.

When I see how time passes from day to night, the fading violet and the silvered hair;

When I see lofty trees barren of leaves, which from the heat sheltered the herd, and summer's green girded in sheaves borne with white and bristly beard,

Then I question my beauty (talents), that it must go among the wastes of time, since sweets and beauties fade, and die as fast as others grow;

Nothing can stand against Time, save breed. (Increase, products.)

SONNET 13.

O, that you were yourself! but, love, you are
No longer yours than you yourself here live:
Against this coming end you should prepare,
And your sweet semblance to some other give.
So should that beauty which you hold in lease
Find no determination; then you were
Yourself again, after yourself's decease,
When your sweet issue your sweet form should bear.
Who lets so fair a house fall to decay,
Which husbandry in honour might uphold
Against the stormy gusts of winter's day
And barren rage of death's eternal cold?
   O, none but unthrifts: dear my love, you know
   You had a father; let your son say so.

O that I were myself! but I am no longer myself than I shall live; against the end I should prepare, and my semblance to some other give. (Perpetuate myself in my poetry.)

So should that beauty (art) which I hold in lease, be not determined (ended); then I were myself again after my death, when my issue (works) should bear my form. (Name.)

Who lets so fair a house fall to decay, which husbandry in honor (by the proper use of wine) might uphold, against winter's (old age's) storms, and death's eternal cold?

None but unthrifts (the foolish)! I had a father; let my son say so. (I inherited capacity, and should leave works in proof of it.)

SONNET 14.

Not from the stars do I my judgement pluck;
And yet methinks I have astronomy,
But not to tell of good or evil luck,
Of plagues, of dearths, or seasons' quality;
Nor can I fortune to brief minutes tell,
Pointing to each his thunder, rain and wind,
Or say with princes if it shall go well,
By oft predict that I in heaven find:
But from thine eyes my knowledge I derive,
And, constant stars, in them I read such art,
As truth and beauty shall together thrive,
If from thyself to store thou wouldst convert;
  Or else of thee this I prognosticate:
  Thy end is truth's and beauty's doom and date.

Not from the stars (astrology) do I obtain my judgment, and yet I think I have astronomy, but not to foretell good or evil luck, or plagues, or dearths or the weather;

Nor can I tell fortunes to brief details, predicting for each his thunder, rain and wind, or whether princes shall fare well, but I often predict what in heaven I find:

But from my own eyes (judgment) I derive my knowledge, and they being constant stars, in them I read such art as, that truth and beauty shall together thrive if I would convert myself (uninspired and unstimulated) to store; (the increase which wine would bring)

Or else of myself this I prognosticate: my end is truth's and beauty's (successful art's) doom and date.

The struggle is about to end, and the Tempter has won. There can now be no doubt, and there will be no turning back. Conscience has been given notice to quit. A while—a little while—and the despoiling tyrant will have usurped the place of Shakespeare's faithful and stubborn conscience, with which he has so persistently plead. With ceaseless iteration Shakespeare seeks to justify his dissipation on the ground that through it he will be able to achieve his end, and perform his mission, and that it would be unpardonable to fail in the performance of his duty to his art, though in order not to fail he must commit another, but lesser, sin in the degradation that such a choice would bring upon himself.

SONNET 15.

When I consider every thing that grows
Holds in perfection but a little moment,
That this huge stage presenteth nought but shows
Whereon the stars in secret influence comment;
When I perceive that men as plants increase,
Cheered and check'd even by the self-same sky,
Vaunt in their youthful sap, at height decrease,
And wear their brave state out of memory;
Then the conceit of this inconstant stay
Sets you most rich in youth before my sight,
Where wasteful Time debateth with Decay,
To change your day of youth to sullied night;
    And all in war with Time for love of you,
    As he takes from you, I engraft you new.

When I consider everything that grows holds in perfection but a little moment, that this huge stage presents nothing but shows, whereon the stars have an unknown influence;

When I perceive that men and plants are checked and cheered under the same conditions, vaunt in their youth, at height decrease and pass out of memory;

Then the thought of this inconstant stay, sets my youth before my sight, while Time debates with Decay to change my day of youth to night;

And in war with Time for love of self, as Time takes from me, I engraft me new.

SONNET 16.

But wherefore do not you a mightier way
Make war upon this bloody tyrant, Time?
And fortify yourself in your decay
With means more blessed than my barren rhyme?
Now stand you on the top of happy hours,
And many maiden gardens, yet unset,
With virtuous wish would bear your living flowers
Much liker than your painted counterfeit:
So should the lines of life that life repair,
Which this, Time's pencil, or my pupil pen,
Neither in inward worth nor outword fair,
Can make you live yourself in eyes of men.
   To give away yourself keeps yourself still;
   And you must live, drawn by your own sweet skill.

But why not use a mightier way to make war upon Time? And fortify myself in my decay, with means more blessed than my barren rhyme. (Uninspired.)

Now stand I on the top of happy hours (the noon time of my life) and many maiden gardens (new opportunities for verse) yet unset, with virtuous wish (consent) would bear my living flowers, (poetry) much more like (my genius) than my painted counterfeit; (my unstimulated verse)

So should the lines of life (products of my mind) repair (perpetuate) my life, which this Time's pencil (decay) nor my pupil pen, (uninspired pen) neither in inward (substantial) worth nor outward (apparent) beauty, can make me live myself in eyes of men. (In fame.)

To give away myself (yield to wine) keeps me still myself, and I must live drawn by my own skill.

SONNET 17.

Who will believe my verse in time to come,
If it were fill'd with your most high deserts?
Though yet, heaven knows, it is but as a tomb
Which hides your life and shows not half your parts.
If I could write the beauty of your eyes
And in fresh numbers number all your graces,
The age to come would say 'This poet lies;
Such heavenly touches ne'er touch'd earthly faces.'
So should my papers, yellowed with their age,
Be scorn'd, like old men of less truth than tongue,
And your true rights be term'd a poet's rage
And stretched metre of an antique song:
    But were some child of yours alive that time,
    You should live twice, in it and in my rhyme.

Who will believe my verse in time to come if it were filled with my most high deserts? (If written at my best), though as yet, heaven knows, my verse is but a tomb which hides my life (does not show my merits), and shows not half my parts.

If I could write the beauty of what I see, and in my verse number all my graces, the age to come would say, "This poet lies, such heavenly touches ne'er touched earthly faces." (My verse would be inspired beyond human quality.)

So should my verse, yellowed with age (if uninspired) be scorned, like old men, less truthful than voluble, and my true rights (uninspired poetry), be termed a poet's rage, and stretched (forced, imperfect), meter of an antique song.

But were some child of mine then alive, I should live twice, in it and in my rhyme.

SONNET 18.

Shall I compare thee to a summer's day?
Thou art more lovely and more temperate:
Rough winds do shake the darling buds of May,
And summer's lease hath all too short a date:
Sometime too hot the eye of heaven shines,
And often is his gold complexion dimm'd;
And every fair from fair sometime declines,
By chance or nature's changing course untrimm'd;
But thy eternal summer shall not fade,
Nor lose possession of that fair thou owest;
Nor shall Death brag thou wander'st in his shade,
When in eternal lines to time thou grow'st:
    So long as men can breathe, or eyes can see,
    So long lives this, and this gives life to thee.

Shall I compare myself to a summer's day? I am more lovely and more temperate: rough winds shake the buds of May, and summer is too short;

Sometimes the sun shines too hot, and often is he dimmed with clouds; and everything that is fair declines from its best through chance or nature's untrimmed (uncontrolled) changes.

But my eternal summer shall not fade, nor lose possession of the beauty (talent) I own; nor shall death brag that I wander in his shade, when in eternal lines to time I grow;

So long as men can breathe or eyes can see, so long live this (my poetry) and it give life (fame) to me.

SONNET 19.

Devouring Time, blunt thou the lion's paws,
And make the earth devour her own sweet brood;
Pluck the keen teeth from the fierce tiger's jaws,
And burn the long-lived phœnix in her blood;
Make glad and sorry seasons as thou fleet'st,
And do whate'er thou wilt, swift-footed Time,
To the wide world and all her fading sweets;
But I forbid thee one most heinous crime:
O, carve not with thy hours my love's fair brow,
Nor draw no lines there with thine antique pen;
Him in thy course untainted do allow
For beauty's pattern to succeeding men.
 Yet do thy worst, old Time: despite thy wrong,
 My love shall in my verse ever live young.

Time, blunt the lion's paws, and make the earth devour (reabsorb) her brood (progeny); pluck the teeth from the tiger's jaws, and burn the phœnix in her blood;

Make seasons of gladness and of sorrow as time fleets, and do whatever else you will to the world and her fading sweets (joys), but I forbid you one most henious crime:

Carve not as you pass my love's brow (genius) nor draw lines (wrinkles) there; him in your course unchanged allow, as a pattern of beauty for succeeding men.

Yet do your worst old Time; despite your wrong (decay) my love shall in my verse ever live young.

SONNET 20.

A woman's face with Nature's own hand painted
Hast thou, the master-mistress of my passion;
A woman's gentle heart, but not acquainted
With shifting change, as is false women's fashion;
An eye more bright than theirs, less false in rolling,
Gilding the object whereupon it gazeth;
A man in hue, all 'hues' in his controlling,
Which steals men's eyes and women's souls amazeth.
And for a woman wert thou first created;
Till Nature, as she wrought thee, fell a-doting,
And by addition me of thee defeated,
By adding one thing to my purpose nothing.
    But since she prick'd thee out for women's pleasure,
    Mine be thy love, and thy love's use their treasure.

A woman's face, painted by nature (red), have you Wine, the master-mistress of my passion; a woman's gentle heart, but not so fickle as is false women'd fashion;

An eye has Wine more bright than woman's, less false in rolling, and gilding (illuminating) the object whereupon it gazes; it is a man in hue (character) all hues in its controlling (seeing all phases of life and nature) which steals men's eyes (senses) and amazes the soul of women.

And for a woman (intoxicating—fascinating) was it first created; till nature, as she created it, fell adoting and by addition me of Wine defeated, by adding one thing (lewdness—sexual excitation) not to my purpose.

But since she pricked you (Wine) out for women's pleasure, your love be mine, and your love's use be women's treasure.

We have now come to see Shakespeare's conscience dethroned, and the dark angel of Intemperance exalted in its place. Heretofore Shakespeare has been addressing his excuses and pleas to his better nature. But he has finally determined that he can find no inspiration except in the cup, and it is that or death to his Muse. Like all who with shame choose a guilty or doubtful course, he does not announce openly his choice, but stealthily abandons the old, and openly takes on the new.

Since Sonnet 14 there has been a marked change in the tone of the sonnets. Up to the 20th wine was a thing which Shakespeare imagined he could use to advantage. Until now he has neither thought or spoken of it as a distinct personality, and has given it no greater importance than he would have given to his food, except that it possessed a stimulating quality. His whole thought has centered on himself and his achievement of fame as a poet. To that end he has considered that wine would give to him that nourishment and exhilaration, which would best fit him for the work he most wished to do. He understood the danger of overindulgence, and realized the risks he was incurring, but has concluded that the risks would be justified, because it would lend to him a power which he did not possess, or if he had, he could not use. Undoubtedly during this time he was not only thinking and talking about wine and its effects, but was indulging in it, and, as he imagined, was gaining advantage through its use, and he had finally concluded that it was indispensable to him.

It has been shown that the Sonnets, up to and including the 18th, can be interpreted by converting them from the third to the first person, and thus making them apply to Shakespeare, himself, and to no one else. But now in the 19th and 20th, such an adaptation will not answer, and it is found that a third person, or thing, has obtruded, and it becomes necessary to revise the manner of reading and construing, and to identity the obtruder, who, of course, is Wine.

After Shakespeare had in the 14th sonnet dismissed his conscience, and surrendered himself to wine, he undertook to extend the sonnets on the same plan, but found his subject had been exhausted. Having won himself over to his plan of indulgence, he no longer had a theme. In 15, 16, 17, 18, and 19 Time and Decay became his subjects, and upon these abstractions he continued to soliloquize, but in a distinct vein from that which had supplied the earlier sonnets. In these last five sonnets it is evident he felt himself committed to the use of wine, and says no more as to the objections to it. On the contrary he is rather inclined to exult that all objections have been overcome, and to look forward to the wonderful quality of the rhyme which he is to produce, and in which he, himself, is to gain an immortality, thus defying and defeating Time in its ravages.

In 15, in speaking of the contest with Time, he says to himself, "As he (Time) takes from you, I engraft you new." Evidently the meaning is, that as he declined with age he would renew his youth with wine. Notice here however that wine was not to make the renewal, but that Shakespeare himself is the engrafter. Likewise in the last two lines of 16, he says, "To give yourself away keeps yourself still," thus declaring that by partaking of wine he would still be himself,—the master or superior—with wine but a stimulant. In the 18th he promises himself, through his fame, the victory over death, but claims the victory all for himself, and does not refer to wine, or award it any of the credit. In the 19th he defies Time again, and in the 9th line speaks of "my love's fair brow," and in the last line says, "my love shall in my verse ever live long." What is meant here by his 'love'? Does Shakespeare mean himself, his poetry, or wine? The answer to the question is not without doubt. At the present time, and considering the position the sonnet occupies with relation to the others, "love" is believed to refer to Shakespeare's genius or poetry. But were the sonnet numbered above 40, it would probably have to be construed to mean wine, as will appear later on.

Since 14 the succeeding sonnets are evidently in a transitory stage. The poet has not yet found his bearings, and does not himself know into what he is drifting. He is exploring for an outlet for the continuance of his verse. Nor does this transition end here, but continues on in the following sonnets developing progressively from the insensate, intoxicating wine, through various stages of "love," "windows to my breast," "lord of my love," "jewel," "light," "sweet love," "dear friend," "the grave where buried love doth live," "sun," "salve," "sweet thief," "worth and truth," "abundance," "tenth Muse," "and all the better part of me," and finally his alter ego, and the author of his poems. The climax is not reached until nearly the 40th Sonnet. Until then, the theme is generally, Wine, and the description of its effects. It is portrayed as an assistant, an auxiliary, and as a helpmate, gradually becoming more or less an entity, with a personality, until it finally becomes a master and superior, and Shakespeare its worshipper and slave. It is thus finally exalted above everything that ought to be dear to Shakespeare, even above his mighty talents.

The 20th Sonnet, the last one reviewed, requires some special consideration. It is most important in the elucidation of our theory. All students of Shakespeare have been much puzzled by it. By none has a construction been suggested that would give it a meaning,—a permissible one,—that is at all acceptable. One critic has construed it as implying a sexual perversion on part of the author.

It is quite certain that while Shakespeare was writing the series of sonnets, which are now being considered, and which have always been construed as having a masculine character, he was also writing the dark woman sonnets, to which he gave, unquestionably, a feminine character. Undoubtedly the two series were progressing at the same time. In one the virtues of Wine are commended, while the dark woman sonnets are on the whole condemnatory. There is nothing by which the time or sequence of construction, can be determined. Although the dark woman sonnets, in the publication are at the conclusion, it is most probable they were not the last in the construction. Two of these sonnets, 138 and 144, were published in the Passionate Pilgrim in 1599, ten years prior to the publication of the Sonnets as a whole. Also in this publication were other sonnets taken from *Love's Labor's Lost,* which will be shown to be of a like character. The play, *Love's Labor's Lost* was published in 1598, and had been acted some time before. It is probable therefore, that the two series of sonnets were being composed contemporaneously. If not, the evidence would indicate that the dark woman sonnets were composed prior to many of the others.

When, therefore, in the 20th Sonnet Shakespeare calls his love, the master-mistress of his passion, he unsexes his love, and declares it neither man nor woman, but gives it the character of both. Henceforth, the reader must remember, a new love sits in the poet's heart, and he, or she, or it, is the one hereafter addressed. His conscience has been thrown out, and is a wanderer, never more to appear. Even in the bitterness of his heart, when he feels himslf betrayed and scorned by his new love, his first true love does not return, nor does he again refer to it, except possibly in Sonnet 144 where he calls it his "better angel."

The reader is now requested to observe closely, that hereafter there are no sufficient suggestions in the first series of Sonnets themselves, to justify the assumption that they are addressed to any living being, male or female. In a few instances which will be noted, a masculine character is ascribed to that to which the Sonnets is addressed, but that is only as any idealized object or thing may be designated as "he" or "she." The addressee in the series of sonnets under consideration, and to follow, will be found to be described as male or female, or both, as the subject requires, and on at least one occasion is described as a neuter. But on the whole the descriptions indicate neither the male or female character, but undoubtedly the neutral,—Wine.

SONNET 21.

So it is not with me as with that Muse
Stirr'd by a painted beauty to his verse,
Who heaven itself for ornament doth use
And every fair with his fair doth rehearse,
Making a couplement of proud compare,
With sun and moon, with earth and sea's rich gems,
With April's first-born flowers, and all things rare
That heaven's air in this huge rondure hems.
O, let me, true in love, but truly write,
And then believe me, my love is as fair
As any mother's child, though not so bright
As those gold candles fix'd in heaven's air:
> Let them say more that like of hearsay well;
> I will not praise that purpose not to sell.

It is not with me now (inspired as I am) as with that Muse, which is stirred by a painted (false) beauty to his verse, who uses heaven itself for ornament (symbol) and rehearses (compares) every fair (all beauty) with his own conceptions.

Making a couplement (coupling them in comparison) with sun and moon, with earth and sea's richest gems, with April flowers and all things rare, that exist in this huge rondure. (heavens)

Let me true in love (inspired by wine) truly write, and then believe me, my love (art) is as fair as any mother's child (as any one's product) though not so bright as those gold candles. (The sun and moon.)

Let them say more (exaggerate) that like of hearsays (imitations); I will not praise that purpose (adopt that plan) not to sell. (Not for gain.)

As Shakespeare has already used all the exalted comparisons in his previous sonnets, which are referred to and condemned in this sonnet, it is quite evident he is referring, not to some other poet whose exaggerations he condemns, but to his methods heretofore used. He imagines, now that he is to be unstinted in wine, that he may discard all his old faults, and write only in the perfection of his art.

Observe too, that in this sonnet Wine in itself is not praised, but Shakespeare takes all credit for what he is to do entirely to himself, awarding none of it to Wine. This sonnet is clearly transitional.

SONNET 22.

My glass shall not persuade me I am old,
So long as youth and thou are of one date;
But when in thee time's furrows I behold,
Then look I death my days should expiate.
For all that beauty that doth cover thee
Is but the seemly raiment of my heart,
Which in thy breast doth live, as thine in me:
How can I then be elder than thou art?
O, therefore, love, be of thyself so wary
As I, not for myself, but for thee will;
Bearing thy heart, which I will keep so chary
As tender nurse her babe from faring ill.
> Presume not on thy heart when mine is slain;
> Thou gavest me thine, not to give back again.

My glass (appearance) shall not persuade me I am old, so long as youth and you Wine, are of one date (so long as you impart the joyousness of youth); but when in you furrows I behold (when your inspiration begins to fail), then look I death my days should expiate (then may I die).

For all that beauty that covers you (that comes through your use) is but the seemly (natural) raiment (affections) of my heart, which lives in my breast as yours in me (as your love lives in me): How can I then be elder than you are? (While you inspire me with youth.)

Therefore Wine, be wary of yourself (be temperate) as I, not for myself, but for you will be, bearing your heart (cherishing your influence) which I will keep chary, (within bounds) as a tender nurse would keep her babe from faring ill.

Presume not on your heart when mine is slain; (do not expect to abandon me when I cannot live without you) You gave me your heart, not to give back again.

Though in this sonnet Shakespeare praises wine, he still maintains an independence, and pleads with wine for moderation, much as heretofore he appealed to his conscience. He has not yet come to recognize wine as his master and sole reliance.

SONNET 23.

As an unperfect actor on the stage,
Who with his fear is put besides his part,
Or some fierce thing replete with too much rage,
Whose strength's abundance weakens his own heart;
So I, for fear of trust, forget to say
The perfect ceremony of love's rite,
And in mine own love's strength seem to decay,
O'ercharged with burthen of mine own love's might.
O, let my books be then the eloquence
And dumb presagers of my speaking breast;
Who plead for love, and look for recompense,
More than that tongue that more hath more express'd.
   O, learn to read what silent love hath writ:
   To hear with eyes belongs to love's fine wit.

As an imperfect actor on the stage, who with fright is put beside his part (forgets his part), or like some fierce thing full of rage, whose strength weakens his own heart;

So I fearing to trust you wine, forget to say the perfect ceremony of love's rite (the marriage ceremony in which one vows for life), and in my own love's strength seem to decay (am overcome by my excessive love), overcharged with the burden (responsibility) of my love for you.

Let my books (as I cannot speak) be the eloquence, and dumb presages (spokesmen) of my breast, which pleads for love, and look for recompense, more than that tongue (wooers) who protest more.

Learn to read what my silent love has writ; to hear with eyes (understand) belongs to love's fine wit.

SONNET 24.

Mine eye hath play'd the painter and hath steled
Thy beauty's form in table of my heart;
My body is the frame wherein 'tis held,
And perspective it is best painter's art.
For through the painter must you see his skill,
To find where your true image pictured lies;
Which in my bosom's shop is hanging still,
That hath his windows glazed with thine eyes.
Now see what good turns eyes for eyes have done:
Mine eyes have drawn thy shape, and thine for me
Are windows to my breast, where-through the sun
Delights to peep, to gaze therein on thee;
   Yet eyes this cunning want to grace their art,
   They draw but what they see, know not the heart.

My eye (thoughts) has steled (verbalized from the noun stele, meaning sculptured or painted) your beauty's form (the love of wine) in the table of my heart; my body is the frame wherein 'tis held, and its perspective is the best that painter's art can do.

For through the painter's eye must you see his skill, to find where your image painted lies (to find your true image); your picture in my bosom's shop (heart) still hangs, and my heart is glazed with your eyes (sees through yours eyes).

Now see what eyes for eyes have done: my eyes have drawn your shape, and your eyes are windows for my breast, through which the sun delights to peep to gaze on you within;

Yet eyes lack this cunning to grace their art,—they draw but what they see, and do not know the heart.

This sonnet is quite involved, when the words of the sonnet are followed literally or nearly so. The following paraphrased condensation is offered as a fair expression of its meaning:

My eye (appetite) has painted your beauty's form (the love of wine) within my heart; my body is the frame (simply the vehicle), and the perspective proves my art; could you see through my eyes you would appreciate how fully you possess me, for in my heart you continue to rule, and your eyes are the windows of my soul. See how we mutually exist: my thoughts dwell on you, and you inspire my thoughts, and through your inspiration comes the light that shows your beauty. My eyes lack only this,—they only know what they can see, and they cannot see your heart. (They are not certain that you are as lovely as you seem.)

SONNET 25.

Let those who are in favour with their stars
Of public honour and proud titles boast,
Whilst I, whom fortune of such triumph bars,
Unlook'd for joy in that I honour most.
Great princes' favourites their fair leaves spread
But as the marigold at the sun's eye,
And in themselves their pride lies buried,
For at a frown they in their glory die.
The painful warrior famoused for fight,
After a thousand victories once foil'd,
Is from the book of honour razed quite,
And all the rest forgot for which he toil'd:
    Then happy I, that love and am beloved
    Where I may not remove nor be removed.

Let those who are in favor with their stars, of public honor and titles boast, whilst I whom fortunes bars of such triumphs, rejoice in what I most honor. (Wine.)

Great prince's favorites spread their leaves, as the marigold in the sun's eye does, and within themselves are without cause for pride, for at a frown they in their glory die.

The warrior famed for worth, after a thousand victories, once foiled, is from the book of honor razed, and all for which he toiled is forgot.

Then happy I that love (wine) and am beloved (by it) where I may not remove, nor be removed. (From it.)

SONNET 26.

Lord of my love, to whom in vassalage
Thy merit hath my duty strongly knit,
To thee I send this written ambassage,
To witness duty, not to show my wit:
Duty so great, which wit so poor as mine
May make seem bare, in wanting words to show it,
But that I hope some good conceit of thine
In thy soul's thought, all naked, will bestow it;
Till whatsoever star that guides my moving,
Points on me graciously with fair aspect,
And puts apparel on my tatter'd loving,
To show me worthy of thy sweet respect:
Then may I dare to boast how I do love thee;
Till then not show my head where thou mayst prove me.

Lord of my love, (Wine) to whom in vassalage my duty is strongly knit, I send this written ambassage, to show my duty, not my wit;

Duty so great that my poor wit may make it seem bare, in wanting words to show it, but I hope some good impulse in your soul will receive it, though it be naked, (not adequately expressed) till the star that guides my moving,

Points on me favorably, and puts apparel on my tattered loving, (covers up my wretched condition of insobriety) to make me appear worthy of your respect.

Then (when I shall be restored) may I boast how I love you; until then not show my head where you may prove (see) me.

In a debauched condition Shakespeare would not assert love for that which had so degraded him, for that would bring disrepute on his beloved wine. But if restored to an appearance of respectability, he could assert his love, like other respectables. He does not make a direct appeal, as he does so often hereafter, but sends his "written ambassage," as if he were restrained and could not come in person, and begs to pay his respects, and hopes that good fortune may restore him before he shows himself. He, in fact, states that he is in "vassalage," which probably means on probation, where abstinence is required. For once he seems to be humiliated, and wanting in respect for his talents, for he says he does not write "to show his wit." If there be any doubt about this construction, the three following sonnets should remove it.

Here his address to wine, as his 'Lord,' is an instance in which the thing addressed is given a masculine character.

SONNET 27.

Weary with toil, I haste me to my bed,
The dear repose for limbs with travel tired;
But then begins a journey in my head,
To work my mind, when body's work's expired:
For then my thoughts, from far where I abide,
Intend a zealous pilgrimage to thee,
And keep my drooping eyelids open wide,
Looking on darkness which the blind do see:
Save that my soul's imaginary sight
Presents thy shadow to my sightless view,
Which, like a jewel hung in ghastly night,
Makes black night beauteous and her old face new.
    Lo, thus, by day my limbs, by night my mind,
    For thee and for myself no quiet find.

Weary with toil I haste to my bed, the dear repose for tired limbs, but there begins a journey in my head, to work my mind when the body's work is done;

Then my thoughts, from where I abide, intend a pilgrimage to you (wine), and keep my eyelids open wide, though the darkness be as complete as blindness:

Save that my imaginary sight (cravings) presents your shadow to my view, which like a jewel hung in ghastly night, makes night beauteous, and her old face new.

By day my limbs, by night my mind, for you (wine) and for myself no quiet find.

This sonnet needs neither paraphrase nor comment. How could it be made more lucid, or convey greater horror? It expresses the tortures of a drunken collapse.

SONNET 28.

How can I then return in happy plight,
That am debarr'd the benefit of rest?
When day's oppression is not eased by night,
But day by night, and night by day, oppress'd?
And each, though enemies to either's reign,
Do in consent shake hands to torture me;
The one by toil, the other to complain
How far I toil, still farther off from thee.
I tell the day, to please him thou art bright,
And dost him grace when clouds do blot the heaven:
So flatter I the swart-complexion'd night;
When sparkling stars twire not thou gild'st the even.
   But day doth daily draw my sorrows longer,
   And night doth nightly make grief's strength seem
     stronger.

How can I return in happy plight (to labor) that am debarred the benefit of rest? When the day's weariness is not eased by night, but my day oppressed by night, and my night by day?

And each though enemy to the other's reign, shake hands (unite) to torture me, the day by toil, the night to complain how far I toil away from you (wine).

I tell the day to please him, that you (wine) are bright, though the clouds darken the heaven, so I flatter the night when stars shine not, that you brighten the evening.

But the day draws my sorrow longer, and the night increases the strength of my grief.

This is a wonderful description of the approaching end of a protracted revel.

SONNET 29.

When, in disgrace with fortune and men's eyes,
I all alone beweep my outcast state,
And trouble deaf heaven with my bootless cries,
And look upon myself, and curse my fate,
Wishing me like to one more rich in hope,
Featured like him, like him with friend possess'd,
Desiring this man's art and that man's scope,
With what I most enjoy contented least;
Yet in these thoughts myself almost despising,
Haply I think on thee, and then my state,
Like to the lark at break of day arising
From sullen earth, sings hymns at heaven's gate;
   For thy sweet love remember'd such wealth brings
   That then I scorn to change my state with kings.

When in disgrace with fortune, and in men's eyes, I alone beweep my outcast state, and cry to heaven and curse my fate,

Wishing I were more hopeful, and featured (constituted) like him who possesses friends, envying this man's art and that man's scope (capacity), with what I most enjoy (Wine) contented least;

Yet in these thoughts myself almost despising, I think on (partake of) you (Wine), and then my state, like the lark at break of day rising, sings hymns at heaven's gate:

For partaking of you brings such wealth, that then I scorn to change my place with kings.

If the reader has no observation or knowledge of such things, and would like to have the construction here put on them verified, let him submit the four preceding sonnets to any physician of experience in such matter, and ascertain whether they lack in any detail of the tortures and delirium that accompany a prolonged debauch.

SONNET 30.

When to the sessions of sweet silent thought
I summon up remembrance of things past,
I sigh the lack of many a thing I sought,
And with old woes new wail my dear time's waste:
Then can I drown an eye, unused to flow,
For precious friends hid in death's dateless night,
And weep afresh love's long since cancell'd woe,
And moan the expense of many a vanish'd sight:
Then can I grieve at grievances foregone,
And heavily from woe to woe tell o'er
The sad account of fore-bemoaned moan,
Which I new pay as if not paid before.
    But if the while I think on thee, dear friend,
    All losses are restored and sorrows end.

When to the sessions of sweet silent thought, (in comfortable meditations) I recall memories of the past, I sigh the lack of many a thing I sought (failures) and regret the waste of time:

Then can I weep for the precious friends now dead, and weep afresh for those whom I have wept before, and moan the expense (expenditure of feelings) of many a vanquished sight. (Unrealized hopes.)

Then can I grieve at grievances foregone, (past failures) and heavily from woe to woe tell o'er (and recall one woe after another) the sad account of what I have already wept, and which I weep again as if not wept before.

But then, if I think on you, dear friend, (inspirit myself with wine) all losses are restored, and sorrows end.

SONNET 31.

Thy bosom is endeared with all hearts,
Which I by lacking have supposed dead;
And there reigns love, and all love's loving parts,
And all those friends which I thought buried.
How many a holy and obsequious tear
Hath dear religious love stol'n from mine eye,
As interest of the dead, which now appear
But things removed that hidden in thee lie!
Thou art the grave where buried love doth live,
Hung with the trophies of my lovers gone,
Who all their parts of me to thee did give:
That due of many now is thine alone:
 Their images I loved I view in thee,
 And thou, all they, hast all the all of me.

Your bosom (the comforts of wine) is endeared with all the hearts, which I have missed, and have supposed were dead, and there, (in your comforts) reigns love and all love's parts, and all the friends I thought were dead.

How many tears have I wept as interest of the dead (as due to the dead) which dead now appear as but removed, and are hidden in you!

You are the grave where my dead love lives, and you are hung with the trophies (remembrance) of my lovers gone, who gave you all they held of me; that due of many now is yours alone: (in loving you I pay them all their due)

What I loved in them I see in you, (lives in you) and you being they, have all there is of me.

SONNET 32.

If thou survive my well-contented day,
When that churl Death my bones with dust shall cover,
And shalt by fortune once more re-survey
These poor rude lines of thy deceased lover,
Compare them with the bettering of the time,
And though they be outstripp'd by every pen,
Reserve them for my love, not for their rhyme,
Exceeded by the height of happier men.
O, then vouchsafe me but this loving thought:
'Had my friend's Muse grown with this growing age,
A dearer birth than this his love had brought,
To march in ranks of better equipage:
 But since he died, and poets better prove,
 Theirs for their style I'll read, his for his love.'

If you survive my well-contented day, (happy day of indulgence) when I shall be dead, and shall happen to re-survey these poor dead lines of your dead lover,

Compare them with the bettering of the time, and though every pen should excel them, reserve (preserve) them for my love, not for their rhyme, which may be exceeded (surpassed) by the poetry of happier men.

Then vouchsafe me but this loving thought: 'Had my friend's muse grown with his age. (improved as promised by his youth) his love would have yielded a dearer birth, (better poetry) to march in ranks of better equipage; (to rank in a higher class).

But since he died, and other poets have proved better, I'll read their's for their style, his for his love!'

Shakespeare did not expect that after his death, wine in the abstract, could survive in the personality with which he had endowed it, and be capable of reading, remembering and perpetuating as set forth in the sonnet. He has evidently associated with wine in his idealizing of it, its votaries and defenders, who were probably his companions in the times of his indulgences. Possibly, as will be noticed hereafter, to some of these friends (probably Mr. W. H., whoever he may have been), the sonnets were delivered as they were written. For more than ten years before their publication, it is known that they, or some of them, were in circulation among his private friends, which shows they were circulated by his permission. It is not unreasonable to conclude that these recipients believed that the sonnets were actually intended to be addressed to them personally. It is the writer's belief that several of the sonnets hereafter to be reviewed were actually written to these bibulous companions, and that Sonnet 26 and this one are the first of such. This sonnet particularly, is not addressed to wine, and has no direct reference to it.

Under 21 it was noted that Shakespeare had declared a reformation in his style, and had avowed to eschew grandiloquence and self-praise. So far he has kept his promise, and in this last sonnet speaks with discouragement of the qualities of his verse. It is evident that he must have realized a deterioration in his poetical faculty, for the last few sonnets are certainly below the level of his best. Possibly he had begun to realize, that an excess of wine is as far from poetical inspiration, as is the lack of it.

SONNET 33.

Full many a glorious morning have I seen
Flatter the mountain-tops with sovereign eye,
Kissing with golden face the meadows green,
Gilding pale streams with heavenly alchemy;
Anon permit the basest clouds to ride
With ugly rack on his celestial face,
And from the forlorn world his visage hide,
Stealing unseen to west with this disgrace:
Even so my sun one early morn did shine
With all-triumphant splendour on my brow;
But, out, alack! he was but one hour mine,
The region cloud hath mask'd him from me now.
    Yet him for this my love no whit disdaineth;
    Suns of the world may stain when heaven's sun staineth.

Many a glorious morning have I seen the sovereign eye (the sun) flatter the mountain tops, kissing the meadows, gilding pale streams with heavenly alchemy;

Anon permit basest clouds to ride on his celestial face, and hide his visage from the forlorn world, stealing unseen to the west with his disgrace (obscured by clouds);

Even so my sun (fame) one early morn (in youth) shone with splendor on my brow; but out alack! he was but one hour mine, the cloud has masked him from me now.

Yet I do not disdain him for this; suns of the world may stain (be obscured) when heaven's sun stains.

SONNET 34.

Why didst thou promise such a beauteous day,
And make me travel forth without my cloak,
To let base clouds o'ertake me in my way,
Hiding thy bravery in their rotten smoke?
'Tis not enough that through the cloud thou break,
To dry the rain on my storm-beaten face,
For no man well of such a salve can speak
That heals the wound and cures not the disgrace:
Nor can thy shame give physic to my grief;
Though thou repent, yet I have still the loss:
The offender's sorrow lends but weak relief
To him that bears the strong offence's cross.
    Ah, but those tears are pearl which thy love sheds,
    And they are rich and ransom all ill deeds.

Wine, why did you promise such a beauteous day (such excellence), and make me travel forth without my cloak (without other reliance), to let clouds (troubles) overtake me, hiding your bravery (promised help) in their smoke?

'Tis not enough that you break through the clouds, to dry the rain (tears) on my storm-beaten face, for one may not speak well of such a salve (assistance) that heals the wound but does not cure the disgrace (the appetite): Nor can your shame give physic (relief) to my grief; though you repent, yet I have still the loss (disgrace): the offender's sorrow lends weak relief to him who bears the offence's cross.

But those tears are pearl, which you love shed (the drops which give relief) and they are rich and ransom (make amends) for all ill deeds.

SONNET 35.

No more be grieved at that which thou hast done:
Roses have thorns, and silver fountains mud;
Clouds and eclipses stain both moon and sun,
And loathsome canker lives in sweetest bud.
All men make faults, and even I in this,
Authorizing thy trespass with compare,
Myself corrupting, salving thy amiss,
Excusing thy sins more than thy sins are;
For to thy sensual fault I bring in sense—
Thy adverse party is thy advocate—
And 'gainst myself a lawful plea commence:
Such civil war is in my love and hate,
    That I an accessary needs must be
    To that sweet thief which sourly robs from me.

No more be grieved, Wine, at that which you have done: roses have thorns, fountains mud, clouds and eclipses dim both sun and moon, and canker destroys the sweetest bud.

All men err, as I have in this, consenting to your trespass with compare (by my example), corrupting myself, salving (condoning) your wrong, excusing your sins more than your sins are (pardoning your sins which were hardly sins);

For to your sensual fault, I bring in sense (my judgment realizes the nature of your fault)—and I your adverse party become your advocate —and against myself a lawful plea commence (I plead by accusing myself): my love and hate of you are at such war,

That I am accessary (accomplice) needs must be to you, the thief that robs me.

SONNET 36.

Let me confess that we two must be twain,
Although our undivided loves are one:
So shall those blots that do with me remain,
Without thy help, by me be borne alone.
In our two loves there is but one respect,
Though in our lives a separable spite,
Which though it alter not love's sole effect,
Yet doth it steal sweet hours from love's delight.
I may not evermore acknowledge thee,
Lest my bewailed guilt should do thee shame,
Nor thou with public kindness honour me,
Unless thou take that honour from thy name:
    But do not so; I love thee in such sort,
    As thou being mine, mine is thy good report.

Let me confess that we two (wine and I) must be twain, although our loves are one (mutual): so those blots that remain with me, I will bear without your help, Wine.

In our two loves there is but one respect, though in our lives there is a separable spite (distrust) which though it alters not love's sole effect (the mutuality of our love), yet does it steal sweet hours from love's delight (being suspicious of each other our happiness is marred).

I may not at all times acknowledge you, lest my guilt should do you shame, nor need you with public kindness honor me, unless that might take honor from your name:

Nor need you do so; for I love you so, that you are mine, as are your praises.

There is a suggestion in this sonnet that Shakespeare avoided public drinking to avoid disgrace to himself, and discredit to his much beloved Wine. He seems quite as solicitous for wine's welfare and character as for his own,—not an uncommon thing among drunkards, who will neither defend or condemn the use of intoxicants.

SONNET 37.

As a decrepit father takes delight
To see his active child do deeds of youth,
So I, made lame by fortune's dearest spite,
Take all my comfort of thy worth and truth;
For whether beauty, birth, or wealth, or wit,
Or any of these all, or all, or more,
Entitled in thy parts do crowned sit,
I make my love engrafted to this store:
So then I am not lame, poor, nor despised,
Whilst that this shadow doth such substance give
That I in thy abundance am sufficed
And by a part of all thy glory live.
    Look, what is best, that best I wish in thee:
    This wish I have; then ten times happy me!

As a decrepit father delights to see his child do deeds of youth, so I made lame (an addict) by fortune's dearest spite (wine), of your worth and truth (inspiration) take all my comfort;

For whether beauty, birth, wealth or wit, or any or all of these, or more (or other virtues) entitled in your parts do crowned sit, (are entitled to be considered of your attributes) I make my love engrafted to this (your) store: (On your qualities whatever they be I have fixed my love.)

So I am not lame, poor nor despised, whilst this your shadow gives such substance, that I in your abundance am sufficed (my cravings satisfied) and I live by having a part of your glory (inspiration).

Look what is best (imagine the best thing in the world), that best thing I wish in you: this wish I have (this wish being granted), then ten times happy me.

SONNET 38.

How can my Muse want subject to invent,
While thou dost breathe, that pour'st into my verse
Thine own sweet argument, too excellent
For every vulgar paper to rehearse?
O, give thyself the thanks, if aught in me
Worthy perusal stand against thy sight;
For who's so dumb that cannot write to thee,
When thou thyself dost give invention light?
Be thou the tenth Muse, ten times more in worth
Than those old nine which rhymers invocate;
And he that calls on thee, let him bring forth
Eternal numbers to outlive long date.
    If my slight Muse do please these curious days,
    The pain be mine, but thine shall be the praise.

How can my Muse want subject to invent, while you that breathe (exist), Wine, pour into my verse your own argument (theme) too excellent for every vulgar paper to rehearse.

Give yourself the thanks, if aught in me is worthy of perusal, that may come to your sight; for who is so dumb (stupid) that cannot write to you, when you yourself given invention light (supply the inspiration). Be you the tenth Muse, ten times more in worth than those old nine, which rhymers invocate; and he that calls on you, let him bring forth eternal numbers.

If my Muse please these days, the pain (care) be mine but yours the praise (it came through your inspiration).

What a contrast now, with those sonnets written before the poet had constructed his god of wine, and while it was yet a cloudy vision without form. Though it has been some time in the forming, not until now has it become a matured fetish. From the servant, it has become the Master—the Usurper.

SONNET 39.

O, how thy worth with manners may I sing,
When thou art all the better part of me?
What can mine own praise to mine own self bring?
And what is't but mine own when I praise thee?
Even for this let us divided live,
And our dear love lose name of single one,
That by this separation I may give
That due to thee which thou deservest alone.
O absence, what a torment wouldst thou prove,
Were it not thy sour leisure gave sweet leave
To entertain the time with thoughts of love,
Which time and thoughts so sweetly doth deceive,
    And that thou teachest how to make one twain,
    By praising him here who doth hence remain!

Wine, how may I sing your worth with manners (without indulging in self-praise) when you are the better part of me? What can I bring to myself by praising myself? And when I praise you what do I more than praise myself?

Therefore that I may praise you let us divided live, and our love lose the name of single one, then may I give that due (praise) to you which you deserve alone.

What a torment would absence from you prove, were it not, your sour leisure (absence) gave leave to entertain the time with thoughts of love, which love, time and thoughts sweetly (agreeably) deceive,

And that you teach how to make one (yourself) twain, by praising him here who remains away. (Absence how tormenting; were it not that I can spend the time in anticipation, thus being deceived by time and thoughts, by making you twain—here in my thoughts, and yet absent.)

It would seem that there were times when Shakespeare was compelled either by compulsion or conditions, to exercise abstinence.

In the last line wine is referred to as 'him.'

SONNET 40.

Take all my loves, my love, yea, take them all;
What hast thou then more than thou hadst before?
No love, my love, that thou mayst true love call;
All mine was thine before thou hadst this more.
Then, if for my love thou my love receivest,
I cannot blame thee for my love thou usest;
But yet be blamed, if thou this self deceivest
By wilful taste of what thyself refusest.
I do forgive thy robbery, gentle thief,
Although thou steal thee all my poverty:
And yet, love knows, it is a greater grief
To bear love's wrong than hate's known injury.
  Lascivious grace, in whom all ill well shows,
  Kill me with spites; yet we must not be foes.

Wine, take all my loves, then what would you have more than you have had before? No love that you may call true love (you have had all that you could call true love); all that was mine was yours before you took this more (this last one).

Then if for my love you have received her whom I love, I cannot blame you that you use my love; but yet be blamed if you deceive this self (her) by wilful taste of what this self (she) refuses. (If you induce her to partake of that which she refuses.)

I forgive your robbery, gentle thief, although you steal all my property; (what little I have? or does it mean I am rich when I am drunk?) and yet, love knows, it is a greater grief to be wronged by ones love than by hate (his enemy).

Lascivious grace (spirit of wine) in whom ill seems good, kill me with spites (though you kill me with wrongs) we must not be foes.

This Sonnet 40 and the following two 41 and 42 are to be construed by themselves, as relating to a subject that is not elsewhere touched upon in the sonnets. They relate the fact that Shakespeare's wife, mistress or some loved female has fallen under the spell of intoxication, as Shakespeare has, and these three sonnets chronicle the deplorable fact.

SONNET 41.

Those pretty wrongs that liberty commits,
When I am sometime absent from thy heart,
Thy beauty and thy years full well befits,
For still temptation follows where thou art.
Gentle thou art, and therefore to be won,
Beauteous thou art, therefore to be assailed;
And when a woman woos, what woman's son
Will sourly leave her till he have prevailed?
Ay me! but yet thou mightst my seat forbear,
And chide thy beauty and thy straying youth,
Who lead thee in their riot even there
Where thou art forced to break a twofold truth,
    Hers, by thy beauty tempting her to thee,
    Thine, by thy beauty being false to me.

Those pretty wrongs that liberty commits, when I am sometimes absent from your heart, Wine, (when I am sometimes sober) well befit your beauty and years, for still temptation follows you.

You are gentle and therefore to be won, beauteous and therefore to be assailed; and when a woman woos what man will leave her till he have prevailed?

But you might my seat forbear (respect) and chide (control) your beauty and your straying youth, who lead you in your riot even there, where you are forced to break a twofold truth,

Hers, by your beauty tempting her to you, yours, by your beauty being false to me.

The sonnet both accuses and condones wine for ensnaring the woman he loves. It is indicated that this happened when the poet was sometimes absent from wine's heart. The only conclusion to be drawn from this is, that Shakespeare and his love indulged together in convivality, but that the present case is exceptional, and that her indulgence in this instance occurred while Shakespeare was soberly absent.

In this sonnet the masculine character of the addressee is indicated.

SONNET 42.

That thou hast her, it is not all my grief,
And yet it may be said I loved her dearly;
That she hath thee, is of my wailing chief,
A loss in love that touches me more nearly.
Loving offenders, thus I will excuse ye:
Thou dost love her, because thou know'st I love her;
And for my sake even so doth she abuse me,
Suffering my friend for my sake to approve her.
If I lose thee, my loss is my love's gain,
And losing her, my friend hath found that loss;
Both find each other, and I lose both twain,
And both for my sake lay on me this cross:
    But here's the joy: my friend and I are one;
    Sweet flattery! then she loves but me alone.

That you, Wine, have her is not all my grief, and yet I loved her dearly, that she has you (has the appetite for you) is my chief complaint, a loss that touches me more nearly (seriously).

Loving offenders, thus I will excuse you: You, Wine, love her because you know I do, and for my sake she abuses me by suffering my friend, Wine, to approve (accept) her.

If I lose you, Wine, that is the gain of her I love, and losing her, my friend Wine gains her; then both find each other, and I lose you both, and both for my sake lay on me this cross:

But here's the joy; Wine and I are one, then she loves but me alone (her love for wine is love for me alone).

SONNET 43.

When most I wink, then do mine eyes best see,
For all the day they view things unrespected;
But when I sleep, in dreams they look on thee,
And, darkly bright, are bright in dark directed.
Then thou, whose shadow shadows doth make bright,
How would thy shadow's form form happy show
To the clear day with thy much clearer light,
When to unseeing eyes thy shade shines so!
How would, I say, mine eyes be blessed made
By looking on thee in the living day,
When in dead night thy fair imperfect shade
Through heavy sleep on sightless eyes doth stay!
    All days are nights to see till I see thee,
    And nights bright days when dreams do show thee me.

I see best when most I wink (when my eyes are closed), for all the day they view things unrespected (without interest); but when I sleep I dream of you Wine, and darkly bright (what is dark in day) are bright in dark (night).

Then you, Wine, whose shadow makes the shadows (gloom) bright, how happy the show which your shadow forms to the clear day with your clearer light, when to unseeing eyes, at night, you shine so!

How would my eyes be blessed by looking on you in the living day, when in dead night your fair, but imperfect shade, though heavy sleep, on my sightless eyes doth stay!

All days are nights, to my sight, till I see you, and nights are bright days when dreams show you to me.

SONNET 44.

If the dull substance of my flesh were thought,
Injurious distance should not stop my way;
For then, despite of space, I would be brought,
From limits far remote, where thou dost stay.
No matter then although my foot did stand
Upon the farthest earth removed from thee;
For nimble thought can jump both sea and land,
As soon as think the place where he would be.
But, ah, thought kills me, that I am not thought,
To leap large lengths of miles when thou art gone,
But that, so much of earth and water wrought,
I must attend time's leisure with my moan;
    Receiving nought by elements so slow
    But heavy tears, badges of either's woe.

If the substance of my flesh were thought, O Wine, distance should not stop my way (separate us), for then despite of space I would be brought from far away to where you stay.

No matter then though I should stand upon the earth, farthest from you; for thought can jump both sea and land as soon as think where you are.

But the thought kills me, that I am not thought, to leap lengths of miles when you are gone, but that there is so much of earth and water, and I must attend (wait) time's leisure with my moan (distress);

Receiving nothing by elements so slow (earth and water) but tears, badges of our woe.

SONNET 45.

The other two, slight air and purging fire,
Are both with thee, wherever I abide;
The first my thought, the other my desire,
These present-absent with swift motion slide.
For when these quicker elements are gone
In tender embassy of love to thee,
My life, being made of four, with two alone
Sinks down to death, oppress'd with melancholy;
Until life's composition be recured
By those swift messengers return'd from thee,
Who even but now come back again, assured
Of thy fair health, recounting it to me:
    This told, I joy; but then no longer glad,
    I send them back again, and straight grow sad.

The other two elements (besides earth and water) air and fire, are both with you wherever I may be; the first (air) my thoughts, the other (fire) my desire, these present-absent (here-there) with swift motion slide (quickly come and go).

For when these quicker elements are gone in tender embassy of love to you, my life being made of four (earth, water, air and fire) with two alone, (earth and water) sinks down to death oppressed with melancholy;

Until life's composition is recured (restored) by those swift messengers (air and fire, thoughts and desires) returned from you, who even now come back again (he takes a drink), assuring me of your fair health:

This told (thus refreshed) I joy; but then no longer glad (desiring more) I send them back again, and straight grow sad (waiting their return).

SONNET 46.

Mine eye and heart are at a mortal war,
How to divide the conquest of thy sight;
Mine eye my heart thy picture's sight would bar,
My heart mine eye the freedom of that right.
My heart doth plead that thou in him dost lie,
A closet never pierced with crystal eyes,
But the defendant doth that plea deny,
And says in him thy fair appearance lies.
To 'cide this title is impanneled
A quest of thoughts, all tenants to the heart;
And by their verdict is determined
The clear eye's moiety and the dear heart's part:
　　As thus; mine eye's due is thine outward part,
　　And my heart's right thine inward love of heart.

My eye (reason) and heart (appetite, cravings) are at war how, Wine, to estimate the conquest of your sight (power). My eye would bar my heart your pictures sight; my heart would bar my eye the freedom of that right.

My heart (cravings) pleads that you Wine, in him do lie, (that it has the right of decision), but the defendant (eye) denies that plea, and says in him (the eye) your fair appearance is a lie.

To decide this title (question) is empanelled an inquest (jury) of thoughts, all, tenants of the heart, and by their verdict they determine what part belongs to the eye, and what to the heart;

Thus: The eye's due is the outward part (the sight, taste and smell) and to the heart your inward love of heart (the effects).

SONNET 47.

Betwixt mine eye and heart a league is took,
And each doth good turns now unto the other:
When that mine eye is famish'd for a look,
Or heart in love with sighs himself doth smother,
With my love's picture then my eye doth feast
And to the painted banquet bids my heart;
Another time mine eye is my heart's guest
And in his thoughts of love doth share a part:
So, either by thy picture or my love,
Thyself away art present still with me;
For thou not farther than my thoughts canst move,
And I am still with them and they with thee;
    Or, if they sleep, thy picture in my sight
    Awakes my heart to heart's and eye's delight.

Betwixt my eye and heart a league (compact) is made, and each does good turns unto the other: When my eye (senses) are famished for a look (are thirsty), or when my heart smothers himself with sighs. With Wine's picture (taste) my senses feast, and to the banquet bids my heart (cravings); another time my eye is my heart's guest and in his (heart's) love shares a part:

So Wine, either by your picture or my love, you thought absent, are present with me; for you cannot move farther than my thoughts, and I am still with my thoughts, and they with you;

Or if my thoughts sleep, your picture awakes my heart to heart's and eye's delight.

SONNET 48.

How careful was I, when I took my way,
Each trifle under truest bars to thrust,
That to my use it might unused stay
From hands of falsehood, in sure wards of trust!
But thou, to whom my jewels trifles are,
Most worthy comfort, now my greatest grief,
Thou, best of dearest and mine only care,
Art left the prey of every vulgar thief.
Thee have I not lock'd up in any chest,
Save where thou art not, though I feel thou art,
Within the gentle closure of my breast,
From whence at pleasure thou mayst come and part;
    And even thence thou wilt be stol'n, I fear,
    For truth proves thievish for a prize so dear.

How careful was I when I made my choice, each trifle under truest bars to thrust (to guard myself against each excess), that to my use, Wine might from hands of falsehood (misuse) stay unused, in sure wards of trust (in strict bounds).

But to you Wine, to whom my jewels are but trifles, my worthy comfort and my greatest grief, best of things that are dearest, and my only care, are left the prey to every vulgar thief (instead of being held in restriction, your use has become an abuse, a continuous theft, in violation of my resolution).

I have not locked you in any chest, save within the closure of my breast, where you are not locked, though I feel you are, but from whence at pleasure you may come and part:

And even from there I fear you will be stolen, for truth (those who would be faithful) proves thievish for a prize so dear.

SONNET 49.

Against that time, if ever that time come,
When I shall see thee frown on my defects,
When as thy love hath cast his utmost sum,
Call'd to that audit by advised respects;
Against that time when thou shalt strangely pass,
And scarcely greet me with that sun, thine eye,
When love, converted from the thing it was,
Shall reasons find of settled gravity;
Against that time do I ensconce me here
Within the knowledge of mine own desert,
And this my hand against myself uprear,
To guard the lawful reasons on thy part:
    To leave poor me thou hast the strength of laws,
    Since why to love I can allege no cause.

If ever the time shall come when I shall see you frown on my defects (disown me for my faults), when your love has cast his utmost sum (has come to a final conclusion), called to that result by advised respect (well considered judgment);

When you shall strangely pass (as a stranger), and scarcely greet me with your eye, when love converted from the thing it was, shall find reasons of settled gravity; (for good cause).

Against that time do I ensconce me here within the knowledge of my own desert, and this my hand against myself upraise (swear) to guard the lawful reasons on your part (to justify your action):

To leave poor me you have the strength of laws (a legal excuse) since why to love me I can allege no cause.

SONNET 50.

How heavy do I journey on the way,
When what I seek, my weary travel's end,
Doth teach that ease and that repose to say,
'Thus far the miles are measured from thy friend!'
The beast that bears me, tired with my woe,
Plods dully on, to bear that weight in me,
As if by some instinct the wretch did know
His rider loved not speed, being made from thee:
The bloody spur cannot provoke him on
That sometimes anger thrusts into his hide;
Which heavily he answers with a groan,
More sharp to me than spurring to his side;
　　For that same groan doth put this in my mind;
　　My grief lies onward, and my joy behind.

How heavily (wearily) I journey on my way, when the end of my travel teaches the ease and repose awaiting me to say, 'Thus far the miles are measured from my friend' (Wine)!

The beast that bears me (my body) tired with my woe, plods dully on, to bear that weight of woe in me, as if by some instinct the wretch knew his rider (cravings) loved not speed, being made from you:

The bloody spur (necessity) that sometimes anger thrusts into his side cannot provoke him on, which spur he answers with a groan, more sharp to me than spurring to his side.

For that groan puts this in my mind; my grief lies onward, and my joy behind.

The journey mentioned in this sonnet is a mental and not a physical one. The poet is being restrained, or is restraining himself in the use of stimulants, and is passing through that trying period of reinstatement to normal, when he can subsist without the help of wine. In such stages the drinker is grievously depressed mentally, and to him undoubtedly the ordeal seems endless, wearisome and full of woe.

SONNET 51.

Thus can my love excuse the slow offence
Of my dull bearer when from thee I speed:
From where thou art why should I haste me thence?
Till I return, of posting is no need.
O, what excuse will my poor beast then find,
When swift extremity can seem but slow?
Then should I spur, though mounted on the wind,
In winged speed no motion shall I know:
Then can no horse with my desire keep pace;
Therefore desire, of perfect'st love being made,
Shall neigh—no dull flesh—in his fiery race;
But love, for love, thus shall excuse my jade;
    Since from thee going he went wilful-slow,
    Towards thee I'll run and give him leave to go.

Thus, can my love, Wine, excuse the slow offense (weary abstinence) of my dull bearer, when from you I speed: from where you are why should I haste me thence? Till I return of posting (hasting) is no need.

What excuse will my poor beast (body) then find when swift extremity can seem but slow? Then should I spur though mounted on the wind, in winged speed, no motion shall I know:

Then can no horse keep pace with my desire, therefore desire (craving) being made of perfectest love, shall neigh in his fiery race; but my love for my love, (Wine) shall excuse my jade;

Since from you going he went wilful slow, towards you I'll run, and give him leave to go.

In his gloom depicted in the preceding sonnet, Shakespeare was 'tapering off' by gradually lessening the use of stimulants. This he likened to a slow and agonizing journey which is bearing him further and further away from his love. In this last sonnet he is looking forward to the time when he may renew his pleasures through a new indulgence. His imagination looks forward to such a time, after a period of abstinence, as full of exhilaration and expectancy. His return to his love he likens to a smooth, magical flight, when he would spur, 'though mounted on the wind,' and 'in winged speed no motion' would he know. He knew his subject well.

SONNET 52.

So am I as the rich, whose blessed key
Can bring him to his sweet up-locked treasure,
The which he will not every hour survey,
For blunting the fine point of seldom pleasure.
Therefore are feasts so solemn and so rare,
Since, seldom coming, in the long year set,
Like stones of worth they thinly placed are,
Or captain jewels in the carcanet.
So is the time that keeps you as my chest,
Or as the wardrobe which the robe doth hide,
To make some special instant special blest,
By new unfolding his imprison'd pride.
   Blessed are you, whose worthiness gives scope,
   Being had, to triumph, being lack'd, to hope.

I am as the rich, whose blessed key can bring him to his locked-up treasure, which he will not every hour survey, lest it should blunt the fine point of seldom pleasure.

Therefore are feasts (drinks) so seldom and so rare, since seldom coming in the long year set, like stones of worth, they are thinly placed, or like captain jewels in the carcanet.

So is the time (of abstinence) that keeps (withholds) you, Wine, as a chest, or as the wardrobe, which hides the robe, to make some special instance (of partaking) specially blest, by a new unfolding of his imprisoned pride, (forbidden wine).

Blessed are you, Wine, whose worthiness gives scope, (has the quality), being had, to triumph; being lacked, to hope.

The sonnet indicates that Shakespeare had been put, or had put himself, upon a limited allowance of wine for a year, and that he was restricted to only an occasional indulgence. When the time came for a drink, then was his triumph, and between drinks he could indulge the pleasure of hope, of anticipation.

SONNET 53.

What is your substance, whereof are you made,
That millions of strange shadows on you tend?
Since every one hath, every one, one shade,
And you, but one, can every shadow lend.
Describe Adonis, and the counterfeit
Is poorly imitated after you;
On Helen's cheek all art of beauty set,
And you in Grecian tires are painted new:
Speak of the spring and foison of the year,
The one doth shadow of your beauty show,
The other as your bounty doth appear;
And you in every blessed shape we know.
    In all external grace you have some part,
    But you like none, none you, for constant heart.

What is your substance Wine, and of what are you made, that you cast millions of strange shadows? Since every one has one shade, and you, who are but one, can lend every shadow.

Describe Adonis and the counterfeit (picture) is a poor imitation of you; adorn Helen with the beauties of all art, and that would be a picture of you in Grecian attire;

Speak of the spring and foison (harvest) of the year,—spring is as your beauty, and the harvest as your bounty;—and you in every blessed shape we know (everything that is blessed is like you).

You have some part in all external grace, but you are like none, and none are like you, for constant heart.

Like in sonnet 20, Shakespeare here gives to wine the combined masculine and feminine attributes, and leaves it a neuter.

SONNET 54.

O, how much more doth beauty beauteous seem
By that sweet ornament which truth doth give!
The rose looks fair, but fairer we it deem
For that sweet odour which doth in it live.
The canker-blooms have full as deep a dye
As the perfumed tincture of the roses,
Hang on such thorns, and play as wantonly
When summer's breath their masked buds discloses:
But, for their virtue only is their show,
They live unwoo'd and unrespected fade;
Die to themselves. Sweet roses do not so;
Of their sweet deaths are sweetest odours made:
　　And so of you, beauteous and lovely youth,
　　When that shall vade, by verse distills your truth

How much more beauteous does beauty seem, when it has the charm
of truth! The rose looks fair, but we deem it fairer for its sweet odour.
The canker-blooms (the dog rose or wild rose) has full as deep a
dye, as the perfumed roses, hang on such thorns, and play as wantonly
when their buds by summer are disclosed:
But their show is their only virtue, they live unwooed and neglected
fade; die to themselves. Not so with sweet roses; of them sweetest
odours are made:
And so of you (my genius), beauteous and lovely youth, when that
(your youth) shall vade, my verse distills your truth.

SONNET 55.

Not marble, nor the gilded monuments
Of princes, shall outlive this powerful rhyme?
But you shall shine more bright in theese contents
Than unswept stone, besmear'd with sluttish time.
When wasteful war shall statues overturn,
And broils root out the work of masonry,
Nor Mars his sword nor war's quick fire shall burn
The living record of your memory.
'Gainst death and all-oblivious enmity
Shall you pace forth; your praise shall still find room
Even in the eyes of all posterity
That wear this world out to the ending doom.
   So, till the judgement that yourself arise,
   You live in this, and dwell in lovers' eyes.

Not marble nor prince's monuments shall outlive this rhyme; but I shall shine more bright in them, than unswept stone, besmeared (corroded) by time.

When war shall statues overturn, and broils destroy masonry, neither the sword of Mars, nor war's fires shall burn this (verses) living record of my memory.

Against death and oblivion shall I pace forth; my praise shall still find room in the eyes of posterity, that wear this world out to the ending doom.

So till the judgment that myself arise (until the resurrection) I live in this rhyme, and dwell in lover's (admirers) eyes.

SONNET 56.

Sweet love, renew thy force; be it not said
Thy edge should blunter be than appetite,
Which but to-day by feeding is allay'd,
To-morrow sharpen'd in his former might:
So, love, be thou; although to-day thou fill
Thy hungry eyes even till they wink with fulness,
To-morrow see again, and do not kill
The spirit of love with a perpetual dulness.
Let this sad interim like the ocean be
Which parts the shore, where two contracted new
Come daily to the banks, that, when they see
Return of love, more blest may be the view;
   Or call it winter, which, being full of care,
   Makes summer's welcome thrice more wish'd, more rare.

Sweet love, Wine, renew your force; let not your edge (effect) be blunter than appetite, which to-day by feeding is satisfied, to-morrow sharpened in his former might;

So love be you; although to-day you fill your hungry eyes till they wink (close) with fulness, to-morrow see again, and do not kill the spirit of love with perpetual dullness. (Do not drink continuously to intoxication, but relieve the dullness of constant drinking with periods of soberness).

Let this sad interim (of soberness) be like the ocean which parts the shore, where two new lovers come daily to the banks, that when they see return of love, more blest may be the view.

Else call it (soberness) winter, which being full of care, makes summer's welcome thrice more wished.

SONNET 57.

Being your slave, what should I do but tend
Upon the hours and times of your desire?
I have no precious time at all to spend,
Nor services to do, till you require.
Nor dare I chide the world-without-end hour
Whilst I, my sovereign, watch the clock for you,
Nor think the bitterness of absence sour
When you have bid your servant once adieu;
Nor dare I question with my jealous thought
Where you may be, or your affairs suppose,
But, like a sad slave, stay and think of nought
Save, where you are how happy you make those.
    So true a fool is love that in your will,
    Though you do any thing, he thinks no ill.

Being your slave, Wine, what should I do but tend upon the times of your desire? I have no time that is precious to spend, nor services to do, till you require.

Nor dare I to complain of the world-without-end hour (the hour of divine service), whilst I watch the clock for you, my sovereign, nor think your absence sour, when you have bid your servant once adieu;

Nor dare I question with my jealous thought where you may be, or speculate on your affairs, but like a slave stay and think of nought, but how happy you make those where you are.

So true a fool is love, that do what you will, he thinks no ill.

The Century Dictionary defines the words "world-without-end," as never ending, and cites this sonnet to support the definition. Notwithstanding, the words have been here defined as the hour of divine service, because of the fact that the Te Deum Laudamus, which is generally read or chanted at church services ends with the words "world without end," and they are universally recognized only in connection with church services. That this is the proper construction is made almost, if not altogether, certain by the fact that at the time the sonnets were written there existed an Act of Parliament prohibiting the sale of liquors during the hours of divine services on Sunday, and also after 9 o'clock in the evening. In this light it is evident why Shakespeare should watch the clock so anxiously, during the hour of church service for the termination of the prohibition. The authority for the statement concerning the act of Parliament is 16 Encyclopaedia Brittannica, Eleventh Ed. under the title "Liquor Laws," at page 761.

SONNET 58.

That god forbid that made me first your slave,
I should in thought control your times of pleasure,
Or at your hand the account of hours to crave,
Being your vassal, bound to stay your leisure!
O, let me suffer, being at your beck,
The imprison'd absence of your liberty;
And patience, tame to sufferance, bide each check,
Without accusing you of injury.
Be where you list, your charter is so strong
That you yourself may privilege your time
To what you will; to you it doth belong
Yourself to pardon of self-doing crime.
    I am to wait, though waiting so be hell,
    Not blame your pleasure, be it ill or well.

That god, Wine, that made me first your slave, forbid that I should in thought (through reason) control your time of pleasure, or that I should crave (ask) and account of your time, I being your vassal and bound to await your leisure!

Let me suffer, being at your beck, the compelled absence of your liberty (the right to indulge); and patience tame to sufferance (obedient) bide each check (restraint) without accusing you of injury.

Be where you list (will) your charter (right) is so strong, that you may do with your time as you will; to you the right belongs to pardon yourself for your own crimes.

I am to wait, though waiting be hell, and not blame your pleasure though it be ill or well.

Shakespeare charges a god of myths, and not God, for making him a slave to wine—a very clear indication of his idea of the manner of his thraldom. That thraldom is so clearly expressed in this and the two preceding sonnets, that nothing less than an open naming of wine could make it clearer, or add to the identification. Shakespeare's liberation for his year of abstinence is not yet complete.

SONNET 59.

If there be nothing new, but that which is
Hath been before, how are our brains beguiled,
Which, labouring for invention, bear amiss
The second burthen of a former child!
O, that record could with a backward look,
Even of five hundred courses of the sun,
Show me your image in some antique book,
Since mind at first in character was done.
That I might see what the old world could say
To this composed wonder of your frame;
Whether we are mended, or whether better they,
Or whether revolution be the same.
   O, sure I am, the wits of former days
   To subjects worse have given admiring praise.

If there be nothing new, but if that which is now, has been before, how are our brains beguiled, which laboring for invention, bear amiss the second burthen of a former child. (Without being conscious of it, we may but repeat what others have written.)

Oh, that a record of the past, even of five hundred years ago, could show me my image in some antique book, since man first began to write.

That I might see what the old world could say of my wonderful composition; whether we or they are better, or whether revolution (change) has left us the same.

I am sure the wits of former days, to worse subjects have given admiring praise.

Does not this sonnet say: That under the suggestion of recurring cycles, nothing occurs which has not occurred before; therefore, if this be true, what Shakespeare has expressed, has been expressed before, and that he would like to look backward to the time when man first began to write, or even five hundred years, and find his image in some antique book, that he might see what the old world could say of his wonderful composition; whether we or they are the better, or whether through change we remain the same? He is sure that the ancients gave admiring praise to worse subjects than his verse.

Beneath the words of the sonnet, but not expressed, but expressly implied, is Shakespeare's desire to look forward, not backward, and know what the future would say of the composed wonder of his poetry. This longing of his cannot be attributed either to egotism or vainglory, for it is evident he was not looking for pretentious honor or fame. He was not writing for his generation, but for the future. His ambition, his passion,—for it was nothing less—was not that he might live for the time but that his poetry might live for eternity. It was not a desire for a personal or individual glory, for the whole tenor of his life shows that William Shakespeare was to him of no importance. What he wished to perpetuate was the thing of marvel, which he had created, for in it, as in nothing else that man has fashioned, had been caught the flash of the vital spark of human passions.

SONNET 60.

Like as the waves make towards the pebbled shore,
So do our minutes hasten to their end;
Each changing place with that which goes before,
In sequent toil all forwards do contend.
Nativity, once in the main of light,
Crawls to maturity, wherewith being crown'd,
Crooked eclipses 'gainst his glory fight,
And Time that gave doth now his gift confound.
Time doth transfix the flourish set on youth
And delves the parallels in beauty's brow,
Feeds on the rarities of nature's truth,
And nothing stands but for his scythe to mow:
And yet to times in hope my verse shall stand,
Praising thy worth, despite his cruel hand.

Like as the waves make towards the shore, so do we to our end; each takes the place of what has gone before, in sequent toil all contend (press) forward.

Those born, once in the main (flood) of light, crawl to maturity, which having gained, crooked eclipses (troubles, ills) gainst his glory fight, and time that gave now confounds the gift.

Time destroys the freshness of youth, and plows furrows in beauty's brow, feeds on the choicest things of nature, and mows all things with his scythe.

And yet to future time my verse shall stand, praising my worth, despite Time's cruel hand.

SONNET 61.

Is it thy will thy image should keep open
My heavy eyelids to the weary night?
Dost thou desire my slumbers should be broken,
While shadows like to thee do mock my sight?
Is it thy spirit that thou send'st from thee
So far from home into my deeds to pry,
To find out shames and idle hours in me,
The scope and tenour of thy jealousy?
O, no! thy love, though much, is not so great:
It is my love that keeps mine eye awake;
Mine own true love that doth my rest defeat,
To play the watchman ever for thy sake:
   For thee watch I whilst thou doth wake elsewhere,
   From me far off, with others all to near.

Is it your will, O Wine, that your image (cravings) should keep my eyelids open to the weary night? Do you desire that my slumbers should be broken, while shadows like to you (thought of you) mock my sight?

Is it your spirit that you send so far from home, to pry into my deeds, to find my shames, and idle hours (mortification and idleness) the scope and tenour of your jealousy?

No, your love though much, is not so great; it is my love of you that keeps my eye awake; it is my own true love of you that defeats my rest, to play the watchman for you.

I watch for you while you are elsewhere, far off from me, with others.

In this, as in several other sonnets, and in the poems to be reviewed, night time seems to be a period of privation to Shakespeare. May this not be because of the law before referred to, which prohibited the furnishing of liquor after nine o'clock at night? (see under Sonnet 57.)

With the last sonnet—61—we are done for a time—until 75 —with Wine. Evidently Shakespeare has after a long and tedious preparation seasoned himself for the year of droughth, which he announced in Sonnet 52. Since then there has been a promiscuous mingling of sonnets treating of wine and other subjects. Sonnets 53, 56, 57, 58 and 61 are devoted to wine, and each and all of these indicate that he is under restraint in its use. The other four, 54, 55, 59 and 60 are devoted to the praise of his verse. The interlarding of these sonnets might indicate that there has been some disarrangement in their order, or it may indicate that in his sobering period he was composing on both lines, and in the order as shown. In one group,—the latter —are the 'deep-brained' or philosophical sonnets, and in the other is shown the ordeal through which he was passing, from an excessive spell of intemperance, to soberness. The order of composition, here, is not important, and there would be no material aid through a rearrangement, even if it were thought that a better one were possible.

Let us look briefly into Shakespeare's life and habits, and from the facts at hand, determine as nearly as may be, something as to his manner of living and writing:

From the first to the twenty-sixth sonnet Shakespeare describes himself as being in the preliminary or initiative stage of drinking. In the 14th he accepted Wine as his helpmate and inspiration, and as is shown, in the 26th and following sonnets, he reached the first recorded collapse. Since then, and up to the 52d, the sonnets would indicate a continuous debauch. This conclusion however, would be an unfair one, for there is no sufficient evidence upon which to form an opinion as to the length of time covered in the composing of the last series of sonnets, nor is it permissible to conclude that there may not have been a considerable lapse of time between the composition of the several sonnets. In other words, the sonnets may not have been, and probably were not, the result of a continuous task. No conclusion, therefore can be drawn that he indulged continuously during the time of the writing of the sonnets.

As is well understood there are two kinds of drunkards. One is the habitual drinker—a man who comes to be known as a "soak"—who lives largely upon intoxicants, and to whom food— other food—is a secondary consideration. With such a man drinking begins with his rising—a "bracer"—and several, or many, are required to prepare the subject for breakfast. With him drink continues before and after meals, and until retiring. He is never drunk, but always full, and, as is well known, is often capable mentally and physically, and may be a well qualified business man. The other kind, or intermittent drinker, is one in whom one drink calls for another, in rapid succession, until complete inebriation ensues, and the drinker becomes wholly incapacitated, mentally and physically. Usually food is not taken nor desired, and the subject hastens to a complete collapse, and if drinking is continued, to delirium. In the last stages the disorder of nerves is terrible, and a man cannot be imagined in a more pitiable plight. The recovery proceeds through constant but lessening stimulation, until there is a complete restoration, and the subject enters on a period of abstinence, more or less prolonged. But, as is well known, while this class of drinkers must have spells of sobriety, periods of drunkenness seem quite as necessary to them. The result is alternating sprees, with the periods of abstinence between, continually growing shorter. The drunkard himself is just as incapable of offering an explanation for his appetite, as is the observer. The craving for drink with him is an irresistible one, and he yields to it fully appreciating the great suffering that must necessarily follow. Shakespeare calls it a lust, and describes it with wonderful effect, as will be seen hereafter.

Sonnets 26, 27 and 28, and 50, 51, and 52, show clearly the character of Shakespeare's weakness. He was what is known as a periodical drinker, and not a constant or perennial drunkard. The constant drinker usually has no such acute mental and nervous depressions as those described in these sonnets, although there is a constant and slow increase in his debility, both mental and physical. The crisis with him is generally long delayed, often for many years, and may not come at all before some organic weakness ends in death.

But, what does all this indicate? Simply this: That Shakespeare's writings, the bulk of them, were not done under the influence of intoxicants, but in his periods of soberness. His sonnets only,—and only some of them—and a very little of the poetry to be reviewed, are the lucubrations of an intoxicated mind. Some of the sonnets are the portrayals of Shakespeare in his periods of insobriety. In those periods, and in those sonnets written while under intoxication, wholly or partially, there is reflected little of the genius of his great verse. Undoubtedly Shakespeare in his cups, like other men, was frivolous, clouded and irresponsible, and probably imagined there was more beauty and depth in his thoughts and speech, than in reality was justified. Like other men, too, his mind may have run, while intoxicated, upon one subjeect, for instance Wine, and its elations, to the exclusion of all other subjects, and he may have believed himself capable of performing any task, however difficult, and may have imagined himself specially inspired by the very agent that, in fact, deprived him of his balance and better judgment.

But Shakespeare's greatest work, written in soberness, themselves show sobriety. Where else can we go to find so much that is truly deep and wise and beautiful? We cannot consent for a moment that this is, or could be, the product of an unbalanced or alcoholic brain. It is too clean and sturdy to have sprung from a tainted source. We know from experience what alcoholism produces, the vulgar, the distorted, the unnatural, the false, the indecent and the ugly, as it is itself, all of these. Never does it yield the true, the natural, the wise, the moral, the just and the beautiful, for it is none of these. It cannot escape from conforming to nature's great ordinance, that decrees that like shall yield its like. Shakespeare made Cassio say: "O, God, that men should put an enemy in their mouths to steal away their brains! that we should with joy, pleasance, revel and applause transform ourselves into beasts." That is sober talk, and was not written by a drunken man, although he may have known what drunkenness was. True, these are Cassio's words, and do not necessarily express Shakespeare's judgment, but he put them in Cassio's mouth, showing he knew the estimate of drunkenness.

Now look at the Sonnets! Are they all the products of a sober mind? Did ever sober men talk, as the author does in some of the Sonnets? In all the world is there a sober and intelligent man who will approve of the spirit of these? Is not every drunken man an exemplar of the sentiments expressed in those sonnets where Wine is lauded? Shakespeare under the influence of drink could, and did, write some of the sonnets, but drunk, could not have written some of the others, nor the great things of his plays. He was at all time, drunk or sober, a poet, and never lost expression, nor the wonderful rhythm of his poetry. Sober he expresseed the feelings and passions of his sober thoughts. Drunk he wrote correspondingly. When drinking, his feelings were joyous in exhilaration, gloomy in depression, wretched when his nerves rebelled, loving to that which yielded relief, and dispelled his misery, and, as will be seen, hating the same thing in his degradation. These were his drunken emotions, and these he found words to express.

Though it would probaly be unsafe to conclude such to be the case, apparently the Sonnets originated in the idea that their author felt that without the impetus which Wine would give, he would be unable to make headway in his literary progress. Whether this was in fact true, we cannot now determine, nor is it probable that Shakespeare himself was able to soberly calculate the effect that Wine would exert in the awakening·of his Muse. Even though it be conceded that at the time he first began the writing of the Sonnets, he was practicing absolute abstention, it is certain that he had not always before that time done so, for had such been the case, he would not have known of the inspiration which he was so sure would prove helpful to him. It is allowable therefore to conclude that he well knew the effects of wine, and that theretofore he had been its votary, and to such an extent, that his own judgment had called him to 'a reform. If that be true, we are justified in concluding that Shakespeare had already contracted an appetite for wine, and that it was not so much a case of wine being originally helpful, as it was that his cravings were demanding to be satisfied, and were crying out so loudly as to distract him from work. It was then a question of stilling the clamours of his cravings, which had already been born, in order that he might be allowed to apply himself to other demands. These conclusions are sustained, not only by inferences from what has gone before, but by detailed facts which will be found hereafter in the Sonnets, and in the poems to be discussed.

As seen, we have already reviewed four sober sonnets, intermixed with others having wine for a subject. All the following sonnets up to and including the 74th are free from allusions to wine, and are doubtless the work of a sober mind. In construing all of these we must revert to the plan adopted in the first series, by reading the sonnets as soliloquies, and by converting all third person references into the first person.

SONNET 62.

Sin of self-love possesseth all mine eye
And all my soul and all my every part;
And for this sin there is no remedy,
Is is so grounded inward in my heart.
Methinks no face so gracious is as mine,
No shape so true, no truth of such account;
And for myself mine own worth do define,
As I all other in all worths surmount.
But when my glass shows me myself indeed,
Beated and chopp'd with tann'd antiquity,
Mine own self-love quite contrary I read;
Self so self-loving were iniquity.
    'Tis thee, myself, that for myself I praise
    Painting my age with beauty of thy days.

My sin of self-love possesses all my eye (thoughts) and soul and every part of me; and for this sin there is no remedy, it is so grounded in my heart.

I think there is no face (verse) so gracious as is mine, no shape (meter) so true, no truth of such account, and for myself praise my own worth, as I surpass all others in all worths.

But when I look upon myself, beated and chopped (worn and wrinkled?), my self-love I value differently; to so love ones self were iniquity.

'T is thee (I), myself, that for myself I praise, painting my age with beauty of my days (with the poetry of my past).

This sonnet gives the key for the interpretation of the sonnets. Here it is expressly stated that the author is not addressing a third person, but himself. The last two lines of the sonnet say this as plainly as words can express it. Heretofore the sonnets have been interpreted by the substitution of a first person pronoun for those of the second and third persons. This is just what is here shown to be the purpose of the writer,

"T, is *thee, myself,* that for myself I praise," and in line 7 he says:
"And for myself my own worth do define,"

In other words his praise is for himself, and for no one else.

SONNET 63.

Against my love shall be, as I am now,
With Time's injurious hand crush'd and o'erworn;
When hours have drain'd his blood and fill'd his brow
With lines and wrinkles; when his youthful morn
Hath travell'd on to age's steepy night,
And all those beauties whereof now he's king
Are vanishing or vanish'd out of sight,
Stealing away the treasure of his spring;
For such a time do I now fortify
Against confounding age's cruel knife,
That he shall never cut from memory
My sweet love's beauty, though my lover's life:
　　His beauty shall in these black lines be seen,
　　And they shall live, and he in them still green.

Against (by the time) my love (my genius) shall be as I (my body) am now, crushed and worn by Time, when Time has impoverished its brow with lines and wrinkles; when its youth

Has reached old age, and all its present beauties are vanishing or vanished out of sight, stealing away the treasure of its spring (youth);

For such a time I now fortify, against age's cruel knife, that he shall never cut from memory, my love's (genius') beauty, though my lover's (genius') life.

Its beauty shall be seen in these black lines, and it shall live in them, still green.

SONNET 64.

When I have seen by Time's fell hand defaced
The rich-proud cost of outworn buried age;
When sometime lofty towers I see down-razed,
And brass eternal slave to mortal rage;
When I have seen the hungry ocean gain
Advantage on the kingdom of the shore,
And the firm soil win of the watery main,
Increasing store with loss and loss with store;
When I have seen such interchange of state,
Or state itself confounded to decay;
Ruin hath taught me thus to ruminate,
That Time will come and take my love away.
    This thought is as a death, which cannot choose
    But weep to have that which it fears to lose.

When I have seen by Time's hand defaced, the rich-proud cost of a buried age; when I see lofty towers razed and eternal brass slave (subject to) mortal rage (Times decay);

When I have seen the ocean gain, advantage on the shore, and the soil win of the sea, increasing gain with loss and loss with gain;

When I have seen such interchange (internal change) of state, or the state itself confounded to decay; ruin has taught me thus to ruminate, that Time will take my love (my genius) away.

This thought is as a death, which cannot choose but weep to have (possess) that which it fears to lose.

SONNET 65.

Since brass, nor stone, nor earth, nor boundless sea,
But sad mortality o'er-sways their power,
How with this rage shall beauty hold a plea
Whose action is no stronger than a flower?
O, how shall summer's honey breath hold out
Against the wreckful siege of battering days,
When rocks impregnable are not so stout,
Nor gates of steel so strong, but Time decays?
O fearful meditation! where, alack,
Shall Time's best jewel from Time's chest lie hid?
Or what strong hand can hold his swift foot back?
Or who his spoil of beauty can forbid?
    O, none, unless this miracle have might,
    That in black ink my love may still shine bright.

Since neither brass, stone, earth nor sea but mortality o'ersways with power, how with this rage (decay) shall beauty hold a plea (contend) whose action (right of action—right to be heard) is no stronger than a flower?

How shall summer's breath hold out against the siege of battering days, when impregnable rocks are not so stout, nor gates of steel so strong, but Time decays?

O fearful meditation! Where shall Times best jewel (product) from Time's chest (coffin) be hid? Or what hand can hold his swift foot (flight) back? Or who can forbid his spoil of beauty?

None, unless this miracle have might, that in black ink (my verse) my love (genius) may still shine.

SONNET 66.

Tired with all these, for restful death I cry,
As, to behold desert a beggar born,
And needy nothing trimm'd in jollity,
And purest faith unhappily forsworn,
And gilded honour shamefully misplaced,
And maiden virtue rudely strumpeted,
And right perfection wrongfully disgraced,
And strength by limping sway disabled,
And art made tongue-tied by authority,
And folly, doctor-like, controlling skill,
And simple truth miscall'd simplicity,
And captive good attending captain ill:
   Tired with all these, from these would I be gone,
   Save that, to die, I leave my love alone.

Tired with all these (what follows) I cry for death, as, to behold the deserving a beggar born, and needy nothing (good-for-nothing) trimmed in jollity, and purest faith forsworn (scoffed at),

And gilded honor shamefully misplaced (exalted), and maiden virtue strumpeted, and right disgraced (dishonored), and strength (character) by limping sway (incompetent rule) disabled,

And art made tongue-tied by authority (censored), and folly controlling skill, and simple truth miscalled simplicity (ignorance), and captive good attending (obeying) captain ill:

Tired with these, I would be gone, save that to die I leave my love (genius) alone. (It must also die.)

SONNET 67.

Ah, wherefore with infection should he live
And with his presence grace impiety,
That sin by him advantage should achieve
And lace itself with his society?
Why should false painting imitate his cheek,
And steal dead seeing of his living hue?
Why should poor beauty indirectly seek
Roses of shadow, since his rose is true?
Why should he live, now Nature bankrupt is,
Beggar'd of blood to blush through lively veins?
For she hath no exchequer now but his,
And, proud of many, lives upon his gains.
    O, him she stores, to show what wealth she had
    In days long since, before these last so bad.

Wherefore with infection should I live, and with my presence grace impiety, that sin should achieve advantage through me, and lace itself with my society?

Why should false painting (imitators) imitate my cheek (poetry) and steal dead seeing (plagiarize what has already been crystallized in my verse) of my living hue (inspired writings)? Why should poor beauty (incompetence) seek roses of shadow (undertake to imitate) since my rose (vision—characterization) is true?

Why should I live, now Nature is bankrupt (since I am Nature's only poet, and my talents are failing) beggared of blood to blush through lively veins (since Nature has no poet to portray her beauties)? For she has no exchequer (treasures) now but mine, and though proud of many, lives upon my gains.

She stores (treasures) my verse to show what wealth she had, in days long since, before these last, so bad.

This and the next sonnet 68, are written in the third person throughout.

It is probable that this and the three succeeding sonnets, were aimed by Shakespeare at Ben Jonson, and that these four sonnets are the 'purge' referred to in the Parnassus, where it is said that Shakespeare gave Ben Jonson a "purge that made him bewray his credit." This will be discussed hereafter, under another head.

SONNET 68.

Thus is his cheek the map of days outworn,
When beauty lived and died as flowers do now,
Before these bastard signs of fair were born,
Or durst inhabit on a living brow;
Before the golden tresses of the dead,
The right of sepulchres, were shorn away,
To live a second life on second head;
Ere beauty's dead fleece made another gay:
In him those holy antique hours are seen,
Without all ornament itself and true,
Making no summer of another's green,
Robbing no old to dress his beauty new;
    And him as for a map doth Nature store,
    To show false Art what beauty was of yore.

Thus is my cheek (poetry) the map of days past, when beauty lived and died as flowers do now, before these bastard signs of fair (false or imitating poets) were born, (came into vogue) or durst inhabit (subsist like vermin) upon a living brow (by plagiarism);

Before the golden tresses of the dead, were shorn away, to live a second life on second head; ere beauty's fleece made another gay: (In these lines Shakespeare likens the theft of his poetry to the wearing of the hair of the dead by the living.)

In my poetry those holy antique hours are seen, without ornament and true, making no summer of another's green, robbing no old to dress my beauty (poetry) new.

My poetry for a map does Nature store (keep) to show false art what beauty was of yore.

SONNET 69.

Those parts of thee that the world's eye doth view
Want nothing that the thought of hearts can mend;
All tongues, the voice of souls, give thee that due,
Uttering bare truth, even so as foes commend.
Thy outward thus with outward praise is crown'd;
But those same tongues, that give thee so thine own,
In other accents do this praise confound
By seeing farther than the eye hath shown.
They look into the beauty of thy mind,
And that, in guess, they measure by thy deeds;
Then, churls, their thoughts, although their eyes were kind,
To thy fair flower add the rank smell of weeds:
    But why thy odour matcheth not thy show,
    The soil is this, that thou dost common grow.

These parts of me that the world sees, want nothing that the heart can mend; All tongues give me that due, uttering bare truth, even as foes commend me.

My outward qualities are openly praised; but those same tongues that thus give me my own, in other accents confound their praise, by seeing further than the eye has shown (by looking beyond my works, and judging my actions).

They look into the beauty of my mind (my poetry) and that they measure by my deeds (my works), then their thoughts, although their eyes were kind, to my fair flower (poetry) add the rank smell of weeds (my weakness for drink):

But why my odour (fame) does not match my show (life), the soil (stain? or solution?) is this, that I grow common (my weakness is commonly known and discussed).

SONNET 70.

That thou art blamed shall not be thy defect,
For slander's mark was ever yet the fair;
The ornament of beauty is suspect,
A crow that flies in heaven's sweetest air.
So thou be good, slander doth but approve
Thy worth the greater, being woo'd of time;
For canker vice the sweetest buds doth love,
And thou present'st a pure unstained prime.
Thou hast pass'd by the ambush of young days,
Either not assail'd, or victor being charged;
Yet this thy praise cannot be so thy praise,
To tie up envy evermore enlarged:
    If some suspect of ill mask'd not thy show,
    Then thou alone kingdoms of hearts shouldst owe.

It is not my defect that I am blamed, for slander's mark was ever the fair; the ornament (possession) of beauty is suspect (beauty is made the mark of the slanderer) (who is) a crow that flies in heaven's sweetest air.

So if I be good, slander but approves my worth the greater, (1) being wooed (approved) of time; (Being good, and approved or wooed by time, I become a more attractive mark for slander); for the canker loves the sweetest buds, and I present a fair unstained prime.

I have passed the ambush (dangers) of young days, either (as a poet) not assailed, or as a victor being charged; yet my praise cannot prevent the growth of envy:

If some suspect of ill mark not my brow (if I were not charged with some ill), then should I own kingdoms of hearts.

It is evident from the foregoing four sonnets that Shakespeare has keenly felt and resented some attack upon him, or some exposure of his weakness. He makes it evident that his poetry has not been assailed or criticized, but that his conduct has been unfavorably depicted or commented upon. It will be attempted hereafter to throw some light upon the conditions which called forth these sonnets, and to give some reasons for suggesting that Ben Jonson was the rival, who had given the offence.

The four following sonnets 71, 72, 73 and 74 are marked with great depression—that depression which in the drunkard usually precedes or accompanies a surrender to his cravings.

SONNET 71.

No longer mourn for me when I am dead
Than you shall hear the surly sullen bell
Give warning to the world that I am fled
From this vile world, with vilest worms to dwell:
Nay, if you read this line, remember not
The hand that writ it; for I love you so,
That I in your sweet thoughts would be forgot,
If thinking on me then should make you woe.
O, if, I say, you look upon this verse
When I perhaps compounded am with clay,
Do not so much as my poor name rehearse,
But let your love even with my life decay;
    Lest the wise world should look into your moan,
    And mock you with me after I am gone.

It would be useless to paraphrase this sonnet, which would mean little other than a copy. The appeal herein is to his readers and admirers, as has been before noted. He releases them from a defense of himself or his verse, both of which in his disconsolate state of mind, he imagines the world will assail.

SONNET 72.

O, lest the world should task you to recite
What merit lived in me, that you should love
After my death, dear love, forget me quite,
For you in me can nothing worthy prove;
Unless you would devise some virtuous lie,
To do more for me than mine own desert,
And hang more praise upon deceased I
Than niggard truth would willingly impart:
O, lest your true love may seem false in this,
That you for love speak well of me untrue,
My name be buried where my body is,
And live no more to shame nor me nor you.
   For I am shamed by that which I bring forth,
   And so should you, to love things nothing worth.

Lest the world should task you to recite what merit lived in me that you should love me after my death, dear love, (admirers) forget me, for you can find nothing in me that is worthy.

Unless you would devise some virtuous lie, to do more for me than I deserve, and award me, when dead, more praise, than the exact truth would impart:

Lest your love may seem false in this, that you speak untruthfully, when you speak well of me, let my name be buried with my body, and live no more to shame you nor me.

For I am shamed by that which I bring forth (his poetry? or his conduct?), and so should you to love things nothing worth.

SONNET 73.

That time of year thou mayst in me behold
When yellow leaves, or none, or few, do hang
Upon those boughs which shake against the cold,
Bare ruin'd choirs, where late the sweet birds sang.
In me thou see'st the twilight of such day
As after sunset fadeth in the west;
Which by and by black night doth take away,
Death's second self, that seals up all in rest.
In me thou see'st the glowing of such fire,
That on the ashes of his youth doth lie,
As the death-bed whereon it must expire,
Consumed with that which it was nourish'd by.
   This thou perceivest, which makes thy love more strong,
   To love that well which thou must leave ere long.

That time of year (autumn) I may in myself behold, when yellow leaves, or few, or none hang upon the boughs which shake in the cold wind, bare ruined choirs where late the sweet birds sang.

In me I see the twilight of such (autumn) day, as after sunset fades in the west, which soon black night takes away, death's second self (night) that seals up all in rest.

In me I see the glowing of such fire, as lie on the ashes of youth, as the death-bed whereon it expires, consumed by that which it was nourished by (wine).

This I perceive which makes my love more strong, to love that well which I must leave ere long.

SONNET 74.

But be contented: when that fell arrest
Without all bail shall carry me away,
My life hath in this line some interest,
Which for memorial still with thee shall stay.
When thou reviewest this, thou dost review
The very part was consecrate to thee:
The earth can have but earth, which is his due;
My spirit is thine, the better part of me:
So then thou hast but lost the dregs of life,
The prey of worms, my body being dead;
The coward conquest of a wretch's knife,
Too base of thee to be remembered.
    The worth of that is that which it contains,
    And that is this, and this with thee remains.

But be contented: When that fell arrest (death) without all bail shall carry me away, my life has in this line (my verse) some interest, which shall stay with me as a memorial.

When I review (consider) this, I review the very part which was consecrated to myself: the earth can have but earth, my spirit is my own, the better part of me:

So then I will have lost the dregs of life, the prey of worms, my body being dead; the coward conquest of a wretch's knife, too base to be remembered.

The worth of that is that which it contains, and that is this (my poetry) and this with me remains.

The literal reading of this sonnet would indicate that Shakespeare had been seriously wounded by a knife, and that he believed the wound would prove fatal. Such may be its true meaning. On the other hand it may be a continuation of the theme of the preceding sonnets, discussing the rival poet, and in his depression Shakespeare may have felt so seriously the injury to his character, as to imagine that morally he had been assassinated.

SONNET 75.

So are you to my thoughts as food to life,
Or as sweet-season'd showers are to the ground;
And for the peace of you I hold such strife
As 'twixt a miser and his wealth is found;
Now proud as an enjoyer, and anon
Doubting the filching age will steal his treasure;
Now counting best to be with you alone,
Then better'd that the world may see my pleasure:
Sometime all full with feasting on your sight,
And by and by clean starved for a look;
Possessing or pursuing no delight,
Save what is had or must from you be took.
    Thus do I pine and surfeit day by day,
    Or gluttoning on all, or all away.

So are you to my thoughts, Wine, as food to life, or as showers are to the ground; and for your peace I hold such strife, as twixt a miser and his wealth is found;

Now proud as an enjoyer, then fearing the filching age will steal my treasure; now counting best to be with you alone, then counting it better that the world may see my pleasure:

Sometimes I am all full with feasting on you, and by and by starved for a look (a drink); possessing or pursuing no delight, save those you give.

Thus do I pine (desire) and surfeit (over indulge) day by day gluttoning on all (using excessively) or all away (having none).

SONNET 76.

Why is my verse so barren of new pride,
So far from variation or quick change?
Why with the time do I not glance aside
To new-found methods and to compounds strange?
Why write I still all one, ever the same,
And keep invention in a noted weed,
That every word doth almost tell my name,
Showing their birth and where they did proceed?
O, know, sweet, love, I always write of you,
And you and love are still my argument;
So all my best is dressing old words new,
Spending again what is already spent:
    For as the sun is daily new and old,
    So is my love still telling what is told.

Why is my verse so barren of new thought, from variation or change? Why with the time do I not glance aside (seek other subjects) to new methods or strange compounds (fancies)?

Why do I write still on one subject, ever the same, and keep invention (thoughts) in a noted weed (in characteristic dress—wine), that every word almost tells my name (shows my thoughts) showing their birth and where they did proceed (showing the cravings of my thoughts and how they were satisfied)?

Know, sweet love, Wine, I always write of you, and you and love are still my theme; so all my best is dressing old words new (saying the same thing over in other words), saying again what is already said:

As the sun is daily new and old, my love still tells what it has told before.

SONNET 77.

Thy glass will show thee how thy beauties wear,
Thy dial how thy precious minutes waste;
The vacant leaves thy mind's imprint will bear,
And of this book this learning mayst thou taste.
The wrinkles which thy glass will truly show
Of mouthed graves will give thee memory;
Thou by thy dial's shady stealth mayst know
Time's thievish progress to eternity.
Look, what thy memory cannot contain
Commit to these waste blanks, and thou shalt find
Those children nursed, deliver'd from thy brain
To take a new acquaintance of thy mind.
    These offices, so oft as thou wilt look,
    Shall profit thee and much enrich thy book.

My glass will show me how my beauties wear, my dial how my minutes waste; the vacant leaves will bear my mind's imprint, and of this book (by referring to it) this learning (what it contains in its notes) may I taste.

The wrinkles which my glass will show of mouthed (open) graves will give me memory; I by my dial's stealth may know Time's thievish progress to eternity.

Look, what my memory cannot contain, commit to these blanks, and I shall find those children (ideas noted) nursed (preserved) which were delivered from my brain, to take a new acquaintance of my mind (to be recalled to mind).

These offices (this use) so often as I look, shall profit me, and much enrich my book.

This sonnet would seem to record that Shakespeare, possibly for the first time, began keeping a note book for jotting down his ideas. When he says, 'what thy memory cannot contain, commit to these waste blanks,' he gives the impression that this was a new experiment, and that he had theretofore been relying upon his memory. Then when he goes further and defines the manner of using the book, suggesting its purpose and helpfulness, it occurs that the ideas were new to him.

SONNET 78.

So oft have I invoked thee for my Muse
And found such fair assistance in my verse
As every alien pen hath got my use
And under thee their poesy disperse.
Thine eyes, that taught the dumb on high to sing
And heavy ignorance aloft to fly,
Have added feathers to the learned's wing
And given grace a double majesty.
Yet be most proud of that which I compile,
Whose influence is thine and born of thee:
In others' works thou dost but mend the style,
And arts with thy sweet graces graced be:
    But thou art all my art, and dost advance
    As high as learning my rude ignorance.

So often have I invoked you for my Muse, Wine, and found such assistance in my verse, that other pens now use my methods, and under your aid dispense their poesy.

Your eyes (inspiration) that taught the dumb (me) to sing, and ignorance (me) to fly, has also added feathers to the learned's wing, and given to (his) grace a double majesty.

Yet be most proud of that which I compile, which is yours and born of you: in others works you but improve the style, and grace the art with your graces:

But you are all my art, and advance my ignorance as high as learning.

Here begins a group of nine sonnets all in the same vein as this, in which the poet pleads piteously with his mistress Wine, not to forsake him for others, although admitting his unworthiness, and the superiority of his rival for his mistress' favor. It is hardly understandable that he could so idealize his love as to address and beseech her as if she were possessed of discrimination, and could at her will decide his fate. And yet so great was his dramatic imagination, that he had the capacity to personify insensate things, and actually endow them with human qualities, and maintain the illusion throughout, logically and consistently. Let it not be insisted upon, that Shakespeare was making this his appeal to some real intelligence—some human creature. That would enormously multiply the intricacies of the situation. What being, human or divine, would answer to his importunities, or fit his ideality? What real flesh in existence could be all of Shakespeare's art, or reach that perfection attributed to him, or her, or it? And why should Shakespeare be ever promising to immortalize an unsexed and unnamed living something, that never establishes an individuality, and never has a name. He calls it the Master-Mistress of his passion. There is no flesh that can be so described, and were there any such, he-she would not be Shakespeare's passion.

These sonnets also, it is believed, refer to Ben Jonson as the rival poet. The reasons for this belief will be given hereafter. It should however now be noted, that the bitterness manifested in sonnets 67 to 70 has disappeared in these last sonnets, and given place to expressions of esteem. This is accounted for by the fact, that between the two poets there existed a mutual friendship, but that the same had been interrupted through a temporary, and short-lived hostility, the reasons for which will be set forth later.

SONNET 79.

Whilst I alone did call upon thy aid,
My verse alone had all thy gentle grace;
But now my gracious numbers are decay'd,
And my sick Muse doth give another place.
I grant, sweet love, thy lovely argument
Deserves the travail of a worthier pen;
Yet what of thee thy poet doth invent
He robs thee of, and pays it thee again.
He lends thee virtue, and he stole that word
For thy behaviour; beauty doth he give,
And found it in thy cheek: he can afford
No praise to thee but what in thee doth live.
 Then thank him not for that which he doth say,
 Since what he owes thee thou thyself dost pay.

Whilst I alone (the only one) called upon your aid, mine was the only verse that had your gentle grace; but now my gracious numbers are decayed, and another takes the place of my sick Muse.

I grant sweet love, Wine, your argument deserves the travail of a worthier pen; yet whatever your poet writes of you, he gets from you, and gives it back to you.

He attributes virtue to you, but he stole the name of virtue from your behavior; he calls you beautiful, but he found the beauty in your cheek: He can say nothing in praise of you more than you already have.

Then do not thank him for what he says, since you yourself pay what he owes.

SONNET 80.

O, how I faint when I of you do write,
Knowing a better spirit doth use your name,
And in the praise thereof spends all his might,
To make me tongue-tied, speaking of your fame!
But since your worth, wide as the ocean is,
The humble as the proudest sail doth bear,
My saucy bark, inferior far to his,
On your broad main doth wilfully appear.
Your shallowest help will hold me up afloat,
Whilst he upon your soundless deep doth ride;
Or, being wreck'd, I am a worthless boat,
He of tall building and of goodly pride:
    Then if he thrive and I be cast away,
    The worst was this; my love was my decay.

O, Wine, how I faint when I write of you, knowing a better spirit uses your names (writes of or to you) and in your praise spends all his might, to make me tongue-tied (to so outdo me that I cannot be heard) speaking of your fame!

But since your worth is as wide as the ocean, and bears the humble as the proudest sail, my saucy bark, inferior far to his, on your broad main wilfully (confidently) appears.

Your shallowest help will hold me up afloat (being of small draft), whilst he upon your soundless sea rides (is capable of sea faring), or, being wrecked, I am a worthless boat (if I am wrecked it is because I am incapable), he is of tall building and goodly pride:

Then if he thrive, and I be cast away, the worst was this; my love (indulgence) was my decay.

SONNET 81.

Or I shall live your epitaph to make,
Or you survive when I in earth am rotten;
From hence your memory death cannot take,
Although in me each part will be forgotten.
Your name from hence immortal life shall have,
Though I, once gone, to all the world must die:
The earth can yield me but a common grave,
When you entombed in men's eyes shall lie.
Your monument shall be my gentle verse,
Which eyes not yet created shall o'er-read;
And tongues to be your being shall rehearse,
When all the breathers of this world are dead;
    You still shall live—such virtue hath my pen—
    Where breath most breathes, even in the mouths of men.

If I shall live to make your epitaph, Wine, or you survive when I am rotten, death cannot take your memory hence, although I be forgotten.

Your name shall have immortal life, though I must die: the earth can yield me but a grave, when you in men's eyes (thoughts) shall lie.

Your monument shall be my verse, which eyes not yet created shall read, and tongues to be (unborn) shall rehearse your being, when all the breathers of this world (those now alive) are dead.

You still shall live—such virtue has my pen—where breath most breathes, even in the mouths of men. (Has the last sentence a double meaning: praise from the mouths of men, and drink in the mouths of men?)

Owing to Shakespeare often confounding wine, and his own talents as a poet, some sonnets like the foregoing may be construed as applying either to one or the other. Owing to the fact that the other accompanying sonnets in this group are so evidently addressed to Wine, this one has also been construed so. The distinction however is so slight, that using either construction means the same thing.

SONNET 82.

I grant thou wert not married to my Muse,
And therefore mayst without attaint o'erlook
The dedicated words which writers use
Of their fair subject, blessing every book.
Thou art as fair in knowledge as in hue,
Finding thy worth a limit past my praise;
And therefore art enforced to seek anew
Some fresher stamp of the time-bettering days,
And do so, love; yet when they have devised
What strained touches rhetoric can lend,
Thou truly fair wert truly sympathized
In true plain words by thy true-telling friend;
    And their gross painting might be better used
    Where cheeks need blood; in thee it is abused.

grant, Wine, you were not married (bound solely) to my Muse, and may without attain o'erlook (without blame accept) the dedicated words that writers use, in praise of subjects of their books.

You are as fair in knowledge (inspiration) as in hue (appearance), and it is beyond my praise to find the limit of your worth; and therefore you are compelled to seek some fresher stamp (more inspired poet) of these better days.

And do so, love, and when they have devised what strained (unmetrical) touches rhetoric can lend, you truly fair, were truly sympathized (feelingly lauded) in true plain words by (me) your true telling friend.

And their gross painting might be better used, where cheeks need blood (lack healthful beauty) in you it is abused.

SONNET 83.

I never saw that you did painting need,
And therefore to your fair no painting set;
I found, or thought I found, you did exceed
The barren tender of a poet's debt:
And therefore have I slept in your report,
That you yourself, being extant, well might show
How far a modern quill doth come too short,
Speaking of worth, what worth in you doth grow.
This silence for my sin you did impute,
Which shall be most my glory, being dumb;
For I impair not beauty being mute,
When others would give life and bring a tomb
    There lives more life in one of your fair eyes
    Than both your poets can in praise devise.

I never saw that you needed painting, Wine, and therefore did not paint your fair (beauty); I found you exceeded all a poet could express;

And therefore have I slept (remained silent) in your report (praise), that you, being extant, (having a present existence) might show how far short, is a modern quill to speak of worth, such worth as in you grows.

You took my silence to be my sin, but being dumb shall be my glory, for being mute, I do not impair your beauty, when others who would give you life, bring a tomb (destroy you with praise).

There lives more life in one of your fair eyes, than both your poets can in praise devise.

Shakespeare's criticism of his rival for praising wine (or whatever the subject of the sonnets may be, if not wine), and his protestations of good taste, in his silence, as proof of his devotions, is rather remarkable in view of the fact, that the sonnets, beautiful as they are, become really tiresome by reason of the fulsome, extravagant and unending praise, that he seems never to tire of expending on his nondescript love. One often stops to wonder if his fund of imagery will ever exhaust itself, and how he can invent so many ways for saying the same thing, and that thing the most extravagant praise of an unworthy object. Possibly Shakespeare means to say, (and upon consideration we may find that he does say) that he never describes the physical qualities of wine by referring to it by name, or to its color, taste, smell or appearance. It is very noticeable that in all the sonnets he never mentions wine or any other intoxicant, nor any of their outward qualities. That his silence, of which he boasts, has reference to this does not seem improbable. In Sonnet 82 he speaks of his rival's gross painting, and says it might be better used, 'when cheeks need *blood*, in thee it is abused.' In 83 he says, 'I never saw that you did *painting* need, and therefore to your fair no *painting* set.' To forestall; in Sonnet 84 he says, 'let him but copy what in you is writ, not making worse what nature made so *clear*.'

These three sonnets all charge the rival poet with exaggeration, and of attempting the impossible. Every one knows that it is impossible to describe color, or taste or smell, further than by name, and all attempts to describe, distinguish, or emphasize them by words are tiresome and unimpressive, as well as futile.

Under another head it will be shown how Jonson in his writings conforms to this condemnation of Shakespeare, by lauding wine, and by continually employing names and phrases to exalt it and its qualities. In these Shakespeare never indulges. He says: "Let him copy what in you is writ," that is the inward quality or effect, and let the outward go, or let it be implied. In another line he says, "to your fair no painting set" indicating that the fair, beauty or inward quality would bear comment, but that there should be no painting, or false coloring.

SONNET 84.

Who is it that says most? which can say more
Than this rich praise, that you alone are you?
In whose confine immured is the store
Which should example where your equal grew.
Lean penury within that pen doth dwell
That to his subject lends not some small glory;
But he that writes of you, if he can tell
That you are you, so dignifies his story.
Let him but copy what in you is writ,
Not making worse what nature made so clear,
And such a counterpart shall fame his wit,
Making his style admired every where.
   You to your beauteous blessings add a curse,
    Being fond on praise, which makes your praises worse.

Who can say most? Who can praise you higher, Wine, than say that you, are you alone? In whose confine immured is the store (in whom does the capacity exist), which should example where your equal grew (to find a comparison that would show your equal)? (Each sentence in the first four lines is doubtless interrogatory, and should be so punctuated.)

Poor is the pen that does not lend some glory to its subject; but if he that writes of you can tell that you are you, he dignifies his story.

Let him copy what is in you expressed, and not by overpraise disguise what nature made so clear, then his counterpart shall fame his wit, making his style admired everywhere.

You, Wine, to your beauteous blessings add a curse, being fond on praise (such as the rival uses) which makes your praises worse (such exaggerations are worse than simply saying, you are you).

SONNET 85.

My tongue-tied Muse in manners holds her still,
While comments of your praise, richly compiled,
Reserve their character with golden quill,
And precious phrase by all the Muses filed.
I think good thoughts whilst other write good words,
And, like unletter'd clerk, still cry 'Amen'
To every hymn that able spirit affords,
In polish'd form of well refined pen.
Hearing you praised, I say ' 'Tis so, 'tis true,'
And to the most of praise add something more;
But that is in my thought, whose love to you,
Though words come hindmost, holds his rank before.
    Then others for the breath of words respect,
    Me for my dumb thoughts, speaking in effect.

My tongue-tied Muse in manners (decorously) keeps still, while comment of your prise, Wine, richly compiled, reserve (preserve?—re-serve?) their character with golden quill, and precious phrase, filed (fitted) by all the Muses.

I think good thoughts, while others write good words, and like an unlettered clerk (I) cry 'Amen' to every hymn that able spirit (the rival poet) affords, in polished form of well refined pen.

Hearing you, Wine, praised I say " 'Tis so, 'tis true," and to the most of praise add something more; but what I add is in my thoughts, whose love to you is first in rank, though words come last.

Then respect others for their words, me for my silent thoughts, speaking in effect.

SONNET 86.

Was it the proud full sail of his great verse,
Bound for the prize of all too precious you,
That did my ripe thoughts in my brain inhearse,
Making their tomb the womb wherein they grew?
Was it his spirit, by spirits taught to write
Above a mortal pitch, that struck me dead?
No, neither he, nor his compeers by night
Giving him aid, my verse astonished.
He, nor that affable familiar ghost
Which nightly gulls him with intelligence,
As victors, of my silence cannot boast;
I was not sick of any fear from thence:
    But when your countenance fill'd up his line,
    Then lack'd I matter; that enfeebled mine.

Was it his great verse (the rival poet's) seeking to win the prize from you, that restrained my ripe thoughts in my brain, making their tomb, of the womb wherein they grew (my brain)?

Was it the spirit of this poet, taught by other spirits to write above a mortal pitch, that struck me dead? No, neither he, nor his compeers (visiting spirits) by night giving him aid, astonished (stunned) my verse.

He nor his familiar (visiting) ghost, which gulls him with intelligence, can boast of having triumphed over my silence, for I fear them not.

But when your countenance, Wine, filled up his line (when he truly portrayed you), then I lacked matter; that enfeebled mine. (Then I felt that I was indeed rivaled.)

This sonnet ends those which are devoted to the rival poet.

SONNET 87.

Farewell! thou art too dear for my possessing,
And like enough thou know'st thy estimate:
The charter of thy worth gives thee releasing;
My bonds in thee are all determinate.
For how do I hold thee but by thy granting?
And for that riches where is my deserving?
The cause of this fair gift in me is wanting,
And so my patent back again is swerving.
Thyself thou gavest, thy own worth then not knowing,
Or me, to whom thou gavest it, else mistaking;
So thy great gift, upon misprision growing,
Comes home again, on better judgment making.
    Thus have I had thee, as a dream doth flatter,
    In sleep a king, but waking no such matter.

Oh Wine, farewell! you are too dear for my possessing, and like enough you know your estimate: (how dear you are): the charter (rights) of your worth release you; my bonds are determinate (may be terminated or ended).

I hold you but by your granting, and how could I deserve such riches? The cause for your gift is wanting in me, and so my patent (right or privilege) back again is swerving (is forfeited or annulled).

When you gave yourself you did not know your worth, or you were mistaken in me, and so your gift upon misprision growing (founded on mistake) comes home again (is annulled) on better judgment making (when you have made your election or choice, on discovering the true facts).

Thus have I had you as a dream, in sleep a king, in waking nothing.

In this sonnet as in many of them Shakespeare applies legal principles. In this one the compact with wine is void on two grounds: First, there was no consideration for the contract, and it is therefore void. Second, it was founded on a mistake of facts, and for that reason also void. In either instance it was subject to be avoided and terminated by the one who had parted with valuable rights.

SONNET 88.

When thou shalt be disposed to set me light,
And place my merit in the eye of scorn,
Upon thy side, against myself I'll fight,
And prove thee virtuous, though thou art forsworn.
With mine own weakness being best acquainted,
Upon thy part I can set down a story
Of faults conceal'd, wherein I am attainted;
That thou in losing me shalt win much glory:
And I by this will be a gainer too;
For bending all my loving thoughts on thee,
The injuries that to myself I do,
Doing thee vantage, double-vantage me.
    Such is my love, to thee I so belong,
    That for thy right myself will bear all wrong.

When you shall be disposed to make light of me, Wine, and place my merits in the eye of scorn, I'll fight upon your side, and prove you virtuous (right) although you are forsworn (perjured)

Knowing best my own weakness, I can testify in your behalf, of concealed faults, of which I am attainted (guilty); and you in losing me shall win much glory (be better off without me)

And I by this will also be gainer; for devoting all my thoughts to you, the injuries that I do to myself, being helpful to you will double-vantage me.

Such is my love, for I so belong to you, that for your right I will bear all wrong.

SONNET 89.

Say that thou didst forsake me for some fault,
And I will comment up that offence:
Speak of my lameness, and I straight will halt,

Against thy reasons making no defence.
Thou canst not, love, disgrace me half so ill,
To set a form upon desired change,
As I'll myself disgrace; knowing thy will,
I will acquaintance strangle and look strange;
Be absent from thy walks; and in my tongue
Thy sweet beloved name no more shall dwell,
Lest I, too much profane, should do it wrong,
And haply of our old acquaintance tell.
  For thee, against myself I'll vow debate,
  For I must ne'er love him whom thou dost hate.

Say, Wine, that you forsook me for some fault, and I will comment upon (admit) that offence: Speak of my lameness (frailty) and I straight will halt (be or do as you say), against your reasons (charges) making no defence.

You cannot disgrace me half so ill, to set a form upon desired change (by making a formal excuse for change), as I will myself disgrace; knowing your will, I will acquaintance strangle, and look strange,

Be absent from your walks (haunts) and not speak your name, lest I should haply tell of our old acquaintance.

Against myself I'll take your part in debate (strife, contest), for I must not love him whom you hate. (I will not love myself, if you hate me.)

Shakespeare here defines the conditions which we have found to exist in the sonnets, namely: the absence of the name of wine, the espousal of its cause, in all discussions, the strangling of all acquaintanceship, his absence from its walks or haunts (none of which are ever mentioned), and his looking strange, lest he might profane it, or do it an injury. If he considered this sonnet as his pledge of fidelity and secrecy, he has kept is conscientiously.

SONNET 90.

Then hate me when thou wilt if ever, now;
Now, while the world is bent my deeds to cross,
Join with the spite of fortune, make me bow,
And do not drop in for an after-loss:
Ah, do not, when my heart hath 'scaped this sorrow,
Come in the rearward of a conquer'd woe;
Give not a windy night a rainy morrow,
To linger out a purposed overthrow.
If thou wilt leave me, do not leave me last,
When other petty griefs have done their spite,
But in the onset come: so shall I taste
At first the very worst of fortune's might;
   And other strains of woe, which now seem woe,
   Compared with loss of thee will not seem so.

If you are to hate me, Wine, hate me now, while the world is bent to cross my deeds, join with misfortune, make me bow (humble me), an do not drop in for an after-loss (do not come after all my sorrows):

Ah, do not when my heart has scaped this sorrow (what sorrow?) come after I have conquered my woe; do not come as a rainy morrow after a windy night (do not follow sorrow with sorrow) to linger out a purposed overthrow (abandonment).

Do not leave me last when I have suffered other petty griefs, but come at first: so that I shall taste at first the worst that fortune has in store.

Other woes coming after loss of you, will not seem woes.

SONNET 91.

Some glory in their birth, some in their skill,
Some in their wealth, some in their body's force;
Some in their garments, though new-fangled ill;
Some in their hawks and hounds, some in their horse;
And every humour hath his adjunct pleasure,
Wherein it finds a joy above the rest:
But these particulars are not my measure;
All these I better in one general best.
Thy love is better than high birth to me,
Richer than wealth, prouder than garments' cost,
Of more delight than hawks or horses be;
And having thee, of all men's pride I boast:
    Wretched in this alone, that thou mayst take
    All this away and me most wretched make.

Some glory in their birth, some in their skill, some in their wealth, some in their body's force (strength); some in their garments; some in their hawks and hounds, some in their horse;

And every humour has its adjunct pleasure, wherein it finds a joy over the rest: but those particulars are not my measure (these are not the pleasures in which I delight); all these I better in one general best (Wine).

Your love, Wine, is better than high birth to me, richer than wealth, prouder than garments cost, of more delight than hawks or horses be; and having you, of all men's pride I boast (I have all that all men prize).

Wretched in this alone, that you may take all this away, and make me wretched.

SONNET 92.

But do thy worst to steal thyself away,
For term of life thou art assured mine;
And life no longer than thy love will stay,
For it depends upon that love of thine.
Then need I not to fear the worst of wrongs,
When in the least of them my life hath end.
I see a better state to me belongs
Than that which on thy humour doth depend:
Thou canst not vex me with inconstant mind,
Since that my life on thy revolt doth lie.
O, what a happy title do I find,
Happy to have thy love, happy to die!
    But what's so blessed-fair that fears no blot?
    Thou mayst be false, and yet I know it not.

But do your worst, O Wine, for you are assured to me for life; and life will stay no longer than your love, for it depends upon that love of yours.

Then I need not fear the worst of wrongs, when in the least of them (taking wine from me) my life has an end. A better state is mine (death), than is life, which depends on you:

You cannot vex me with your inconstant mind, since should you revolt death would ensue. How happy is my state, being happy in your love, happy to die!

But my happiness is not without fears, for you may be false, and I know it not.

This is the first sonnet in which Shakespeare has shown any defiance towards wine.

SONNET 93.

So shall I live, supposing thou art true,
Like a deceived husband; so love's face
May still seem love to me, though alter'd new;
Thy looks with me, thy heart in other place:
For there can live no hatred in thine eye,
Therefore in that I cannot know thy change.
In many's looks the false heart's history
Is writ in moods and frowns and wrinkles strange,
But heaven in thy creation did decree
That in thy face sweet love should ever dwell;
Whate'er thy thoughts or thy heart's workings be,
Thy looks should nothing thence but sweetness tell.
    How like Eve's apple doth thy beauty grow,
    If thy sweet virtue answer not thy show.

So, Wine, shall I live, supposing you are true, like a deceived husband; so love's face though newly altered may still seem love; your looks with me, your heart in some other place:

For there can live no hatred in your eye, therefore by your looks I cannot know your change. In the looks of many the false heart's history is expressed in moods and frowns and wrinkles,

But heaven in your creation decreed that in your face love should forever dwell; whatever your thoughts or your heart's workings might be, your looks should indicate nothing but sweetness.

How like Eve's apple (temptation) does your beauty grow, if your virtue is not indicated by your show.

SONNET 94.

They that have power to hurt and will do none,
That do not do the thing they most do show,
Who, moving others, are themselves as stone,
Unmoved, cold and to temptation slow;
They rightly do inherit heaven's graces
And husband nature's riches from expense;
They are the lords and owners of their faces,
Others but stewards of their excellence.
The summer's flower is to the summer sweet,
Though to itself it only live and die,
But if that flower with base infection meet,
The basest weed outbraves his dignity:
 For sweetest things turn sourest by their deeds;
 Lilies that fester smell far worse than weeds.

Those that have the power to hurt and will not, that do not do what they most show they could do, though they move others, are themselves unmoved, cold and to temptation slow;

They inherit heaven's graces and husband nature's riches from expense (waste); they are the lords and owners of their faces (fortunes), while others are but stewards (servants) of their excellence (mastery)

The summer's flower is to the summer sweet, though it may live and die to itself, but if the flower meet with infection, the basest weed (outlives surpasses) his dignity (charm)

For sweetest things turn sourest by their deeds, Lilies that fester smell far worse than weeds.

Shakespeare tries to placate his love with flattery, accompanied by a picture of results should it prove untrue. If it have power to injure and will not; if it does not the wrongs that are feared; if it influences others, but is itself stable and true; if it does not yield to temptation, but is faithful to those who love it,—then having all these qualities it has heavenly graces, and will accumulate nature's riches, and others will become its stewards, servants and dependents. Like the flower, though it bloom to itself, it will be loved and cherished, but if infected or soiled, the basest weed would have more charm. Thus he declaims to Wine, that while it simply inspires, and performs a proper and moral function, it will retain a virtuous reputation, but if it besots and degrades it will become a stench to morals.

SONNET 95.

How sweet and lovely dost thou make the shame
Which, like a canker in the fragrant rose,
Doth spot the beauty of thy budding name!
. O, in what sweets dost thou thy sins inclose!
That tongue that tells the story of thy days,
Making lascivious comments on thy sport,
Cannot dispraise but in a kind of praise;
Naming thy name blesses an ill report.
O, what a mansion have those vices got
Which for their habitation chose out thee,
Where beauty's veil doth cover every blot
And all things turn to fair that eyes can see!
    Take heed, dear heart, of this large privilege;
    The hardest knife ill used doth lose his edge.

O Wine, how sweet you make the shame which like the canker in the rose mars your budding name (the inspiration of your bud or promise, before the expanded bloom)! In what sweets do you inclose your sins!

That tongue that tells your story, making lascivious comments on your sport, while dispraising you, gives you a kind of praise; naming you, blesses an ill report.

What a mansion have those vices got, which chose you for their habitation, where your veil (disguise) of beauty covers every blot, and all things turn to fair that eyes can see.

Take heed, dear heart, of this large privilege; the hardest knife ill used loses its edge. (Excesses will destroy your beauty.)

SONNET 96.

Some say, thy fault is youth, some wantonness;
Some say, thy grace is youth and gentle sport;
Both grace and faults are loved of more and less:
Thou makest faults graces that to thee resort.
As on the finger of a throned queen
The basest jewel will be well esteem'd,
So are those errors that in thee are seen
To truths translated and for true things deem'd.
How many lambs might the stern wolf betray,
If like a lamb he could his looks translate!
How many gazers mightst thou lead away,
If thou wouldst use the strength of all thy state!
But do not so; I love thee in such sort,
As thou being mine, mine is thy good report.

Some say your fault is youth, and some say it is wantonness; some say your grace is youth and sport; both your faults and graces are beloved, more or less: You make faults that resort to you, graces.

On the fingers of a queen the basest jewel is esteemed, so are your errors esteemed as truths.

How many lambs might the wolf betray, if he could look like a lamb! How many gazers might you lead away if you should employ all your arts.

But you do not so; for being mine, I love you, and your good report (reputation) is mine (it will cover my faults).

This group of ten sonnets from the 87th to and including the 96th, are all in one strain of loving, condemning, accusing and excusing, and of warning and threatening. They mark that particular stage in all illicit excesses, that follows mutual confidence and passion, and presages hatred and distrust in the future.

In these sonnets Shakespeare shows an awakening, and begins to estimate wine in its true character. He still loves it, but doubts its love for him, or rather its devotion to his ideals, and he has come to be suspicious that it is playing him false. His was, so he would have us believe, a case of true, and relatively pure love. He espoused wine believing it to be virtuous, and capable of inspiring him to nobler things, and took it as a partner and helpmate. But now he begins to suspect that he may have overvalued wine's character, and that it is false to their union—that instead of inspiring, he fears that it is degrading and destructive, and that it will debauch him and his intellect, and leave him an abandoned outcast.

It is noticeable with what vision he bears out the likeness of the overpowering mistress of his appetite, to an embodied mistress of his passion—beginning in illicit love and continuing through all its stages, and to end ultimately in the inevitable tragedy.

After these sonnets Shakespeare took another leave of wine, and devoted himself, let us believe, to something more useful than the worship of his enchantress. The next sonnet tells of his abstention.

SONNET 97.

How like a winter hath my absence been
From thee, the pleasure of the fleeting year
What freezings have I felt, what dark days seen!
What old December's bareness every where!
And yet this time removed was summer's time;
The teeming autumn, big with rich increase,
Bearing the wanton burthen of the prime,
Like widowed wombs after their lords' decease:
Yet this abundant issue seem'd to me
But hope of orphans and unfather'd fruit;
For summer and his pleasures wait on thee,
And, thou away, the very birds are mute;
    Or, if they sing, 'tis with so dull a cheer
    That leaves look pale, dreading the winter's near.

How like winter has my absence been from you, Wine, you who are
the pleasure of the fleeting year; what freezings have I felt, and dark
days seen—December's bareness everywhere!

Yet my absence was in summer's time, and autumn big with increase,
bearing the burden of the prime (the growing season), like widowed
wombs after their lords' decease:

Yet this abundant issue (harvest) seemed to me but hope of
orphans and unfathered fruit (as if there had been no season to produce
it); for you are the summer's pleasure, and without you the birds are
mute;

Or if they sing 'tis with so dull a cheer, that leaves look pale dread-
ing the winter's near.

SONNET 98.

From you have I been absent in the spring,
When proud-pied April, dress'd in all his trim,
Hath put a spirit of youth in every thing,
That heavy Saturn laugh'd and leap'd with him.
Yet nor the lays of birds, nor the sweet smell
Of different flowers in odour and in hue,
Could make me any summer's story tell,
Or from their proud lap pluck them where they grew:
Nor did I wonder at the lily's white,
Nor praise the deep vermilion in the rose;
They were but sweet, but figures of delight,
Drawn after you, you pattern of all those.
    Yet seem'd it winter still, and, you away,
    As with your shadow I with these did play.

I have been absent from you in April, Wine, (probably not a part of the period mentioned in 97) when there was the spirit of youth in everything; when Saturn laughed and leaped with this spirit.

Yet not the song of birds, nor the smell nor hue of flowers could make it summer time to me, or make me pluck the flowers where they grew:

Nor did I wonder at the lily's white, nor praise the color of the rose; they were but sweet, figures of delight, imitations of you, who are the pattern of all these.

It was winter, and you away, and with your shadow I played with these.

SONNET 99.

The forward violet thus did I chide:
Sweet thief, whence didst thou steal thy sweet that smells,
If not from my love's breath? The purple pride
Which on thy soft cheek for complexion dwells
In my love's veins thou hast too grossly dyed.
The lily I condemned for thy hand,
And buds of marjoram had stol'n thy hair;
The roses fearfully on thorns did stand,
One blushing shame, another white despair;
A third, nor red nor white, had stol'n of both,
And to his robbery had annex'd thy breath;
But, for his theft, in pride of all his growth
A vengeful canker eat him up to death.
    More flowers I noted, yet I none could see
    But sweet or colour it had stol'n from thee.

The early violet, thus I chided: 'Sweet thief where did you steal your odour, if not from my love's breath? The purple complexion of your cheeks in my love's veins you have too grossly dyed' (you have too grossly dyed to imitate my love's veins. The text does not bear this construction exactly, but that is probably what it means).

The lily I condemned for stealing the color of your hands, and buds of marjoram for stealing your hair; the roses grew on fearful thorns; one's blush was shame, another's white despair;

A third neither red nor white, had stolen both colors, and had also stolen your breath, but for his theft, a canker ate him up.

I noted other flowers, but all had stolen both sweet and color from you.

SONNET 100.

Where art thou, Muse, that thou forget'st so long
To speak of that which gives thee all thy might?
Spend'st thou thy fury on some worthless song,
Darkening thy power to lend base subjects light?
Return, forgetful Muse, and straight redeem
In gentle numbers time so idly spent;
Sing to the ear that doth thy lays esteem
And gives thy pen both skill and argument.
Rise, resty Muse, my love's sweet face survey,
If Time have any wrinkle graven there;
If any, be a satire to decay,
And make Time's spoils despised every where.
    Give my love fame faster than Time wastes life;
    So thou prevent'st his scythe and crooked knife.

Where are you Muse, that you forget so long to speak of that (my own art) which gives you all your might? Do you spend your efforts on some worthless song, exhausting your art to lend base subjects light? (why have you neglected the sonnets so long, and devoted yourself to base subjects?).

Return (to the sonnets) and redeem in gentle numbers the time so idly spent; sing to the ear (my own) that appreciates your lays, and which gives your pen both skill and theme.

Rise and look on my love's face (my art), and see if Time has grown any wrinkles there (if it has deteriorated); if any, be you a satire to Time's decay, and make its spoils despised. (Show that your poetry is as vigorous as it has ever been).

Give my love (my art) fame, faster than Time can waste it; and prevent Time's scythe.

Beginning here with the 100th sonnet and ending with the 108th, we find a group of sonnets written in soberness, or near soberness. In several of them there would seem to be an allusion to wine, but it is not certain that such is the case,—on the contrary, taking these sonnets altogether, it is more likely that Shakespeare is addressing himself, and not his alter ego, Wine. But the sonnets may be read either way, and do no great violence to the meaning which they were intended to express. At first they were unhesitatingly read as being addressed to Wine, but upon more careful study, that conclusion has given way to the other construction, and the readings as here given, which in turn may prove to be the worser choice.

Evidently there has been a considerable time during which the sonnets have been neglected, and their composition suspended, and Shakespeare is now returning to them. He speaks of having spent his 'fury' on 'worthless song', and of darkening his power 'to lend base subjects light' and of having idly spent his time. It may be a mistaken idea, but throughout the sonnets one cannot avoid the thought that Shakespeare himself felt that his fame was to rest on the Sonnets, and that his other poetry was being devoted to base subjects,—simply a means for livelihood. In all his promises of an enduring fame to both Wine and himself, if those promises are to have a literal construction, that fame was to be founded upon the Sonnets alone. So far as any reference is contained in the Sonnets, it could not be imagined that Shakespeare had written anything else, or if he had, that he had put the slightest value upon such writings.

SONNET 101.

O truant Muse, what shall be thy amends
For thy neglect of truth in beauty dyed?
Both truth and beauty on my love depends;
So dost thou too, and therein dignified.
Make answer, Muse: wilt thou not haply say,
'Truth needs no colour, with his colour fix'd;
Beauty no pencil, beauty's truth to lay;
But best is best, if never intermix'd'?
Because he needs no praise, wilt thou be dumb?
Excuse not silence so, for 't lies in thee
To make him much outlive a gilded tomb
And to be praised of ages yet to be.
 Then do thy office, Muse; I teach thee how
 To make him seem long hence as he shows now.

Truant Muse, what amends shall you make for this neglect of truth in beauty dyed (Shakespeare's art)? Both truth and beauty depend on my love (my art): and so Muse do you, and therein are you dignified.

Make answer, Muse, and you will say: 'Truth needs no color, his color is fixed; beauty no pencil, to draw beauty's truth; But best is best, if never intermixed (if never confused by trying to improve it)?

Because my love (art) needs no praise, will you be dumb? That is no excuse for silence, for it is your duty to make him outlive the tomb, and to be praised of ages yet to be.

Then to your duty Muse; I'll teach you to make him (my art) seen, in the future, as he is now.

SONNET 102.

My love is strengthen'd, though more weak in seeming;
I love not less, though less the show appear:
That love is merchandized whose rich esteeming
The owner's tongue doth publish every where.
Our love was new, and then but in the spring,
When I was wont to greet it with my lays;
As Philomel in summer's front doth sing,
And stops her pipe in growth of riper days:
Not that the summer is less pleasant now
Than when her mournful hymns did hush the night,
But that wild music burthens every bough,
And sweets grown common lose their dear delight.
    Therefore, like her, I sometime hold my tongue,
    Because I would not dull you with my song.

My love (art) is strengthened, though weaker in seeming (having been idle); I love not less, though less the show appear (I am not less inspired, though I fail to write): that love is merchandised (commercialized, made a commodity) when its owner's esteeming publishes it everywhere.

Our love (the mutual love between him and his art) was new, but in the spring, when I was wont to greet it with my lays; as philomel sings in the early summer, and stops her voice with the growth of riper days:

Not that the summer is less pleasant now, (as it grows older) than when her mournful hymns hushed the night, but that wild music burdens every bough, and sweets grown common lose their delight.

Like her I sometimes hold my tongue, because I would not dull you with my song.

SONNET 103.

Alack, what poverty my Muse brings forth,
That having such a scope to show her pride,
The argument, all bare, is of more worth
Than when it hath my added praise beside!
O, blame me not, if I no more can write!
Look in your glass, and there appears a face
That over-goes my blunt invention quite,
Dulling my lines and doing me disgrace.
Were it not sinful then, striving to mend,
To mar the subject that before was well?
For to no other pass my verses tend
Than of your graces and your gifts to tell;
    And more, much more, than in my verse can sit,
    Your own glass shows you when you look in it.

What poverty my Muse brings forth, when there is so much of which to sing, the bare theme is of more worth than when my praise is added!

Blame me not if I can write no more! Look in my glass (mind), and there appears a face (thoughts) that over-goes (overwhelms) my blunt invention, dulling my lines, and disgracing my art.

Were it not sinful then, by striving to improve, to mar the subject, that before was well? For to no other result do my verses tend than to tell of my graces and gifts;

And more than in my verse can sit (can be expressed) my own glass shows me, when I look in it. (My own thoughts conceive.)

While Shakespeare feels that his mental strength is unweakened, he finds, or imagines he finds, that his poetical expression lacks his former inspiration, and that whenever he undertakes to expand his theme, he ends in praising his own gifts. His criticism, if not his judgment, is well founded.

SONNET 104.

To me, fair friend, you never can be old,
For as you were when first your eye I eyed,
Such seems your beauty still. Three winters cold
Have from the forests shook three summers' pride,
Three beauteous springs to yellow autumn turn'd
In process of the seasons have I seen,
Three April perfumes in three hot Junes burn'd,
Since first I saw you fresh, which yet are green.
Ah, yet doth beauty, like a dial-hand,
Steal from his figure, and no pace perceived;
So your sweet hue, which methinks still doth stand,
Hath motion, and mine eye may be deceived:
    For fear of which, hear this, thou age unbred;
    Ere you were born was beauty's summer dead.

To me, fair friend, (my art) you never can be old, for as you were when first your eye I eyed, (when first I felt your inspiration) so are you still. Three winters have from the forests shook three summer's leaves.

Three springs have turned to autumns, and I have seen the perfumes of three Aprils burned in three hot Junes, since first I saw you fresh, and you are yet green.

And yet beauty, like the hands of the dial, moves (ages) without perceptible motion, and my eye may be deceived.

For fear of which, hear this, you unbred age, ere you were born, beauty's summer (the height of my art) was dead (past).

It is not evident what is meant by Shakespeare in referring to the lapse of three years, as set out in this sonnet. Is he referring to the beginning of his poetical career? Or to the beginning of the sonnets? Or, to probably what amounts to the same thing, the beginning by him of the use of intoxicants, as an inspiration? Even were these questions answered, we would still be in ignorance as to when this particular sonnet was written. Therefore without further information, this reference can give us but little definite information.

SONNET 105.

Let not my love be call'd idolatry,
Nor my beloved as an idol show,
Since all alike my songs and praises be
To one, of one, still such, and ever so.
Kind is my love to-day, to-morrow kind,
Still constant in a wondrous excellence;
Therefore my verse to constancy confined,
One thing expressing, leaves out difference.
'Fair, kind, and true,' is all my argument,
'Fair, kind, and true,' varying to other words;
And in this change is my invention spent,
Three themes in one, which wondrous scope affords.
    'Fair, kind, and true,' have often lived alone,
    Which three till now never kept seat in one.

Let not my love be called idolatry, nor my beloved art an idol, since my songs and praises are all alike 'To one, of one, still such, and ever so' (suggestive of the Te Deum, 'As it was in the beginning, is now, and ever shall be').

Kind is my love (art) to-day and to-morrow, still constant in its excellence; therefore my verse is confined to constancy, expressing one thing, it leaves out difference.

Fair, kind and true (beauty, love and truth) varying to other words (equivalent words); and in this change (of words) is my invention spent, three themes in one, afford a wondrous scope.

Each of these has often been treated alone, but never till now have all been treated by one poet.

SONNET 106.

When in the chronicle of wasted time
I see descriptions of the fairest wights,
And beauty making beautiful old rhyme
In praise of ladies dead and lovely knights,
Then, in the blazon of sweet beauty's best,
Of hand, of foot, of lip, of eye, of brow,
I see their antique pen would have express'd
Even such a beauty as you master now.
So all their praises are but prophecies
Of this our time, all you prefiguring;
And, for they look'd but with divining eyes,
They had not skill enough your worth to sing:
>   For we, which now behold these present days,
>   Have eyes to wonder, but lack tongues to praise.

When in chronicles of the past, I see descriptions of fairest wights, and poets making beautiful old rhymes, in praise of ladies and knights, now dead.

In display of their beauty of hand, foot, lip, eye, or brow, I see their pen would have expressed, even such beauty as my art now possesses.

Their praises are but prophecies of our times, foretelling my art, and while they foresaw these things, they had not art enough to sing my worth (to express what my art expresses);

For we, which now behold these present days, have eyes to wonder, but lack tongues to praise.

In the last two lines Shakespeare evidently intends to say, or to convey the impression, that his art, at the present time has lost the power of expression, and that while he has the same conception, he lacks the 'tongue to praise' of his prime.

SONNET 107.

Not mine own fears, nor the prophetic soul
Of the wide world dreaming on things to come,
Can yet the lease of my true love control,
Supposed as forfeit to a confined doom.
The mortal moon hath her eclipse endured,
And the sad augurs mock their own presage;
Incertainties now crown themselves assured,
And peace proclaims olives of endless age.
Now with the drops of this most balmy time
My love looks fresh, and Death to me subscribes,
Since, spite of him, I'll live in this poor rhyme,
While he insults o'er dull and speechless tribes:
    And thou in this shalt find thy monument,
    When tyrants' crests and tombs of brass are spent.

Neither my fears, nor the prophetic soul of the world, dreaming on things to come, can terminate the lease of my true love (art), supposed as forfeit to a confined doom (supposed to be mortal).

The mortal moon has been eclipsed, and the augurs find their presages false; incertainties have become assured (certain), and an endless age of peace is proclaimed.

Now with the drops (dews) of this balmy time, my love (art) looks fresh, and death subscribes (yields) to me, since spite of him I'll live in this rhyme, while he insults (triumphs) over dead tribes.

And my art in this shall find its monument, when tyrants crests and tombs are spent.

SONNET 108.

What's in the brain, that ink may character,
Which hath not figured to thee my true spirit?
What's new to speak, what new to register,
That may express my love, or thy dear merit?
Nothing, sweet boy; but yet, like prayers divine,
I must each day say o'er the very same;
Counting no old thing old, thou mine, I thine,
Even as when first I hallowed thy fair name.
So that eternal love in love's fresh case
Weighs not the dust and injury of age,
Nor gives to necessary wrinkles place,
But makes antiquity for aye his page;
    Finding the first conceit of love there bred,
    Where time and outward form would show it dead.

What's in the brain that ink may write, that has not been figured (imagined) by my true spirit? What can I say or write, that's new, that may express my art, or its dear merit?

Nothing, sweet boy, (my art), yet like prayers I must each day repeat the same, counting nothing old, though it be old; you mine, I yours, as when at first I began your praises.

So eternal love is ever fresh, weighs (regards) not the dust and injury of age, nor becomes wrinkled, but keeps antiquity always a page (youth).

Finding the first conceit (inspiration) of love there bred (continued), when time and outward form would show it dead (when by time and form it should be dead).

SONNET 109.

O, never say that I was false of heart,
Though absence seem'd my fame to qualify
As easy might I from myself depart
As from my soul, which in thy breast doth lie:
That is my home of love: if I have ranged,
Like him that travels, I return again;
Just to the time, not with the time exchanged,
So that myself bring water for my stain.
Never believe, though in my nature reign'd
All frailties that besiege all kinds of blood,
That it could so preposterously be stain'd,
To leave for nothing all thy sum of good;
    For nothing this wide universe I call,
    Save thou, my rose; in it thou art my all.

Never say that I was false of heart, though absence seemed my flame to qualify (to indicate my love had cooled). I might as easily depart from myself, as from my soul, which lies in your breast, Wine.

That, Wine, is my home of love: If I have been absent I return again; promptly to the time, and unchanged by time, unstained, except by water. (A declaration that water has been his only beverage?)

Never believe though I possess all frailties of flesh and blood, that I could be so stained (so false) as to leave your sum of good, for nothing.

For I call nothing in this universe, but you, Wine, my rose; you are my all.

Shakespeare again returns to his Wine, after an absence of what duration is not told.

SONNET 110.

Alas, 'tis true I have gone here and there,
And made myself a motley to the view,
Gored mine own thoughts, sold cheap what is most dear,
Made old offences of affections new;
Most true it is that I have look'd on truth
Askance and strangely: but, by all above,
These blenches gave my heart another youth,
And worse essays proved thee my best of love.
Now all is done, have what shall have no end:
Mine appetite I never more will grind
On newer proof, to try an older friend,
A god in love, to whom I am confined.
    Then give me welcome, next my heaven the best,
    Even to thy pure and most loving breast.

'Tis true Wine, I have gone here and there and made myself a motley (conspicuous) to the view, gored my own thoughts (humiliated myself), sold cheap what is most dear (sacrificed my self respect), made old offenses of affections new (repeated old offenses in new indulgences, substitutes,);

Even truer it is that I have looked on truth askance and strangely (I have questioned my love for you with doubts and misgivings): but by all above, these blenches (nauseating experiences) gave my heart another youth (these trials renewed my love for you), and worse essays (efforts that failed) proved you my best of love:

Now all is done, have what shall have no end (I accept what must be to the end): I never more will grind (punish) my appetite, on newer proof, to try an older friend, (With new experiments to replace an older friend) a god in love to whom I am confined.

Then give me welcome, next my heaven the best, to your pure and most loving breast.

Nearly all the expressions in this sonnet are vague, and their meanings can only be guessed. The foregoing construction is submitted, as probably a correct one, but it is realized that other reading might be even more satisfactory.

This and several sonnets following have usually been construed as referring to Shakespeare's calling as an actor, and as expressing his feelings towards that calling. This is not believed to be correct. In the first place, the proof is not satisfactory that Shakespeare was a professional actor, or so far as known, that he actually made a business of appearing upon the stage. In the second place, the sonnet seems to indicate that Shakespeare is describing his experiences in his efforts to find a cure for, or relief from, the appetite which is enslaving him, and that he had been experimenting with some of the supposed remedies of his times.

Heretofore, it is probable, he had passed his periods of drinking in privacy, and that now his efforts to apply a remedy has necessitated the surrender of his seclusion, and exposed him to the view of the public, and to the consequent humiliation, which is so plainly recorded in this and the succeeding sonnets. Some of the references in the sonnets to follow make this even plainer than the present one does.

It is suggested that the cure referred to, and which he undertook, consisted of a visit to some of the thermal springs, probably a popular resort, somewhere in continental Europe. Just as in our own day hot springs are resorted to by inebriates, on account of their reputed qualities. That Shakespeare made such a visit, and that it failed to give the desired relief, is plainly stated in the last two of the Sonnets, Nos. 153 and 154. The reference in the sonnet under review seems quite pertinent, in the line where it is said, 'And worse essays proved thee my best of love'. The same thing in effect is said in the last two sonnets.

It is considered a likely surmise, that these two last Sonnets 153 and 154, had they been placed in their proper sequence, should have been incorporated in this group of sonnets, which are now under consideration, as it is believed they were written while Shakespeare was sojourning at these springs.

The sonnet also suggests that while Shakespeare was seeking relief at the springs, he was also trying out some substitute for his usual beverage, such as light wines or ales in the place of the stronger alcoholic drinks. This is more plainly stated in the sonnets to follow. In this sonnet it is suggested by the expression of 'affections new' and 'Mine appetite I never more will grind on newer proof'. That these substitutes proved unsatisfactory to him he plainly indicates by pledging himself to his 'older friend, a god in love, to whom I am confined'.

"Proof" as used here is a well known technical word commonly used in expressing the percentage of alcohol in wines. Nothing contained in the sonnets comes so near to defining in express words the subject, as alcoholic, as does the use of this word in its otherwise suggestive surroundings.

SONNET 111.

O, for my sake do you with Fortune chide,
The guilty goddess of my harmful deeds,
That did not better for my life provide
Than public means which public manners breeds.
Thence comes it that my name receives a brand,
And almost thence my nature is subdued
To what it works in, like the dyer's hand:
Pity me then and wish I were renew'd;
Whilst, like a willing patient, I will drink
Potions of eisel 'gainst my strong infection;
No bitterness that I will bitter think,
Nor double penance, to correct correction.
    Pity me then, dear friend, and I assure ye
    Even that your pity is enough to cure me.

O, Wine, for my sake chide with Fortune, guilty goddess (authoress) of my harmful deeds, that did not provide better for my life, than public means, which public manners breeds (which makes my actions public).

From such conditions my name receives a brand, and because of it my nature is subdued (mortified), and like the dyer's hand is stained, by what it works in (associates with): pity me then, and wish I were renewed (restored to you).

I will drink like a willing patient, potions of eisel (vinegar—sour wines) against my strong infection (as a substitute for stronger drink), and will not think any exaction bitter, and will do double penance to correct what I have done.

Pity me, dear friend, Wine, and I assure you your pity will cure me.

Shakespeare's complaint that Fortune had not made better provision for his life, than public means, is taken to mean that he was not able to afford the privacy of the rich, and consequently with only ordinary accommodations was exposed to the public gaze, from which his name received a brand, and his nature was subdued.

The reference to eisel—vinegar—in this sonnet is the basis for the suggestion made in the previous sonnet, that Shakespeare had undertaken the use of light, sour wines as a substitute for stronger drink. This is strongly suggested, if not actually stated in this sonnet.

As Shakespeare in the previous sonnet had renounced all cures, and pledged himself to his 'older friend', and as in this, a subsequent and immediately following sonnet, he declares himself willing to make a substitution, and to do anything necessary to correct what he had done, it is concluded that these two sonnets have been interchanged, and that this one should have preceded the former one.

SONNET 112.

Your love and pity doth the impression fill
Which vulgar scandal stamp'd upon my brow;
For what care I who calls me well or ill,
So you o'er-green my bad, my good allow?
You are my all the world, and I must strive
To know my shames and praises from your tongue;
None else to me, nor I to none alive,
That my steel'd sense or changes right or wrong.
In so profound abysm I throw all care
Of others' voices, that my adder's sense
To critic and to flatterer stopped are.
Mark how with my neglect I do dispense:
    You are so strongly in my purpose bred
    That all the world besides methinks are dead.

Your love and pity, Wine, fill the impression (hurts) which vulgar scandal stamped upon my brow; for what care I for what others say, if you excuse what's bad in me and allow what's good.

You are all the world to me, and I must strive to know my shames and praises from your tongue (in my troubles I must come to you for comfort); no opinion except yours is ought to me, nor am I alive to the censure of any one, that can change my hardened sense, either for good or bad. (It is impossible to construe lines 7 and 8 with certainty).

I am so profoundly careless of others' opinions, that my adder's (deaf) sense, to either critic or flatterer is stopped. Mark how with my neglect I do dispense: (mark how unconcerned I am):

So strongly are you intrenched in my thoughts, that I think all the world besides are dead.

SONNET 113.

Since I left you mine eye is in my mind,
And that which governs me to go about
Doth part his function and is partly blind,
Seems seeing, but effectually is out;
For it no form delivers to the heart
Of bird, of flower, or shape, which it doth latch:
Of his quick object hath the mind no part,
Nor his own vision holds what it doth catch;
For if it see the rudest or gentlest sight,
The most sweet favour or deformed'st creature,
The mountain or the sea, the day or night,
The crow or dove, it shapes them to your feature:
    Incapable of more, replete with you,
    My most true mind thus maketh mine untrue.

Since I left you my eye is in my mind (I am absent minded, preoccupied through thinking of you), and my sight divides its function, and is partly blind, seems to see but not effectually (clearly).

For there is no inspiration in seeing bird or flower or shape, which the eye catches; what it does see the mind does not realize, nor does the eye appreciate;

For if it see the rudest or gentlest sight, the sweetest favor or the most deformed creature, the mountain, sea, day or night, the crow or dove, it shapes them all to your features (it can see or think of nothing but you):

Incapable of seeing otherwise, and being possessed by you, my most true mind, thus maketh mine untrue (my mind being true, therefore my eye must be untrue).

SONNET 114.

Or whether doth my mind, being crown'd with you,
Drink up the monarch's plague, this flattery?
Or whether shall I say, mine eye saith true,
And that your love taught it this alchemy,
To make of monsters and things indigest
Such cherubins as your sweet self resemble,
Creating every bad a perfect best,
As fast as objects to his beams assemble?
O, 'tis the first; 'tis flattery in my seeing,
And my great mind most kingly drinks it up:
Mine eye well knows what with his gust is 'greeing,
And to his palate doth prepare the cup:
    If it be poison'd, 'tis the lesser sin
    That mine eye loves it and doth first begin.

Or does my mind being full of you, Wine, flatter (give beauty to) what it sees? Or shall I believe my eye sees true, and that your love taught it this alchemy (the magic of transforming everything to beauty),

To make of monsters and unnatural things such cherubins as resemble you, creating every bad a perfect best, as fast as objects are seen?

O 'tis the first; 'tis flattery in my seeing, and my great mind drinks it up (as a king does flattery): my eye well knows what agrees with my mind's gust (desires), and prepares the cup to my mind's taste.

If it be poisoned (distorted) it is the lesser sin that my eye loves it, and first begins the deception (itself first takes the poison that it offers to the mind).

This group of sonnets show that Shakespeare in his cups is becoming less clear in his conceptions, or if not that, he is less clear in his expressions of them.

SONNET 115.

Those lines that I before have writ do lie,
Even those that said I could not love you dearer:
Yet then my judgement knew no reason why
My most full flame should afterwards burn clearer.
But reckoning Time, whose million'd accidents
Creep in 'twixt vows, and change decrees of kings,
Tan sacred beauty, blunt the sharp'st intents,
Divert strong minds to the course of altering things;
Alas, why, fearing of Time's tyranny,
Might I not then say 'Now I love you best,'
When I was certain o'er incertainty,
Crowning the present, doubting of the rest?
    Love is a babe; then might I not say so,
    To give full growth to that which still doth grow?

The lines that I have before written lie, even those that said I could not love you dearer, Wine; yet I had no reason then to know that my love should afterwards burn clearer.

But the happenings of Time creep in 'twixt vows, and change decrees of kings, mar beauty, blunt the sharpest intent, and change strong minds to conform to changed conditions;

Why fearing of Time's tyranny (his power to change) might I not then say 'Now I love you best', when I was certain beyond doubting, praising you in the present, and doubting the future?

Love is a babe; then (in the past) might I not say, I could not love you better, to give full growth to that which still grows (and my love grow with the object it loves)?

SONNET 116.

Let me not to the marriage of true minds
Admit impediments. Love is not love
Which alters when it alteration finds,
Or bends with the remover to remove:
O, no! it is an ever-fixed mark,
That looks on tempests and is never shaken;
It is the star to every wandering bark,
Whose worth's unknown, although his height be taken.
Love's not Time's fool, though rosy lips and cheeks
Within his bending sickle's compass come;
Love alters not with his brief hours and weeks,
But bears it out even to the edge of doom.
    If this be error and upon me proved,
    I never writ, nor no man ever loved.

Let me not to the marriage of true minds admit impediments. Love is not love which alters (lessens) with changes, or bends (adjusts) itself to him who would remove (terminate) it.

It is a fixed mark that tempests cannot shake; the star to every bark, whose worth (material qualities) is unknown, though his heights (movements) be taken.

Love is not Time's fool, though lips and cheeks come within the compass of Time's sickle; love alters not with Time's hours and weeks, but continues to the edge of doom.

If in this I be proven in error, I have never written, and no one has ever loved.

SONNET 117.

Accuse me thus: that I have scanted all
Wherein I should your great deserts repay.
Forgot upon your dearest love to call,
Whereto all bonds do tie me day by day;
That I have frequent been with unknown minds,
And given to time your own dear-purchased right;
That I have hoisted sail to all the winds
Which should transport me farthest from your sight.
Book both my wilfulness and errors down,
And on just proof surmise accumulate;
Bring me within the level of your frown,
But shoot not at me in your waken'd hate;
    Since my appeal says I did strive to prove
    The constancy and virtue of your love.

Accuse me thus: that I have scanted in repaying your great deserts, forgot upon your dearest love to call, whereto I am bound day by day;

That I have often been with unknown minds, and given to time what belonged to you; that I have hoisted sails to all the winds which could take me farthest from you (have sought for methods which would abate my cravings).

Charge me with wilfulness and errors, and on just proof increase your surmises (suspicions); bring me within the aim of your frown but do not shoot at (endanger) me with your hate;

Since I declare my purpose was to prove the constancy and virtue of your love.

Shakespeare returns to Wine in complete servility, and dares not admit the truth, but explains his desertion by falsely declaring that he was only trying to make her jealous.

SONNET 118.

Like as, to make our appetites more keen,
With eager compounds we our palate urge;
As, to prevent our maladies unseen,
We sicken to shun sickness when we purge;
Even so, being full of your ne'er-cloying sweetness,
To bitter sauces did I frame my feeding;
And sick of welfare found a kind of meetness
To be diseased, ere that there was true needing.
Thus policy in love, to anticipate
The ills that were not, grew to faults assured,
And brought to medicine a healthful state,
Which, rank of goodness, would by ill be cured:
    But thence I learn, and find the lesson true,
    Drugs poison him that so fell sick of you.

As we try to make our appetites keener with eager (acrid) compounds; or to prevent (relieve) our maladies, we sicken ourselves with purges;

So being full of your ne'er cloying sweetness, I fed on bitter sauces (antidotes, substitutes), and sick of welfare (good fare, wine), found a kind of meetness to be diseased (by medicines or substitutes) before it was needed (before alcoholism had come to an acute stage).

Thus love's policy—to anticipate ills that were not yet—grew to ills assured (actual ills) and brought to medicine a healthful state, which rank of goodness (excess of wine) would by ill (medicine) be cured:

Through this lesson I learn, that drugs poison him who falls sick of you.

Shakespeare here describes his efforts by substitutes and antidotes to forestall and prevent the final collapse that follows alcoholic excesses. The next sonnet, 119, shows the failure of the experiment.

SONNET 119.

What potions have I drunk of Siren tears,
Distill'd from limbecks foul as hell within,
Applying fears to hopes and hopes to fears,
Still losing when I saw myself to win!
What wretched errors hath my heart committed,
Whilst it hath thought itself so blessed never!
How have mine eyes out of their spheres been fitted,
In the distraction of this madding fever!
O benefit of ill! now I find true
That better is by evil still made better;
And ruin'd love, when it is built anew,
Grows fairer than at first, more strong, far greater.
    So I return rebuked to my content,
    And gain by ill thrice more than I have spent.

What potions have I drunk, distilled from limbecks foul as hell, fearing in hope and hoping in fears, still losing when I saw myself to win (when I thought I would succeed)!

What wretched errors my heart has committed (by drinking) whilst it felt itself blessed (in intoxication)! How have my eyes with fits started from their spheres, in the distraction of the madding fever!

O, benefit of ill (relief through wine)! Now I find that better is by evil still made better (relief through wine is improved by more wine); and ruined love (delirium) when built anew (restored through wine) grown fairer than at first, stronger, greater.

So I return rebuked to my content (comfort of wine) and gain by ill (sickness) thrice more than I have spent.

SONNET 120.

That you were once unkind befriends me now,
And for that sorrow which I then did feel
Needs must I under my transgression bow,
Unless my nerves were brass or hammer'd steel.
For if you were by my unkindness shaken,
As I by yours, you've pass'd a hell of time;
And I, a tyrant, have no leisure taken
To weigh how once I suffer'd in your crime.
O, that our night of woe might have remember'd
My deepest sense, how hard true sorrow hits,
And soon to you, as you to me, then tender'd
The humble salve which wounded bosoms fits!
    But that your trespass now becomes a fee;
    Mine ransoms yours, and yours must ransom me.

That you, Wine, were unkind once (denied to me) befriends me now, and for the sorrow of that time, needs I under my transgression bow (succumb) unless my nerves were brass or hammered steel (such nerves as could have come through such ordeal without collapse).

If you were shaken by my unkindness as I by yours, you've passed a hell of time; and I have no leisure taken (have not ceased the use of stimulant) to realize how I suffered in your crime.

O, that our night of woe might have remembered (realized) my deepest sense (cravings), how hard true sorrow hits (how I suffered), and soon to you, as you to me (permitted you sooner, as you did later, to relieve me), then tendered the humble salve which wounded bosoms fits!

But that your trespass now becomes a fee; (a legal meaning, indicating that under the statutes of Limitations a trespass continued ripens into an absolute title, or fee); mine (all I have) ransoms yours (is given for you) and yours must ransom me (you must give all you have for me).

The last two sonnets describe such a condition of nervous frenzy as is unmistakable. They were written in the fearful and lingering memory of the horrors of delirium tremens.

SONNET 121.

'Tis better to be vile than vile esteemed,
When not to be receives reproach of being;
And the just pleasure lost, which is so deemed
Not by our feeling, but by others' seeing:
For why should others' false adulterate eyes
Give salutation to my sportive blood?
Or on my frailties why are frailer spies,
Which in their wills count bad what I think good?
No, I am that I am, and they that level
At my abuses reckon up their own:
I may be straight, though they themselves be bevel;
By their rank thoughts my deeds must not be shown;
Unless this general evil they maintain,
All men are bad and in their badness reign.

'Tis better to be vile, than to be thought vile, when one who is not vile is reproached for being so; and the pleasure of being honest is lost, not in fact, but by others thinking it lost:

For why should the false and impure thoughts of others salute (make light of) my sportive blood (weakness)? Or why do frailer ones than I spy on my frailties, and judge that bad which I think good?

No, I am what I am, and they that level (point) at my abuses, reckon up their own (are pharisaical): I may be straight and they be bevel; by their rank thoughts my deeds must not be shown;

Unless they maintain all men are bad, and in their badness reign.

SONNET 122.

Thy gift, thy tables, are within my brain
Full character'd with lasting memory,
Which shall above that idle rank remain,
Beyond all date, even to eternity:
Or, at the least, so long as brain and heart
Have faculty by nature to subsist;
Till each to razed oblivion yield his part
Of thee, thy record never can be miss'd.
That poor retention could not so much hold,
Nor need I tallies thy dear love to score;
Therefore to give them from me was I bold,
To trust those tables that receive thee more:
    To keep an adjunct to remember thee
    Were to import forgetfulness in me.

Your gifts, Wine, your tables (inspiration, knowledge) are in my brain written in my memory, and shall remain above that idle rank, even to eternity; (Idle rank is taken to refer to Shakespeare's detractors, mentioned in sonnet 121, where he calls their thought 'rank', and here plays upon the word, as is his custom when drinking. Here he seems to say, that notwithstanding his degraded condition, and their raillery, he considers they are and will remain beneath his talents).

Or at least so long as men shall live; till each to oblivion yields his part of you, your records (tables) never can be missed (lost).

That poor retention (the minds of his detractors) could not so much hold, but I need no tallies thy dear love to score; therefore was I bold to give them from me (forget them while drunken) and to trust those (service) tables that receive you more:

To keep an adjunct (assistance) to remember you were to impart forgetfulness in me.

The foregoing construction is not adopted without some misgivings. The writer has no doubt that the 'tables' referred to in the first line means his own capacity and genius, and the inspiration or assistance that the poet believed he was receiving from his intoxicant; he is equally certain that it does not mean any written or blank memoranda. If this conclusion be correct then Shakespeare could not part with memory, which constituted his tables, except to forget or become oblivious, as in drunkenness. Therefore he was bold enough to give them away that he might 'trust those tables that receive thee more', the tables on which wine was served. If service tables are meant it is a very light and frivolous turn to give the sonnet, but when it comes to playing on words Shakespeare is never dignified.

SONNET 123.

No, Time, thou shalt not boast that I do change:
Thy pyramids built up with newer might
To me are nothing novel, nothing strange;
They are but dressings of a former sight.
Our dates are brief, and therefore we admire
What thou dost foist upon us that is old;
And rather make them born to our desire
Than think that we before have heard them told.
Thy registers and thee I both defy,
Not wondering at the present nor the past,
For thy records and what we see doth lie,
Made more or less by thy continual haste.
    This I do vow, and this shall ever be,
    I will be true, despite thy scythe and thee.

Time, you shall not boast that I change; your pyramids, (wonders) built with newer might, are not novel or strange to me, they are but the dressings of a former sight.

Our lives are short and therefore we admire what is old, and rather make them born (new) to our desire (pleasure), than think we have heard them told before.

I defy you and your records, wondering at neither the present or the past, for your records and what we see are lies, made more or less by your continual haste (consequently not complete enough to tell the truth).

This I vow, and this shall ever be (eternal), I will be true, despite your scythe and you.

SONNET 124.

If my dear love were but the child of state,
It might for Fortune's bastard be unfather'd,
As subject to Time's love or to Time's hate,
Weeds among weeds, or flowers with flowers gather'd.
No, it was builded far from accident;
It suffers not in smiling pomp, nor falls
Under the blow of thralled discontent,
Whereto the inviting time our fashion calls:
It fears not policy, that heretic,
Which works on leases of short-number'd hours.
But all alone stands hugely politic,
That it nor grows with heat nor drowns with showers
    To this I witness call the fools of time,
    Which die for goodness, who have lived for crime.

If my dear love, Wine, were but the child of state (under state control), it might for Fortune's bastard be unfathered (by the state controlled and condemned), as subjects to Time's love or hate, weeds among weeds (when haters control), or flowers with flowers gathered (when lovers control).

No, it was builded far from accident (not subject to popular favour); it suffers not in smiling pomp (the mighty), nor falls under the blow of thralled discontent (the oppressed), whereto the inviting time our fashion calls.

It fears not policy which works on short leases (is of short duration), but stands alone hugely (extremely) politic (discreet), and grows not with heat (under favorable conditions) nor drowns with showers (public clamours).

To this I call as witness the fools of time, which die for goodness, who have lived for crime.

Fools of time: Those who have lived drunkards and die reformers, who have favored and opposed Wine, but have not changed results.

Throughout this sonnet Shakespeare's love is designated as 'it', showing plainly that it is of neuter sex. While neuter things may be designated as 'he' or 'she' the respectful designation of the human masculine or feminine as 'it', is under no circumstances admissible.

SONNET 125.

Were't aught to me I bore the canopy,
With my extern the outward honouring,
Or laid great bases for eternity,
Which prove more short than waste or ruining?
Have I not seen dwellers on form and favour
Lose all, and more, by paying too much rent,
For compound sweet forgoing simple savour,
Pitiful thrivers, in their gazing spent?
No, let me be obsequious in thy heart,
And take thou my oblation, poor but free,
Which is not mix'd with seconds, knows no art
But mutual render, only me for thee.
    Hence, thou suborn'd informer! a true soul
    When most impeach'd stands least in thy control.

Were't ought to me I bore the canopy with my extern the outward honoring (what mattered it to me whether I be acclaimed with outward honoring), or laid great bases for eternity (or whether by my writings I laid great bases for eternity), which (in either case) prove more short than waste or ruining?

Have I not seen dwellers on form and favor (pets of fortune) lose all and more by paying too much rent (getting nothing for their devotions) foregoing simplicity for display, pitiful thrivers in their gazing (worshipping) spent?

No, let me be obsequious in your heart, Wine, and receive you my poor but free oblation, which is not mixed with seconds (depends not on time but is eternal), knows not art (craft), but mutually give me for you (with the comforts of Wine I care nothing for honors or favors).

Hence suborned informer (fools of time, betrayers)! a true soul when most impeached, stands least in your control.

SONNET 126.

O thou, my lovely boy, who in thy power
Dost hold Time's fickle glass, his sickle, how'er;
Who hast by waning grown, and therein show'st
Thy lovers withering as thy sweet self grow'st;
If Nature, sovereign mistress over wrack,
As thou goest onwards, still will pluck thee back,
She keeps thee to this purpose, that her skill
May time disgrace and wretched minutes kill.
Yet fear her, O thou minion of her pleasure!
She may detain, but not still keep, her treasure:
    Her audit, though delay'd answer'd must be
    And her quietus is to render thee.

O, Wine, my lovely boy, who in your power (perennial youth) hold
Time's fickle glass, which is his sickle howe'er; who by waning (being
consumed) grows, and therein show your lovers withering as you grow:
If nature, sovereign mistress over rack (restorer), as you go onward
still pulls you back (continues to restore as you strive to destroy), she
keeps you to show that her skill may time disgrace (everrule) and
wretched minutes kill (by comforting those you make miserable).
Yet fear her, O minion of her pleasure! She may detain but not
keep her treasure (her creatures, you, Wine, among the others); her
audit (accounting) though delayed, must be answered, and her quietus
(acquittance, final result) is to render (destroy) you.

Thus, with an unfinished sonnet (two lines short of the usual)
Shakespeare ends his panegyric on Wine. Several sonnets, pre-
ceding this last one, indicate a change. Where before there had
been nothing but the most extravagant praise, even in the throes
of his misery, a less infatuated tone becomes evident. Then, in
the last, with almost supernatural tones, Wine is warned that
it too will be the subject of time's devastating power.

The first 18 sonnets were addressed, in form, to a male objec-
tive. After that, and particularly after the twentieth sonnet,
the sex of the addressee is, at least, in doubt as to whether it is
male, female or neuter. It is believed that the contention has
been established, that the sex of that which has been addressed,
is neuter. At any rate, it may be said, that if it has been shown
that Wine is the object addressed, there is nothing after the
twentieth sonnet that would do violence to such a construction.

THE DARK WOMAN SONNETS.

The Sonnets, yet remaining to be construed, are those which are sometimes referred to as the Dark Woman Sonnets. This, too, is a misnomer. These sonnets, except one, are not addressed to a woman. Shakespeare's dark or black, Mistress, is Wine—Wine in its debasing or degrading character.

While these sonnets have been segregated and published as a distinct series, it is hardly doubtful that they were written either before or during the composition of the series which has just been reviewed. It must therefore be concluded that Shakespeare was never wholly deluded as to Wine's character. But had he not written these last sonnets, we should not have suspected that he had come to realize the true and vicious character of Wine, but would have been left to think of him, as of Omar, ever rejoicing, and suffering, in the embraces of his Siren.

It is not altogether plain, why the author should have given to Wine the masculine or neuter character when he was wooing it as his virgin love, and praising it as his helpmate and companion, and exalting it as his master and inspirer, and, then when defining it as a debaucher, betrayer and wrecker, to give it the character and guise of a woman. We have seen his treatment of it as a neuter, and we shall now see how in his degradation and humiliation, he discovers it to be feminine. If there is no reason for this difference of view, it is not at all complimentary to the feminine sex. There is however a possible reason why it should have been so distinguished. This is to be noticed hereafter.

SONNET 127.

In the old age black was not counted fair,
Or if it were, it bore not beauty's name;
But now is black beauty's successive heir,
And beauty slander'd with a bastard shame:
For since each hand hath put on nature's power,
Fairing the foul with art's false borrow'd face,
Sweet beauty hath no name, no holy bower,
But is profaned, if not lives in disgrace.
Therefore my mistress' eyes are raven black,
Her eyes so suited, and they mourners seem
At such who, not born fair, no beauty lack,
Slandering creation with a false esteem:
    Yet so they mourn, becoming of their woe,
    That every tongue says beauty should look so.

In former times black was not counted fair, or if it were, it bore not beauty's name (was not called beautiful); but now black is beauty's heir, and beauty is slandered with a bastard (illegitimate or undeserved) shame (likeness):

For since each hand has put on nature's power (makes beauty, which only nature can make), fairing the foul (making the foul fair) with art's (deceits) false borrowed face, sweet beauty has no name nor bower, but is profaned, if lives not in disgrace (discredited).

Therefore (under like conditions) my mistress' (Wine's) eyes are raven black, and are so suited (dressed) and they seem mourners, at such who, not born fair, no beauty lack (like those, who though not born fair, no beauty lack, foulness being her beauty), thus slandering creation with a false esteem.

Yet so they mourn becoming of their woe (the woe they cause), that every tongue says beauty should look so (all agree that her evil ways are beautiful).

It is admitted that lines 9 to 12, literally construed do not bear the above construction, but if they do not mean that, they are madness and meaningless.

SONNET 128.

How oft, when thou, my music, music play'st,
Upon that blessed wood whose motion sounds
With thy sweet fingers, when thou gently sway'st
The wiry concord that mine ear confounds,
Do I envy those jacks that nimble leap
To kiss the tender inward of thy hand,
Whilst my poor lips, which should that harvest reap,
At the wood's boldness by thee blushing stand
To be so tickled, they would change their state
And situation with those dancing chips,
O'er whom thy fingers walk with gentle gait,
Making dead wood more blest than living lips.
   Since saucy jacks so happy are in this,
   Give them thy fingers, me thy lips to kiss.

How oft when you play music on the virginal, and with your fingers sway the wiry concord that confounds (charms) my ear,

Do I envy the jacks (keys) that leap to kiss the inward of your hand, whilst my lips that should that harvest reap, stand blushing at the boldness of the wood (keys)!

So to be tickled (kissed) they would change places with the dancing chips (keys) over which your fingers gently move, making dead wood more blessed than living lips.

Since saucy jacks so happy are in this, give them your fingers, me your lips to kiss.

This sonnet has no apparent relation with the others, and should be entitled: 'Sonnet written on seeing a beautiful woman playing upon the virginal.' Like several of the sonnets it was no doubt composed upon some occasion, or suggested by some incident.

This is the one, and only sonnet that is actually addressed to a woman.

SONNET 129.

The expense of spirit in a waste of shame
Is lust in action; and till action, lust
Is perjured, murderous, bloody, full of blame,
Savage, extreme, rude, cruel, not to trust;
Enjoy'd no sooner but despised straight;
Past reason hunted; and no sooner had,
Past reason hated, as a swallowed bait,
On purpose laid to make the taker mad:
Mad in pursuit, and in possession so;
Had, having, and in quest to have, extreme;
A bliss in proof, and proved, a very woe;
Before, a joy proposed; behind, a dream.
    All this the world well knows; yet none knows well
    To shun the heaven that leads men to this hell.

The expenditure of spirit in shame's waste (shameful waste, drinking) is lust in action; until in action (while simply craving) lust is perjured, murderous, bloody etc.; (A well known fact that a lustful craving, unindulged, and especially the lust for drink, stops at nothing short of being satiated.)

No sooner enjoyed, than the indulgence is despised; hunted beyond reason; and no sooner had than it is hated beyond reason, as if it were a bait prepared to make the taker mad, when swallowed:

Mad in pursuit and in possession; extreme (unreasonable) when it has been had, when it is being indulged, and when in quest of it; a bliss in proof (anticipation), and proved (a reality), a very woe; before obtaining it, a joy proposed; behind (after) a dream.

The world knows all this; yet none knows well enough to shun the heaven (indulgence) that leads men to this hell.

SONNET 130.

My mistress' eyes are nothing like the sun;
Coral is far more red than her lips' red:
If snow be white, why then her breasts are dun;
If hairs be wires, black wires grow on her head.
I have seen roses damask'd, red and white,
But no such roses see I in her cheeks;
And in some perfumes is there more delight
Than in the breath that from my mistress reeks.
I love to hear her speak, yet well I know
That music hath a far more pleasing sound:
I grant I never saw a goddess go,
My mistress, when she walks, treads on the ground:
    And yet, by heaven, I think my love as rare
    As any she belied with false compare.

My mistress' (Wine's) eyes are nothing like the sun; coral is redder than her lips; if snow be white her breasts are dun; if hairs be wires, black wires grow on her head. (There is a possibility that the color 'dun' and 'black wires' may give a clue to what particular liquors Shakespeare indulged in. The dun of course refers to color, and it is suspected the black wires refer to the retainer in which the liquor was sold or delivered. If so, the reference is probably to the manner in which the top or cork was secured.)

I have seen roses damasked, red and white, but no such roses in her cheeks; and there's more delight in some perfumes, than in her reeking breath.

I love to hear her speak, but music is more pleasing; I never saw a goddess go, but my mistress treads upon the ground.

And yet I think my love as rare, as any she, belied (exaggerated) by false comparisons.

Shakespeare has discovered that his mistress is altogether of the earth, earthy, and without the divinity with which he had endued her.

SONNET 131.

Thou art as tyrannous, so as thou art,
As those whose beauties proudly make them cruel;
For well thou know'st to my dear doting heart
Thou art the fairest and most precious jewel.
Yet, in good faith, some say that thee behold,
Thy face hath not the power to make love groan:
To say they err I dare not be so bold,
Although I swear it to myself alone.
And to be sure that is not false I swear,
A thousand groans, but thinking on thy face,
One on another's neck, do witness bear
Thy black is fairest in my judgement's place.
    In nothing art thou black save in thy deeds,
    And thence this slander, as I think, proceeds.

You, Wine, are as tyrannous as those whose beauties make them cruel; for you know to my doting heart, you are the fairest and most precious jewel.

Yet some say that behold your face, that it has not the power to make love groan (suffer): I do not dare to say they err (to contradict them), though I swear it to myself alone.

And to be sure that I swear not falsely, I swear it makes a thousand groans, to but think on your face; one (other face) on another's neck (I) witness bear, your black is fairest in my judgment.

In nothing are you black save in your deeds, and thence this slander (that you are black), I think proceeds.

Students of the sonnet seem to find no difficulty in construing this one, for there seems to be no comments on the construction of the 9th to the 12th lines, thus indicating that they need no elucidation. It is not certain that the construction above given is the one intended by the poet, but it seems probable, and having no other suggestions, it was formulated.

SONNET 132.

Thine eyes I love, and they, as pitying me,
Knowing thy heart torments me with disdain,
Have put on black and loving mourners be,
Looking with pretty ruth upon my pain.
And truly not the morning sun of heaven
Better becomes the grey cheeks of the east,
Nor that full star that ushers in the even
Doth half that glory to the sober west,
As those two mourning eyes become thy face:
O, let it then as well beseem thy heart
To mourn for me, since mourning doth thee grace,
And suit thy pity like in every part.
   Then will I swear beauty herself is black,
   And all they foul that thy complexion lack.

Your eyes, Wine, I love, and they pitying me, knowing your heart torments me with disdain, have put on black and are mourners, looking with pity on my pain.

And truly, the morning sun does not become the east, nor that full star that ushers in the evening, does half that glory to the west,

As your two mourning eyes become your face: let it then as well beseem your heart to mourn for me, since mourning graces you, and suits (dresses) your pity like in every part.

Then will I swear beauty is black, and all are foul that lack your complexion.

SONNET 133.

Beshrew that heart that makes my heart to groan
For that deep wound it gives my friend and me!
Is't not enough to torture me alone,
But slave to slavery my sweet'st friend must be?
Me from myself thy cruel eye hath taken,
And my next self thou harder hast engrossed:
Of him, myself, and thee, I am forsaken;
A torment thrice threefold thus to be crossed.
Prison my heart in thy steel bosom's ward,
But then my friend's heart let my poor heart bail;
Whoe'er keeps me, let my heart be his guard;
Thou canst not then use rigour in my gaol:
    And yet thou wilt; for I, being pent in thee,
    Perforce am thine, and all that is in me.

Beshrew that heart that makes my heart to groan (suffer), for that wound it gives my friend (his genius or source of his poetry, his art) and me! Is't not enough to torture me alone, but that my friend must also be enslaved?

You, Wine, have taken me from myself, and my next self (my art) you have engrossed (absorbed): of him (my art) myself and you am I forsaken, a torment thrice three fold thus to be crossed.

Prison my heart in your steel bosom, but then my friend's heart (my art) has gone my poor heart's bail; whoever keeps me (you or my other self) let my heart be his guide; you cannot then use rigor in my gaol. (If my heart is on guard I shall not be denied indulgences.)

And yet you will; for I being pent in you, am yours, and all that is in me.

Now the poet realizes that his inspiration which he has all along professed to believe was due to wine, like his mind and body, has been enslaved and destroyed.

SONNET 134.

So, now I have confess'd that he is thine
And I myself am mortgaged to thy will,
Myself I'll forfeit, so that other mine
Thou wilt restore, to be my comfort still:
But thou wilt not, nor he will not be free,
For thou art covetous and he is kind;
He learn'd but surety-like to write for me,
Under that bond that him as fast doth bind.
The statute of thy beauty thou wilt take,
Thou usurer, that put'st forth all to use,
And sue a friend came debtor for my sake;
So him I lose through my unkind abuse.
   Him have I lost; thou hast both him and me:
   He pays the whole, and yet am I not free.

So now I have confessed that he (my art) is yours, and I am mortgaged to your will (power), I'll forfeit myself if that other mine (my art) you will restore to be my comfort still:

But you will not, nor will he be free, for you are covetous, and he is kind; he learned but surety-like to write (sign) for me, on the bond that binds him fast.

The statute (rights? penalty?) of your beauty you will take, you usurer, that lets all you have to use (interest), and sue a friend came debtor for my sake, (as my surety) so I lose him through my abuse.

I have lost him, and you have both him and me: he pays the whole and still I am not free.

It would be difficult to find a better elucidation of the truth, that Shakespeare intoxicated was but an echo of Shakespeare sober, than is shown in this sonnet, for it is a strict adaptation of the story of Shylock and the two friends, one the debtor and the other surety, with much the same adaptation of ideas throughout.

SONNET 135.

Whoever hath her wish, thou hast thy 'Will,'
And 'Will' to boot, and 'Will' in overplus;
More than enough am I that vex thee still,
To thy sweet will making addition thus.
Wilt thou, whose will is large and spacious,
Not once vouchsafe to hide my will in thine?
Shall will in others seem right gracious,
And in my will no fair acceptance shine?
The sea, all water, yet receives rain still,
And in abundance addeth to his store;
So thou, being rich in 'Will,' add to thy 'Will'
One will of mine, to make thy large 'Will' more.
    Let no unkind, no fair beseechers kill;
    Think all but one, and me in that one 'Will.'

Whoever has her wish, you have your 'Will' and 'Will' to boot (kick) and 'Will' in overplus; more than enough am I that vex you still, to your sweet will (temper) making addition thus (making myself a nuisance).

Will you whose will (love) is large and spacious, not vouchsafe to hide my will (weakness) in yours? Shall will (joy) in others seem right gracious, and in my will (desire) no acceptance shine?

The sea all water, yet receives rain, and in abundance adds to his store; so you being rich in 'Will,' add to your 'Will' one will of mine (to indulge), to make your large 'Will' more.

Let no unkind (ones), or fair beseechers (votaries) kill (me in your love); think all (of us) but one, and me in that one 'Will.' (Me your only 'Will.')

There is no ground for believing that 'Will' wherever used, is other than Shakespeare himself.

SONNET 136.

If thy soul check thee that I come so near,
Swear to thy blind soul that I was thy 'Will,'
And will, thy soul knows, is admitted there;
Thus far for love, my love-suit, sweet, fulfil.
'Will' will fulfil the treasure of thy love,
Ay, fill it full with wills, and my will one.
In things of great receipt with ease we prove
Among a number one is reckon'd none:
Then in the number let me pass untold,
Though in thy store's account I one must be;
For nothing hold me, so it please thee hold
That nothing me, a something sweet to thee:
    Make but my name thy love, and love that still,
    And then thou lovest me, for my name is 'Will.'

If your soul check (annoy) when I come near, swear to your soul
that I was your 'Will' (your love), and will (love) your soul knows,
is admitted there (in your soul); thus for love, fulfil my love-suit,
sweet. (Wine.)

'Will' (I) will fulfill the treasure of your love, will it full with wills
(love), and my will (love) one. In things of great receipt we prove
among a number one is reckoned none: (Evidently referring to com-
putations by addition and subtraction. Thus, to 27 add 10 and the sum
will be 37, yet counting and beginning at 27 and ending with 37, we
shall have 11. In order to arrive at a correct result one of the numbers
must be counted out, or 'reckoned none.') Then in the number (of your
lovers) let me pass untold, though in your stores account (affections)
I must be one; for nothing hold (count) me, so you hold (count) that
nothing me, and that a something sweet to you.

Make but my name your love, and love that still, and then you love
me, for my name is 'Will.'

SONNET 137.

Thou blind fool, Love, what dost thou to mine eyes,
That they behold, and see not what they see?
They know what beauty is, see where it lies,
Yet what the best is take the worst to be.
If eyes, corrupt by over-partial looks,
Be anchor'd in the bay where all men ride,
Why of eyes' falsehood hast thou forged hooks,
Whereto the judgement of my heart is tied?
Why should my heart think that a several plot
Which my heart knows the wide world's common place?
Or mine eyes seeing this, say this is not,
To put fair truth upon so foul a face?
   In things right true my heart and eyes have erred,
   And to this false plague are they now transferred.

You blind fool love, Wine, what do you to my eyes, that they behold and see not what they see? They know what beauty is, see where it lies (see and understand it) yet take the best to be the worst.

If eyes corrupt (misinterpret) by over-partial looks, be anchored in the bay where all men ride (must exist where all men exsit, and under the same conditions) why of eye's falsehoods (misinterpretations) have you forged hooks, whereto the judgment of my heart is tied? (That holds my judgment to these false ideas.)

Why should my heart think that a several (exclusive) plot, which my heart knows is the whole world's common place (open to all the world)? Or my eyes seeing this (falsehood), say this is not (done) to put truth upon so foul a face?

In things true my heart and eyes have erred, and to this false plague (deception) are they now transferred (converted).

SONNET 138.

When my love swears that she is made of truth,
I do believe her, though I know she lies,
That she might think me some untutor'd youth,
Unlearned in the world's false subtleties.
Thus vainly thinking that she thinks me young,
Although she knows my days are past the best,
Simply I credit her false-speaking tongue:
On both sides thus is simple truth suppress'd.
But wherefore says she not she is unjust?
And wherefore say not I that I am old?
O' love's best habit is in seeming trust,
And age in love loves not to have years told:
  Therefore I lie with her and she with me,
  And in our faults by lies we flatter'd be.

When Wine, my love, says she is made of truth I believe her, though I know she lies; she treats me as though I were an untutored youth unlearned in the world's subtleties.

Thus pretending that she thinks me young, although she knows my days are past the best, simply (foolishly) I credit her false-speaking tongue: thus on both sides is truth suppressed.

But why does she not say she is unjust? And why do I not say I am old? O love's best habit is to pretend to trust, and love does not like to have years told.

Therefore I lie with her and she with me, and each by lies is flattered.

SONNET 139.

O call not me to justify the wrong
That thy unkindness lays upon my heart;
Wound me not with thine eye, but with thy tongue;
Use power with power, and slay me not by art.
Tell me thou lovest elsewhere; but in my sight,
Dear heart, forbear to glance thine eye aside:
What need'st thou wound with cunning, when thy might
Is more than my o'er-pressed defence can bide?
Let me excuse thee: ah, my love well knows
Her pretty looks have been mine enemies;
And therefore from my face she turns my foes,
That they elsewhere might dart their injuries:
    Yet do not so; but since I am near slain,
    Kill me outright with looks, and rid my pain.

O, Wine, ask me not to justify the wrong, that your unkindness lays upon my heart; wound me not with your eye (thoughts) but with your tongue; use power with power (strength with determination) and slay me not with art. (Subterfuge.)

Tell me you love others, but in my presence forbear to glance your eye aside; why wound me with cunning when your might is more than I can defend against?

Let me excuse you: my love well knows how pretty looks (wine's fascinations) has been my enemies, and therefore from my face she turns my foes, (artfully disguising her attacks) that they elsewhere (than to my face) might dart their injuries.

Yet do not so; but since I am so near slain, kill me outright with looks, (openly) and rid my pain.

SONNET 140.

Be wise as thou art cruel; do not press
My tongue-tied patience with too much disdain;
Lest sorrow lend me words, and words express
The manner of my pity-wanting pain.
If I might teach thee wit, better it were,
Though not to love, yet, love, to tell me so;
As testy sick men, when their deaths be near,
No news but health from their physicians know;
For, if I should despair, I should grow mad,
And in my madness might speak ill of thee:
Now this ill-wresting world is grown so bad,
Mad slanderers by mad ears believed be.
    That I may not be so, nor thou belied,
    Bear thine eyes straight, though thy proud heart go wide.

Wine, be wise as you are cruel; do not press my tongue-tied (uncomplaining) patience with too much disdain; lest sorrow lend me words to express the manner of your pitiless inflictions.

If I might be permitted to teach you wit, it were better, though you do not love, to tell me that you do, as dying men are encouraged by their physicians;

For if I should despair, I should grow mad, and in my madness might speak ill of you: now this ill-wresting world has grown so bad, that mad slanderers are believed.

That I may not be so (a slanderer) nor you belied, bear your eyes straight, (pretend to be honest) though your proud heart go wide.

SONNET 141.

In faith, I do not love thee with mine eyes,
For they in thee a thousand errors note;
But 'tis my heart that loves what they despise,
Who, in despite of view, is pleased to dote;
Nor are mine ears with thy tongue's tune delighted;
Nor tender feeling, to base touches prone,
Nor taste, nor smell, desire to be invited
To any sensual feast with thee alone:
But my five wits nor my five senses can
Dissuade one foolish heart from serving thee,
Who leaves unsway'd the likeness of a man,
Thy proud heart's slave and vassal wretch to be:
    Only my plague thus far I count my gain,
    That she that makes me sin awards me pain.

Wine I do not love you with my eyes (thoughts), for they note in you a thousand errors; but 't is my heart that loves what they despise, who in despite of view (reason) dotes on you;

Nor are my ears with your tongue delighted, nor my feelings to your base touches prone, nor taste, nor smell, desire to be invited to any sensual feast with you alone.

But neither my five wits nor senses, dissuade my heart from serving you, who leave me, the likeness of a man, your slave and vassal wretch unswayed (constant)

Only my plague I count my gain, that she that makes me sin awards me pain.

SONNET 142.

Love is my sin, and thy dear virtue hate,
Hate of my sin, grounded on sinful loving:
O, but with mine compare thou thine own state,
And thou shalt find it merits not reproving;
Or, if it do, not from those lips of thine,
That have profaned their scarlet ornaments
And seal'd false bonds of love as oft as mine,
Robb'd others' beds' revenues of their rents.
Be it lawful I love thee, as thou lovest those
Whom thine eyes woo as mine importune thee:
Root pity in thy heart, that, when it grows,
Thy pity may deserve to pitied be.
    If thou dost seek to have what thou dost hide,
    By self-example mayst thou be denied!

Love is my sin, and your hate of my sin is your virtue, grounded on sinful loving: but with my state compare your own, and you shall find mine merits no reproving;

Or if it do, not from your lips, that have profaned their scarlet ornaments, (red lips that are unfaithful) and sealed false bonds of love as oft as mine, robbed others' beds' revenues of their rents. (Cheated prostitutes.)

Be it lawful I love you as you love those, whom you woo as I woo you; root pity in your heart, that when it (pity) grows, your pity may deserve to be pitied. (Have pity that you may deserve to be pitied.)

If you seek to have what you hide (pity) may you by self-example be denied it.

SONNET 143.

Lo, as a careful housewife runs to catch
One of her feather'd creatures broke away,
Sets down her babe, and makes all swift dispatch
In pursuit of the thing she would have stay;
Whilst her neglected child holds her in chase,
Cries to catch her whose busy care is bent
To follow that which flies before her face,
Not prizing her poor infant's discontent:
So runn'st thou after that which flies from thee,
Whilst I thy babe chase thee afar behind;
But if thou catch thy hope, turn back to me,
And play the mother's part, kiss me, be kind:
    So will I pray that thou mayst have thy 'Will,'
    If thou turn back and my loud crying still.

As a housewife runs to catch one of her feathered creatures, sets down her babe and pursues the fowl;

Whilst the child follows her as she follows the flying fowl, she not prizing (considering) the infant's discontent:

So you, Wine, run after that which flies from you, whilst I your babe chase far behind: But if you catch your hope turn back to me and play the mother's part, kiss me and be kind.

So will I pray that you may have your 'Will,' if you turn back and still my crying.

SONNET 144.

Two loves I have of comfort and despair,
Which like two spirits do suggest me still:
The better angel is a man right fair,
The worser spirit a woman colour'd ill.
To win me soon to hell, my female evil
Tempteth my better angel from side,
 And would corrupt my saint to be a devil,
Wooing his purity with her foul pride.
And whether that my angel be turn'd fiend
Suspect I may, yet not directly tell;
But being both from me, both to each friend,
I guess one angel in another's hell:
    Yet this shall I ne'er know, but live in doubt,
    Till my bad angel fire my good one out.

Two loves I have of comfort and despair, which like two spirits suggest (direct) me still; the better angel is a man right fair (conscience), the worser spirit a woman, colored ill (wine).

To win me to hell, my female evil, tempts my better angel from my side, and would corrupt my saint (conscience) to be a devil, wooing his purity with her foul pride (spirit)

And whether my angel be turned fiend I may suspect, yet not say; but when both are away from me, each is to the other friend; I guess the angel (is) in the others hell:

But this I shall never know, but live in doubt, till my bad angel fire my good one out. (And it comes back to me.)

SONNET 145.

Those lips that Love's own hand did make
Breathed forth the sound that said 'I hate,'
To me that languish'd for her sake:
But when she saw my woeful state,
Straight in her heart did mercy come,
Chiding that tongue that ever sweet
Was used in giving gentle doom;
And taught it thus anew to greet;
'I hate' she alter'd with an end,
That follow'd it as gentle day
Doth follow night, who, like a fiend,
From heaven to hell is flown away;
    'I hate' from hate away she threw,
    And saved my life, saying 'not you.'

Those lips that Love's own hand did make, said 'I hate' to me who languished for her sake, but when she saw my woeful state,

Straight mercy came in her heart, chiding that tongue that was used in giving doom, and taught it thus anew to greet:

'I hate,' she altered with an end, that followed as day follows night, who (night) like a fiend from heaven to hell is flown away.

'I hate,' from hate away she threw, and saved my life by saying 'not you.'

This sonnet suggests an occurrence that is not unusual with drunkards: Those who serve liquors frequently become annoyed with the overintoxicated, and express temper and impatience by saying 'I hate you,' or similar words. Upon realizing that the one addressed, or one among a number addressed, is a person of refinement, or a sensitive person, the expression is modified by assuring such a person, that the remark was not intended for him.

SONNET 146.

Poor soul, the centre of my sinful earth,
...... these rebel powers that thee array,
Why dost thou pine within and suffer dearth,
Painting thy outward walls so costly gay?
Why so large cost, having so short a lease,
Dost thou upon thy fading mansion spend?
Shall worms, inheritors of this excess,
Eat up thy charge? is this thy body's end?
Then, soul, live thou upon thy servant's loss,
And let that pine to aggravate thy store;
Buy terms divine in selling hours of dross;
Within be fed, without be rich no more:
    So shalt thou feed on Death, that feeds on men,
    And Death once dead, there's no more dying then.

The second line of this sonnet is imperfect. In the quarto the last words of the first line were repeated in the second, so that the second line read:

"My sinful earth these rebel powers that thee array." Evidently there was a mistake made in the printing. Omitting the first two lines, the sonnet continues:

My soul, why do you pine and suffer dearth, (by being deprived of wine) painting the outward walls (the body) so costly gay?

Why so large cost, having so short a lease (life being so short) do you upon your fading mansion (enfeebled body) spend? Shall worms eat up your charge? is this your body's end?

Then soul live upon your servant's (body's) loss, and let the body pine to aggravate (increase) your store; buy terms divine (exhilaration) by selling hours of dross, (by abandoning temperance). Within be fed (be stimulated), without be rich no more. (Sacrifice the body to intoxication.)

So shall you feed on death, and death feeds on men, and once dead there is no more dying.

The poet is trying to convince himself, that he hasn't long to live, and that the prolongation of life through temperance is the aggravation of the soul, and that life itself is not worth the sacrifice, and therefore it would be better to drink and die, than to abstain and live.

No clue is given in the sonnet as to what is meant by 'painting the outward walls so costly gay,' and 'why so large cost.' The tone of the sonnet clearly indicates that the poet was undergoing some regimen that required the discontinuance of intoxicants. Possibly the two final sonnets indicating his resort to restorative springs may explain the allusions. Or it might be, some cure in vogue in Shakespeare's times would make the references still more pointed.

SONNET 147.

My love is as a fever, longing still
For that which longer nurseth the disease;
Feeding on that which doth preserve the ill,
The uncertain sickly appetite to please.
My reason, the physician to my love,
Angry that his prescriptions are not kept,
Hath left me, and I desperate now approve
Desire is death, which physic did except.
Past cure I am, now reason is past care,
And frantic-mad with evermore unrest;
My thoughts and my discourse as madmen's are,
At random from the truth vainly express'd;
   For I have sworn thee fair, and thought thee bright,
   Who are as black as hell, as dark as night.

My love is a fever, longing for that (Wine) which nurses the disease; feeding on that which preserves the ill, to please the sickly appetite (cravings).

My reason, physician to my love, angry that his prescriptions are not kept, has left me, and I desperate now approve desire is death, which physic did except. (If this means anything, it certainly has not been expressed.)

Past cure I am, now reason is past care (does not care), and frantic mad with evermore unrest; my thoughts and my discourse, as madmen's are, at random from the truth (distracted), vainly (incoherently) expressed;

For, Wine, I have sworn you fair, and thought you bright, who are as black as hell and dark as night.

SONNET 148.

O, me, what eyes hath Love put in my head,
Which have no correspondence with true sight!
Or, if they have, where is my judgement fled,
That censures falsely what they see aright?
If that be fair whereon my false eyes dote,
What means the world to say it is not so?
If it be not, then love doth well denote
Love's eye is not so true as all men's no,
How can it? O, how can Love's eye be true,
That is so vex'd with watching and with tears?
No marvel then, though I mistake my view;
The sun itself sees not till heaven clears.
    O cunning Love! with tears thou keep'st me blind,
    Lest eyes well-seeing thy foul faults should find.

What eyes has Love, (Wine) put in my head, which have no correspondence with true sight! or if they have where is my judgment fled, that censures, (judges) falsely what my eyes see right?

If that (wine) be fair whereon my false eyes dote, what means the world to say it is not fair? If it be not fair, then love denotes that love's eye is not so true as all mens: no.

How can love's eye be true, that is so vexed with watching and with tears? No marvel then, that I should mistake my view; the sun sees not till heaven clears.

O Wine, with tears you keep me blind, lest seeing well I should find your foul faults.

SONNET 149.

Canst thou, O cruel! say I love thee not,
When I against myself with thee partake?
Do I not think on thee, when I forgot
Am of myself, all tyrant, for thy sake?
Who hateth thee that I do call my friend?
On whom frown'st thou that I do fawn upon?
Nay, if thou lour'st on me, do I not spend
Revenge upon myself with present moan?
What merit do I in myself respect,
That is so proud thy service to despise,
When all my best doth worship thy defect,
Commanded by the motion of thine eyes?
    But, love, hate on, for now I know thy mind;
    Those that can see thou lovest, and I am blind.

Can you, O cruel wine! say I love you not, when I partake of you against myself? Do I not think on you, when I, forgotten, (forgetting myself) am all tyrant of myself for your sake?

Who hates you, that I call friend? on whom do you frown, that I fawn upon? If you lour (frown) on me, do I not punish myself with moaning?

What do I respect in myself, that is so proud as to despise your service, when all my best worships your defect, at your eyes command?

But, Wine, hate on for now I know your mind; you love those that can see, and I am blind.

SONNET 150.

O, from what power hast thou this powerful might
With insufficiency my heart to sway?
To make me give the lie to my true sight,
And swear that brightness doth not grace the day?
Whence hast thou this becoming of things ill,
That in the very refuse of thy deeds
There is such strength and warrantise of skill,
That, in my mind, thy worst all best exceeds?
Who taught thee how to make me love thee more,
The more I hear and see just cause of hate?
O, though I love what others do abhor,
With others thou shouldst not abhor my state:
    If thy unworthiness raised love in me,
    More worthy I to be beloved of thee.

From what power have you this might, Wine, to sway my heart with your insufficiency (lack of qualities)? to make me give the lie to my true sight, and swear that brightness does not grace the day?

Whence have you this becoming of things ill (the quality of fitness to all things ill), that in the refuse (foulness) of your deeds, there is such strength and warrantise (assurance) of skill, that in my mind your worst exceeds all best?

Who taught you how to make me love you more, the more I hear and see just cause of hate? Though I love what others abhor, you, with others, should not abhor my state:

If I love your unworthiness, I am more worthy to be loved by you.

SONNET 151.

Love is too young to know what conscience is;
Yet who knows not conscience is born of love?
Then, gentle cheater, urge not my amiss,
Lest guilty of my faults thy sweet self prove:
For, thou betraying me, I do betray
My nobler part to my gross body's treason;
My soul doth tell my body that he may
Triumph in love; flesh stays no farther reason,
But rising at thy name doth point out thee
As his triumphant prize. Proud of this pride,
He is contented thy poor drudge to be,
To stand in thy affairs, fall by thy side.
    No want of conscience hold it that I call
    Her 'love' for whose dear love I rise and fall.

Love is too young to know what conscience is; yet who does not know that conscience is born of love? Then cheater, Wine, urge not my amiss, (errors) lest you prove yourself guilty of my faults:

For through your betraying me, I betray my nobler part to my body's treason (excesses); My soul tells my body he may triumph in love; flesh stays (to hear) no further reason,

But rising at your name (love) points you out as his triumphant prize. Proud of this pride (achievement) he is contented to be your drudge, stand in your affairs, and fall by your side.

No want of conscience hold it that I call wine 'love,' for whose love I rise and fall.

SONNET 152.

In loving thee thou know'st I am forsworn,
But thou art twice forsworn, to me love swearing;
In act thy bed-vow broke, and new faith torn,
In vowing new hate after new love bearing.
But why of two oaths' breach do I accuse thee,
When I break twenty! I am perjured most;
For all my vows are oaths but to misuse thee,
And all my honest faith in thee is lost:
For I have sworn deep oaths of thy deep kindness,
Oaths of thy love, thy truth, thy constancy;
And, to enlighten thee, gave eyes to blindness,
Or made them swear against the thing they see;
   For I have sworn thee fair; more perjured I,
   To swear against the truth so foul a lie!

In loving you you know I am forsworn (perjured), but you are twice forsworn swearing love to me; (first) in act, your bed vow broke; and (second) your new faith torn (broken) in vowing new hate after new love bearing.

But why do I accuse you of the breach of two oaths, when I break twenty? I am perjured most; for all my vows are oaths but to misuse you (misdescribe you, vowing you qualities you have not), and all my honest faith in you is lost;

For I have sworn oaths of your kindness, your love, your truth, your constancy; and, to enlighten (exalt) you, gave eyes to blindness (pretending to see what did not exist), and made them swear against the thing they see;

For I have sworn you fair; more perjured I, to swear falsely so foul a lie.

SONNET 153.

Cupid laid by his brand and fell asleep:
A maid of Dian's this advantage found,
And his love-kindling fire did quickly steep
In a cold valley-fountain of that ground;
Which borrow'd from this holy fire of Love
A dateless lively heat, still to endure,
And grew a seething bath, which yet men prove
Against strange maladies a sovereign cure.
But at my mistress' eye Love's brand new-fired,
The boy for trial needs would touch my breast;
I, sick withal, the help of bath desired,
And thither hied, a sad distemper'd guest,
    But found no cure: the bath for my help lies
    Where Cupid got new fire, my mistress' eyes.

Cupid laid by his brand and fell asleep; a maid of Dian's this advantage (brand) found, and quickly steeped it in a cold spring of that land;

Which spring borrowed from this fire of love a dateless (continuing) heat, which still endures, and grew to a hot bath which men prove a cure against strange maladies.

But Love's brand being newly fired, (heated after having become cooled) at my mistress's eyes (wine), the boy (Cupid) for trial needs would touch my breast; I sick withal desired the help of baths, and thither hied a sad distempered guest.

But found no cure: the bath for my help lies, where Cupid got new fire—my mistress' (Wine's) eyes.

This and the following sonnet are identical in sense with a different word dressing. In these two Shakespeare expressly sets forth a visit to some hot springs, seeking relief as a 'distempered guest,' but failing to find it.

These two sonnets were referred to in suggestions under 110, and there it was stated that the springs visited were probably situated in Continental Europe. This conclusion is founded on the fact that the reference to mythological Dian and Cupid indicated some classical place, and in Shakespeare's day England was hardly considered such. In addition to this, and it is the stronger evidence, the fourth line of the sonnet would seem to certainly exclude England from consideration. That line reads, 'In a cold valley-fountain of *that* ground.' A fair construction of 'that ground' or land, means Cupid and Dian's ground—a land nearer to the Mediterranean.

SONNET 154.

The little Love-god lying once asleep
Laid by his side his heart-inflaming brand,
Whilst many nymphs that vow'd chaste life to keep
Came tripping by; but in her maiden hand
The fairest votary took up that fire
Which many legions of true hearts had warm'd;
And so the general of hot desire
Was sleeping by a virgin hand disarm'd.
This brand she quenched in a cool well by,
Which from Love's fire took heat perpetual,
Growing a bath and healthful remedy
For men diseased; but I, my mistress' thrall,
    Came there for cure, and this by that I prove.
    Love's fire heats water, water cools not love.

This sonnet being so evidently a repetition in substance of 153, but little comment is required. In line 12 it is declared that he was the thrall of his mistress, whom of course it is assumed was Wine, and it was for this that he came to the springs for cure, but he found that while Love's fire heats water, 'water cools not love,' and consequently it failed to quench his thrist for Wine.

The task of reviewing the sonnets is now ended, and but little remains to be said concerning the construction which has been put upon them. It is contended that they have not been construed, but simply interpreted. In the suggestions which have been made the purpose has been to lend some aid in the reading of the sonnets with the meaning that was in Shakespeare's mind in writing them. It has not been the purpose to add to them anything that was not in the mind of Shakespeare, and which he undertook to express in them. In so far as the suggestions which have been made may be considered as interpolations they should be disregarded, for it has not been the intent in a single instance to introduce any unwarranted, or even doubtful, translation.

No sonnet has been omitted from the review, and but a very few of them have been left without each line and sentence having received attention. In every case it has been the effort to clearly define the intended meaning, which meaning, though always obscure, becomes clearly obvious in the light of interpretation. In a few of the sonnets some obscurity still continues, but it is believed that this is owing to a lack of clarity in the use of words, or possibly from errors or omissions that have befallen the text as it has come down to us. In one particularly, the 146th, the omission is evident and indisputable. In the case of the few unintelligible sonnets suggestions have been offered, in which a considerable license has been taken in arriving at a solution of the difficulty. Whether these suggestions be accepted or not makes but little difference in the reading of the remaining sonnets for so far as can be discerned the construction of the others is not at all dependent on these.

SHAKESPEARE THE MAN

SHAKESPEARE THE MAN.

Of no author, living or dead, has the world so high an opinion as of Shakespeare. As he has become the ideal in literature, so is it the general desire to believe him ideal in his personality. Those who have investigated what little there is of his history, and have made a study of conditions existing at the time of his living, have sought to convince themselves, and their readers, to the belief that Shakespeare was really a prosperous and esteemed gentleman in his lifetime, and that he held a station not far removed from nobility, itself. Without tiring have they sought to find records of his recognition and entertainment among those in high places. To them, and to all of us, it seems incredible that the world's greatest genius could live in one of the most enlightened periods of the world's history and not receive his due of respect.

Furthermore, all of us long to believe, and often profess to be convinced, that one who knew, and so fully comprehended the depths of the human mind and heart, as Shakespeare did, must have been himself the perfection of man, in his bearing, his associations, his habits, his aspirations, his appetites and his devotions. What, less than a man above us all, and not much beneath the god-like, could fill this measure of admiration and expectations? And yet, had he been all that we so devoutly wish he might have been, is it possible that such a giant could have strode the streets of London and breathed its air for twenty years, or longer, without leaving a track, or creating some mild commotion that would be recorded in the history of his times? Would it not be possible, to-day, to trace the lives, and a fairly complete record of action, of thousands of persons who lived in London three hundred years ago? who did nothing in their lifetime worthy to be preserved of record, and of whom no person now living has ever thought? How can it be then, that this man eludes our search so completely? He who of all men, then living, commands now the most attention, and excites the greatest interest!

The answer must be, that there was no such individual then alive as we imagine. Shakespeare occupied no exalted place. He did not associate with those who were in the public mind and eye, or who impress themselves upon their times. He was not a part of those who were courted and honored, and who became the subject of envy and of notoriety. He was not a part of the current, genteel upper class of citizenry of his time, to say nothing of royalty and nobility, and only of such is preserved the record of their actions. It is as a part of these that all attempts have been made to identify Shakespeare, and there he was non-existent. If any record of Shakespeare exists it will be found as a part of the lowly, the profane and the vulgar, and of these it is the bad and not the good that is preserved. Perhaps a search of the records of the criminal courts might discover the identity of the wretch whose knife is referred to in Sonnet 74, or perhaps we might discover other evidence, than he himself has given, of the misery that beset him through his frailties.

It would not be fair to charge this lack of recognition of Shakespeare to his contemporaries. The conditions were such that they could have done little to mend his affairs, and it is rather to their credit, that in their kindly consideration they made no mention of him or his weakness. Shakespeare must indeed have been a kindly and lovable man, and one who enlisted the sympathy and kindest consideration of all who knew him, or of him, to have escaped, as he has done all calumny, and even the slightest hint or reference to his degrading affliction. For it must not be overlooked, but that for Shakespeare's own admissions all of this would have been forever excluded from our knowledge. This sentiment of fondness on the part of his friends, may account for their silence with reference to all matters of his history, for his condition was certainly so extreme, that no fair treatment of his life could be proposed which would conceal his weakness.

Nor would Shakespeare himself, in his lifetime, have desired personal honor. He fully realized the impossible position of a personal fame coupled with his unfortunate appetite. His weakness required indulgence, and indulgence would render honors worse than burdensome. He felt, as all addicts come to feel, a desire to escape publicity, and to shun old companions and acquaintances, and to be only with those, who through long experience, could tolerate his frailty. This limited his companionship to those engaged in the liquor traffic. He felt keenly the disgrace which overcame him, and which excluded him from the society of friends, and in his Sonnets has plainly expressed his chagrin and shame. (See Sonnets 29, 34, 36, 49, 89, 90, 111, 112, 121.) In the 89th Sonnet while addressing Wine, he really expresses his feeling towards his friends and the world, when he says: 'Knowing thy will I will acquaintance strangle and look strange; be absent from thy walks; and in my tongue thy sweet beloved name no more shall dwell.' Again in 111: 'Thence comes it that my name receives a brand, and almost thence my nature is subdued, to what it works in like the dyer's hand.' So universally does the confirmed drunkard feel and act, and in his wretched state of mind becomes from choice ostracized from all the world that he respects.

Under these and other adverse conditions we may realize his longing, his yearning, his passion for the perpetuation of himself in his poetry. Alone, deserted by the world, and himself the world deserting, and yet realizing the surpassing beauty of all he wrote, all that was left him, beside the inspiration of wine, was the hope and desire that his lines might become deathless, and therein he might be forever enshrined. Having abandoned all hope of attaining the honors of place and wealth, he clung to the one cherished joy, that he should live in generations yet unborn in his immortal rhyme. Indeed this is the burden of the Sonnets. From the 1st to the 126th Sonnet it is the theme, the absorbing thought and passion. After the 126th the thought is abandoned, or if still entertained, is given no further expression.

It is not reasonable to conclude that Shakespeare was highly prosperous. Certainly he was not rich. His habits were such as to preclude a considerable accumulation, and there is little to indicate that his possessions at the time of his death were more than very moderate. His sonnets support the idea of the lack of wealth, while they hardly indicate an actual poverty. (See Sonnets 25, 29, 91.)

In Sonnet 105 Shakespeare defines the rules which had governed him in all his aspirations as a poet. His motto, as therein stated is, 'fair, kind and true.' Or 'varying to other words,' as he puts it, he sought to have his writings conform to beauty, love and truth. We need not hesitate to say that he completely accomplished his purpose, by always adhering strictly to these 'three themes in one, which wondrous scope affords.' Nor can we conclude otherwise from what he has written and from what we know of him, that he, in person and in thought was not all that his motto implies. Nor does the Shakespeare, as he exposes himself in the Sonnets belie these qualities. Shall we love him less, or esteem him less highly when he divulges to us his very soul in his human weakness? Is he still not beautiful, loving and true, and even more marvellous than we had conceived him, because notwithstanding his human frailties, he shows forth such an imperishable glory? In him we find a brother in weakness, and a master in art,—a superlative genius molded from the common clay. Let him condemn who has not known some gentle soul, beautiful, loving and true, that has worn the galling shackles that Shakespeare bore. Who has not known the greatest intellects and the choicest spirits slave to this self same appetite, which we cannot understand, nor they control? We have seen him, the outcast, with rain upon his 'storm-beaten face,' drinking his potions of 'Siren tears,' in the distraction of the 'madding fever'; tortured in a 'hell of time,' yet confessing that it was beyond his strength 'to shun the heaven that leads men to this hell.' Yet, through all this, drifting into utter darkness, we find in him no unkindness, no ugliness, no falsity. He knew his own sin, if sin it was, and sought not to excuse it, nor to reproach others for the degradation into which he had fallen. Though he had well nigh deified wine as the inspirer of his highest visions, he came to see its evil nature, and as he closed the matchless volume of all literature, he declared it 'as black as hell, as dark as night.' His very last and parting denunciation was, 'For I have sworn thee fair; more perjured I, to swear against the truth so foul a lie.'

Shall we condemn Shakespeare as a drunkard, and call him immoral? Rather shall we not conclude that he was sincere and honest above all men? Who among us would have laid his frailties bare as he has done? He who feels that he cannot still honor and reverence this immortal intellect—drunkard though he was—does not realize, and will not consider, that in spite of his affliction, his achievements were, among men, the nearest approach to the preternatural. As the Sonnets have been heretofore read, and misunderstood, it has been necessary to concede that Shakespeare's life was given to moral laxity, and to such abjectness as robbed him of his manhood. With the true reading all this disappears, and so far as we now know, or probably shall ever know, his life was spotless, and he himself as gentle, kindly and loveable as our most exacting morals could require. That he was unfortunate appeals to our sympathy, and should not provoke our condemnation. That Shakespeare was gentle, kind and much beloved he himself believed. In speaking of himself in the 10th Sonnet, he says, 'grant if thou wilt, thou art beloved of many,' and again, 'Be, as thy presence is, gracious and kind.' And in the 70th he says, 'If some suspect of ill (drunkenness) mask'd not thy brow, then thou alone kingdoms of hearts shouldst owe.' The Sonnets throughout show him to have been of the tenderest feelings, even taking upon himself all blame and shame, and exonerating others. In defending himself against criticism he shows how deeply stung he was by them, but if the conclusions that have been drawn are correct, he soon forgot all vindictiveness, and made ample amends.

In considering Shakespeare's weakness, the surrounding in which he lived should be taken into account. His was an age of unlicensed drunkenness, such as the world has probably never seen, either before or since. All classes, both high and low, were given to the greatest excess in the use of alcoholic liquors. Not only was indulgence to great excess permissible, but by a great majority, it was considered highly respectable. Both gentlemen and ladies indulged without restraint, and to such a degree as to induce orgies indescribable, and almost beyond what could be now believed. Drinking was not only tolerated, but by many it was believed to be actually beneficial, and as Shakespeare himself thought, inspiring. Some were boastful of their capacity for indulgence, and were considered rather superior by reason thereof. It was thought to be a necessity in all conviviality, and as is natural, young gentlemen were rather proud than otherwise in being able to hold their own at drinking bouts. The polite morals of the times did not frown on the custom, and the result was, that young men were rather ashamed to refuse to indulge, and imagined it more manly to acquiesce in indulgence, even to excess, than to decline.

Under the prevailing conditions few were the young men who escaped exposure to the dangers of drunkenness, and generally, only those prevailed against it who were so fortunately constituted that their physical nature rebelled against its encroachments, making alcoholic drinks distasteful, and the effects hateful. Morals had little or nothing to do with immunity. Unfortunately Shakespeare was not favored, and it was without moral fault that he succumbed to an appetite which is so unaccountable, and to some so irresistible. From his own account he did not freely or willingly surrender, but waged a resolute and determined defense, until his famishing art could no longer resist, and live.

So prevalent and menacing had drunkenness become at this time that sentiment began to rise against it, and demands were made for legislation to put the traffic in liquors under legal restraint, and this was the very incipiency of prohibition laws. In Sonnet 124 there is a defense of Wine, and probably a reference to the proposal to regulate its use. It is there that Shakespeare called reformed drunkards, 'fools of time,' and in the next sonnet, 'suborned informer.'

WERE THE SONNETS ADDRESSED TO ANYONE?

Were the Sonnets addressed to any one in particular? Probably this question can never be answered with positiveness. It is not credible that the sonnets in their true and deep meaning, were to be read as applying to any individual. It can hardly be doubted that the construction or interpretation which has been given to them in this review, is the one intended. The only mystery remaining is the reason for the disguise in which the meaning was dressed. That disguise becomes the truly perplexing part of the Sonnets. Was it Shakespeare's purpose to so obscure the meaning that it might not be discovered? That is not for a moment admissible. To so believe would be to hold the Sonnets excuseless, and to find that the writer had gone to infinite pains to produce something without a purpose—to propound an unsolvable puzzle. On the contrary, it is certain that Shakespeare himself was under the impression that the sonnets could be easily read to express the meaning hidden in them. In the 76th sonnet he declares as much. There he says, 'Why write I still all one, ever the same, and keep invention in a noted (well-known) weed, that every word doth almost tell my name, showing their birth, and where they did proceed?' And in the 62d he gives a clear key to the construction, when he says: 'Tis thee, myself, that for myself I praise, painting my age with beauty of thy (my) days.' The Sonnets are a history of the predominating feature of his life, in almost endless repetition, each expression telling his 'name' (divulging his meaning). All of his invention, or verse, is in the same familiar vein, or 'weed,' showing the origin or 'birth,' and 'where they did proceed,' or result, of his passionate appetite. In the beginning of the Sonnets the disguise is perfect, and can scarcely be penetrated, but as they proceed the inward meaning becomes more and more evident, until in the last 25 sonnets, the disguise is practically discarded.

It is the writer's belief, that it was Shakespeare's purpose in the beginning to express the truth, as it has been shown to have been expressed, and at the same time to delude some one, an addressee, into believing that the Sonnets were actually addressed to him.

The Elizabethan poet lacked very much of earning a sufficient living from his writings. His life was a struggle for existence, and he was compelled to seek the favor and patronage of wealthy men, rather than rely upon the sale of his literary products. Copyright was then unknown to the law, and the only value which accrued to a writer was such as he might be able to obtain by direct sale of his works to some publisher. Once published, any literary work, became liable to be pirated by any one who might care to make other publications of it.

In 1623, seven years after the death of Shakespeare, two friends of his, John Heminge and Henry Condell, published all of Shakespeare's plays in one volume, which is now known as the 'first folio.' In a preface they condemn all previous publications of separate plays as, "stolen and surreptitious copies, maimed and deformed by the frauds and stealths of injurious impostors." It is thus evident how slight was the value of one's composition, and if the facts are as stated, Shakespeare received nothing at all from the publication of his plays. His pecuniary rewards, and they must have been comparatively small, must have come altogether from proprietors of the theatres. This was in the form of an outright purchase, after which no returns would be likely.

How much was paid to the author by the theatres we have no means of knowing. Undoubtedly the amount was small and varied with the reputation of the author, and the character of the play. Ben Jonson, who was the literary celebrity of Shakespeare's time, and who undoubtedly was better known and more highly appreciated than was Shakespeare, is reported as saying that for all of his numerous plays he had not received as much as two hundred pounds. That his plays were highly esteemed is certain, and is evidenced by the numerous encomiums, in verse and otherwise, with which they were received, while so far as known Shakespeare's plays received but scant notice.

Notwithstanding the high and almost universal regard in which Jonson was held, his remuneration came not from the sale of his works either to the theatres or publishers, but from pensions granted by the state through the influence of royalty and those in high places, and also from the patronage of the rich. He was granted annuities and pensions, and lavished with gifts, and received handsome rewards for many masques which were written expressly for the celebration of royal and noble functions. Even with all these he was frequently in very straitened circumstances, and besought aid from his patrons to relieve his necessities. It is therefore very improbable that Shakespeare, much less favorably situated was ever easy financially, and undoubtedly he like others of his time was glad enough to receive patronage from those able to grant it.

It is concluded therefore that Shakespeare was willing to have some wealthy noble believe that the Sonnets were addressed to him, and through the apparent praise therein expressed may have profited, but to what extent it is useless to speculate. The fact that 'Mr. W. H.' is mentioned in the dedication is a strong indication that he was the person deluded into believing that Shakespeare saw in him the wonderful qualities which were ascribed to the apparent addressee. That he was the recipient and depository of the Sonnets seems almost certain, for that fact is the only excuse appearing for the mention of his name in connection with the Sonnets. The first 18 sonnets, had they not been supplemented by others, could very well have misled any one into believing that he was really the object of Shakespeare's interest and devotions, as indeed he may have been in one sense, for there must have been intimacy and a companionship between them to have justified the endearing terms that are used. Possibly, even probably, they were convivial friends during the whole of the period of three years mentioned in Sonnet 104, and may have continued so throughout the continuance of the composition of the Sonnets. All this however must be admitted to be pure speculation.

Shakespeare could not have indulged his abnormal appetite without a considerable burden of expense, and it seems a very reasonable suggestion that he purposely cultivated the friendship of 'W. H.', who may have been William Herbert, a wealthy young nobleman, in order that he, Shakespeare, might be supplied with funds for his necessary indulgements. Such ample

and fulsome praise as he seemed to be bestowing would certainly
have brought some response, or would have been discontinued.
Few wealthy young men could have received such evidence of
devotion without feeling a deep interest in their author, and with-
out responding with substantial gifts.

At this distance, and viewing the matter disinterestedly, it
would not seem likely that any sensible man could have received
Shakespeare's idolatrous praises without a sense of their exces-
sive exaggerations, but let it be remembered that this praise
began in a rather modest and flattering way, by advising the
young man that his high qualities and beauty were such that he
owed it to the world to perpetuate himself in his offspring, and
therefore advising him that his marriage was in wisdom his duty.
This young man, we may imagine, was a youth of high breeding
and station, who might, especially in his youth, be possessed of
great confidence and esteem in himself, and might readily
imagine himself to be all that his worshipper saw in him. That
the addressee might have been honestly misled, by thinking him-
self the subject, is evidenced by the fact that many investigators
since have insisted that such a construction was justified. Very
naturally the praises seem to grow in intensity with a growing
companionship, that companionship being constantly cemented
with the provisions for entertainment, which the noble youth was
able to supply.

Shakespeare, let us further speculate, came to feel that his
existence and his art actually depended upon the youth, and this
may have been expressed, not only in his verse, but in his con-
descending conversations. He may have felt and often expressed
himself to the effect, that his young patron was his sole inspira-
tion, and that but for him his art would languish and die. In
this, considering the conditions, the poet may have been sincere,
and the patron may have become convinced of his great influence
and power, and that Shakespeare was awarding to him nothing
but his due. Shakespeare, in order to hold his patron's good will
and favor, may not have bestowed on him unheard of praise
only, but in his conversations and sonnets (let us still continue to
indulge our imaginations), was promising to perpetuate him and
his fame for all future time in his wonderful verse. This verse,
his sonnets, was being delivered as written to this patron who
was disseminating them among his friends, where they were being
received with applause. The young recipient may have felt per-

haps (as even older heads might feel) that he was receiving with the author, an equal share of fame and reputation. Under these conditions he would naturally be little inclined to criticism, if indeed it should occur to him at all, that the praises were beyond what could be due to any mortal. Or if he realized that they were beyond his worth, he might well believe them to be the exaggerated expressions of a devoted friend's admiration and love.

But throughout it all, though Shakespeare may have deceived others, he never deceived himself. If the Sonnets were addressed to an individual, to Shakespeare, that individual personified Wine, as he saw it in its changing effects. That was his star for guidance, through the long and devious course of the Sonnets, and with his dramatic soul he was able to impersonate in an individual the spirit of wine, as he was to create in his mind an abstract nothing and endow it with the soul of a Hamlet, Macbeth or Lear.

But does not this reflect upon Shakespeare's moral character, that he could so purposely deceive a friend by such false pretenses, and by such doubtful means, extracting from him gifts and patronage which would not have been forthcoming had the truth been known? Yes, as it was morally wrong in Shakespeare to be a drunkard, it was morally wrong in him to practice this deception. But in the circumstances it was necessary that he should so live in order to be able to live at all. None knew the moral side of the question better than did Shakespeare. Read the 129th Sonnet, and there find the condition discussed as only this master could discuss it. It was the lust of drink. In action this lust is an "expense of spirit in a waste of shame; and until action lust is perjured, murderous, bloody, full of blame, savage, extreme, rude, cruel, not to trust." There is the answer. The slave to drink knows no moral law, and cannot be expected to respect it. When urged on by the cravings he becomes perjured, full of blame, savage, extreme, rude, cruel and not to be trusted, and he is "mad in pursuit, and in possession so."

So, we may believe that Shakespeare wrote 126 sonnets, nominally or pretendedly addressed to an individual, deluding him into believing that he was worshipping him as an individual, for qualities beyond a man's possessing. In all of these sonnets, while they are not without some blame attached to the addressee, there is above all, a most servile devotion and faithfulness that is not understandable to a normal man, and that is only made clear when the addressee has been pushed aside, and there has been found behind him the coiled serpent that has been the mesmerizing agency in these enigmatical verses. But, at the same time, while he was finding so much to praise, the poet was not blind to the defects and horrors of the serpent that had enchanted him, and realizing how poisonous its sting, he was resolutely attempting to make amends by setting his heel upon its head.

The 26 dark woman sonnets are aimed at Wine, as a horrid despoiler. In these he changes its sex, and calls it feminine. The cause for this seems simple enough, in the light of what has been discussed. While he mingles his love of Wine with hatred, he wishes still to retain his patron, for the patron, as well as wine, is still necessary to the poet's existence. He realizes fully the error of his habits, but cannot loosen the bands that pinion him, and he has no intention of breaking with the young man, who so well administers to his needs, and whose further support will prove both valuable and necessary. Wine has been given its meed of praise, but he is set upon it that it shall receive its deserved denunciation, as well. But to intermix sonnets of praise with those of discredit, without some distinguishing difference, would be offensive to his patron, and would probably result in his estrangement. Therefore, there was no way to better accomplish his purpose, than to change the sex of the addressee, in those sonnets importing blame. Such sonnets could be submitted to his patron without explanation or offense. That they were so received, approved and published we have every reason to believe. It is therefore concluded that this change in the sex of the addressee does not reflect Shakespeare's sentiments towards womankind, but that the change was one of expediency, and without other meaning or implication.

THE DEDICATION.

Some of the imaginings indulged in as to the relations between Shakespeare and his supposed patron, are not altogether without some support, but are to some extent suggested by the dedication which accompanied the first publication of the Sonnets. There is no reason, whatever, to think that Shakespeare had anything to do with this dedication. In it he is referred to as *"our ever living poet,"* showing beyond doubt that those who were privy to the publication, either wrote or directed the dedication. As printed the dedication would appear to be signed by "T. T." This at first, would give the impression that it was written by him. But it must not be overlooked, that "Mr. W. H.", and not "T. T." is the one who wishes happiness and eternity to the adventurer in setting forth. This indicates, quite conclusively, that Mr. W. H. wrote the dedication, and that the adventurer was T. T.

In the original title page of the 1609 publication it is stated that the publication is printed by "G. Eld for T. T." It is not at all unlikely that the history of the Sonnets and their publication, are briefly this: As they were written they were presented to Mr. W. H., who under the conditions already discussed received them, believing that Shakespeare had addressed them to him, and that he was actually the subject of them. He retained them and may have had them privately printed, from time to time, for we know they were circulated among Shakespeare's friends. Undoubtedly W. H. prized them highly, and we may well believe read them to his friends, and circulated copies of them. Thereby they became well known, although not offered for sale to the public.

Shakespeare's work at the time of the publication of the Sonnets had come to an end, or nearly so. All of his poetry, and some of his plays had been published, and many of his plays had been acted on the stage, and had become public property. The Sonnets however remained to be made known. Mr. W. H. and his group of friends, we may assume, were Shakespeare's readers and admirers, and naturally desired that the Sonnets should be preserved and published.

Whether T. T. was one of Shakespeare's friends, or an adventurer, who imagined there might be profit in the publication of the Sonnets, is of but little importance. All that we need to assume is, that it was agreed that T. T. should publish the Sonnets. W. H. having the custody of them would necessarily supply the copy for the printer, and probably wrote and submitted the dedication. Why it should have been printed wholly without punctuation, is an anomaly without apparent reason or explanation. In that lies largely the confusion in its construction. Accept the foregoing suggestions, and supply punctuation, and the dedication may be given quite a reasonable and simple construction. Let us try it:

"To (Shakespeare) the onlie begetter of these ensuing Sonnets.

"Mr. W. H. all happinesse, and that eternitie promised by our ever-living poet (Shakespeare), wisheth the well-wishing adventurer in setting forth—T. T."

T. T. is the adventurer who is setting forth to have the Sonnets published. The happiness that W. H. wishes him comes from W. H. himself, but the eternity promised by the 'ever-living poet' is what W. H. thought Shakespeare was promising him, when in the Sonnets he was so constantly repeating the thought that the addressee of the Sonnets should live for all time in his lines. It is suspected that W. H. was impressed with the hope that he would find lasting fame in the Sonnets. We may also suspect that his desire for their publication was not so much to enhance Shakespeare's fame, as it was to bring out the fact that he, W. H., was the man to whom they were addressed, and to call attention to the fact that the 'ever-living poet' had promised him perpetuation in them. From first to last Shakespeare never identified the addressee of the Sonnets, or gave the slightest clue by which he could be identified. Is it not probable that W. H. sought to supply Shakespeare's omission, through this puzzling dedication, and at the same time obscure his purpose by leaving the author of the dedication in doubt? As an excuse for referring to Shakespeare's promise, and emphasizing it, he wishes the same eternity to T. T. the 'well-wishing adventurer' in his setting forth on the undertaking of the publication. But it cannot be claimed that the eternity promised by Shakespeare was a promise of future life. By no implication could any of Shakespeare's promises be so construed. All that he promises in the Sonnets is a perpetuation of name and fame. How would it be possible then for the 'well-wishing adventurer,' whoever he may have been, to share in what Shakespeare had promised, however much W. H. might be willing to wish it?

Little did W. H. think that T. T. would receive quite as much fame as he through the Sonnets, for it is the irony of fate that one, Thorpe, is conceded to be T. T., while W. H. must remain, probably, for all time, unknown.

OTHER POEMS

OTHER POEMS

There are others of Shakespeare's poems which have proved quite as difficult to construe satisfactorily and understandingly, as the Sonnets. Strangely enough these poems respond, by yielding the same meaning as do the Sonnets, when the same formula for their solution is applied to them. This corroborating evidence, should it be adduced, should be conclusive in removing all doubt, if any still exists, of the correctness of the interpretation which has been applied to the Sonnets, and to all of them without exception, and which has in no instance failed.

How extraordinary it would be, if so much of what Shakespeare has written could be read, by any manner of distortion, and yield the same concealed meaning, and that continually reiterated, unless it had been the purpose of the author to impregnate them with that meaning. If these same writings could be construed to express some other well defined and definite idea or train of thought, it would still be beyond probability that another and entirely distinct thread of construction could be read through and into them, from end to end, unless the hidden thread had been purposely woven in in the composition of the fabric. But it is submitted that no other clear cut and well defined meaning has been, or can be, extracted from these writings, save only the one that has been, and here is, contended for.

To emphasize this point: Let any one take Shakespeare's *Venus and Adonis*, or *The Rape of Lucrece* and try by any manner of forced construction to find a secret or hidden meaning concealed therein that can be followed through them, or any considerable part of them,—for instance, let it be shown, however subtly, that wine and its effect are the burdens of these poems,—and it will soon be seen how difficult, not to say impossible, is the effort.

Can it be considered possible, then, that a scarcely secreted vein of hidden meaning, in its long course, and which can anywhere in that long course be uncovered and found, in fact does not exist, because it is not in the plan and purpose of its creator? Nothing less than plan and purpose could have put it there,— chance never creates a consistent design.

The poems which it is proposed to review for the purpose of this further exposition, are *The Phoenix and the Turtle,* selections from, but not all of, *The Passionate Pilgrim,* and *The Lover's Complaint.* These will be reviewed in the order named, because it is believed that is the order in which they were written.

THE PHOENIX AND THE TURTLE.

This poem was first published in 1601, as one of the poems in Robert Chester's *Love's Martyr; or Rosalin's Complaint.* Shakespeare's name was appended to this poem, indicating that he was its author. There is very little known concerning the poem, other than the meager facts here stated.

The first task in construing this poem is to ascertain as nearly as possible, who or what is the phœnix? and who or what is the turtle dove? Both are birds, one, the phœnix, is altogether fabulous and poetical. It is represented as of great beauty, and of extreme longevity; it prepares its own funeral pile of gums and spices, and with its own wings fans it into flame, and is itself thereon consumed, but again rises renewed and youthful from its own ashes. Whether the myth justifies the conclusion or not, it has become symbolical of immortality and of spirituality. The other bird, the turtle dove, is a common and ordinary wild bird, a native of England, and of many other countries. In this poem it is used to represent the physical or bodily life. It is believed that the poem itself bears out these symbolisms, and represents the spiritual or poetic in union with the physical life. If so, as will be shown, the phœnix is Shakespeare's genius, and the turtle dove is Shakespeare's physical self. (To forestall as to what is contained in the *Lover's Complaint:* The phœnix is there identified clearly as representing Shakespeare's art.)

The poem describes the funeral service over these two 'dead birds,' or the failure of Shakespeare's poetical aspirations. If this point can be maintained, it necessarily follows from the fact that Shakespeare achieved his greatest literary fame thereafter, that the poem must have been produced relatively early in his career, and after he had tasted fame and was assured of his capacity, but for some reason had come to the conclusion that he was not to reach the heights to which his great talents entitled him to ascend—that through some lack he had prematurely decayed.

As has been shown in the treatment of the Sonnets, Shake-speare in the first Sonnet begins his appeal to his moral side to relax its severity, and permit his success through the necessary indulgements in wine, without which he was convinced he could not further expand in his work. Here, in *The Phoenix and the Turtle* it is indicated that he had finally concluded to resolutely refuse to succumb to stimulation through wine, and thereby for-ever abandon his art,—it was dead. It is therefore concluded that the condition of hopelessness and death, here set forth, were the conditions existing when the Sonnets were begun, and there-fore *The Phoenix and the Turtle* is the earlier and older poem.

As in the case of the Sonnets, suggestions will be made as to the interpretation of the stanzas, which for the purpose of a more ready reference will be numbered.

1.

Let the bird of loudest lay,
On the sole Arabian tree,
Herald sad and trumpet be,
To whose sound chaste wings obey.

Let the bird of loudest lay, (the nightingale, taken as the symbol of excellence and fame) be the sad herald and trumpeter, (of the obsequies) whose voice will be heard, and will assemble the chaste. (The worthy ones, the true mourners.)

2.

But thou shrieking harbinger,
Foul precurrer of the fiend,
Augur of the fever's end,
To this troop come thou not near!

But thou shrieking harbinger, (the screech-owl, symbolical of noisy, rioutous drinkers) foul precurrer (forerunner) of the fiend (drunken-ness) and augur of the fever's end (the collapse after drinking) come thou not near (you have nothing to mourn).

3.

From this session interdict
Every fowl of tyrant wing,
Save the eagle, feather'd king:
Keep the obsequy so strict.

From the obsequies exclude every fowl of tyrant wing (those who trade and live on others, merchants, tradesmen, etc.), save the eagle, feathered king (the ruling class, the upper class).

4.

Let the priest in surplice white,
That defunctive music can,
Be the death-divining swan,
Lest the requiem lack his right.

Let the priest be the death-divining swan. (Give the services a religious aspect and tone, out of respect for religious morals, as Shakespeare's abstinence had been.)

5.

And thou treble-dated crow,
That thy sable gender makest
With the breath thou givest and takest,
'Mongst our mourners shalt thou go.

The crow, that outlives three generations, and has the power of changing its sex while living, (typifying the busybodies, the gossips and the curious) shall be among the mourners.

6.

Here the anthem doth commence:
Love and constancy is dead;
Phœnix and the turtle fled
In a mutual flame from hence.

Here the anthem doth commence: Love and constancy (the mutual relations between the phoenix and the turtle) is dead, and they are fled.

7.

So they loved, as love in twain
Had the essence but in one;
Two distincts, division none:
Number there in love was slain.

Mutually they loved, as if they were twain (divided), but in essence
they were one; they were two distincts, but no division; number there
in love was slain (in love they were but one).

8.

Hearts remote, yet not asunder;
Distance, and no space was seen
'Twixt the turtle and his queen:
But in them it were a wonder.

Hearts remote (through different desires and appetites) yet they
were not parted; there was distance, but no space between the turtle
and his queen (the mortal and his genius); But in them, (in any others)
it were a wonder.

9.

So between them love did shine
That the turtle saw his right
Flaming in the phœnix' sight;
Either was the other's mine.

Between them love so shown, that the turtle saw his right (his own,
what belonged to him), flaming in the phœnix' sight (genius); either
was the others mine (each belonged to the other).

10.

Property was thus appalled,
That the self was not the same;
Single nature's double name
Neither two nor one was called.

Property (ownership, rights) were thus appalled (confused), that
the self, (each self) was not the same; single nature's double name
(single by nature but double in name) they could be called neither one
nor two.

11.

Reason, in itself confounded,
Saw division grow together,
To themselves yet either neither,
Simple were so well compounded;

Reason in itself confounded (reason thus was contradicted), saw division grow together (saw two become one); to themselves yet either neither (they were either and at the same time neither), they were simple (each an element), yet well compounded (blended).

12.

That it cried, How true a twain
Seemeth this concordant one!
Love hath reason, reason none,
If what parts can so remain.

Reason cried, How true a twain (how evidently divided) seems this concordant one! Love has reason, but reason none (but there is no reason), if what parts can still remain.

13.

Whereupon it made this threne
To the phœnix and the dove,
Co-supremes and stars of love,
As chorus to their tragic scene.

Whereupon it (reason?) made this threne to the phœnix and the dove, co-supremes and stars of love, as chorus to their tragic scene (end).

(The same intangible ideas attempted to be expressed in this poem, of a single though dual soul, or nature, or being, is found in the Sonnets. Here the two are Shakespeare and his art, while in the Sonnets it is Shakespeare and Wine. See Sonnets 86, 88, 89 and 42. But as has been so often repeated, Shakespeare in the Sonnets makes so little difference between Wine and his Genius, that the change between here and there, is an indistinct one, rather of ideas than of substance.)

THRENOS.

14.

Beauty, truth and rarity,
Grace in all simplicity,
Here enclosed in cinders lie.

Beauty, truth and rarity, grace in all simplicity (the qualities and guiding spirits of Shakespeare's poetry) here lie inclosed in cinders.

15.

Death is now the phœnix' nest;
And the turtle's loyal breast
To eternity doth rest,

The phœnix and the loyal turtle rest in eternity,—in death.

16.

Leaving no posterity:
'Twas not their infirmity,
It was married chastity.

They left no posterity (no living poetry). Not because of their infirmity (they were capable) But because of married chastity (abstinence from wine the inspiritor).

17.

Truth may seem, but cannot be;
Beauty brag, but 'tis not she;
Truth and beauty buried be.

Truth may seem, but cannot be (in its perfection), beauty brag, but 'tis not she (an imperfect imitation); truth and beauty (poetry) are buried.

18.

To this urn let those repair
That are either true or fair;
For these dead birds sigh a prayer.

To this urn let those repair (as worshippers) that are either true or fair (possessed of either of the elements of true poetry), for these dead birds sigh a prayer.

(In sonnet 105 Shakespeare says "fair, kind and true" (beauty, love and truth) is all the argument of his poetry. Here in *The Phoenix and the Turtle* he defines the spirits of his poetry as "beauty, truth and rarity." Rarity, it is assumed refers to his individual excellence and style. At a later age, in the Sonnets, he drops 'rarity,' and substitutes 'kind,' which undoubtedly should be defined as 'love,' or 'consideration,' or 'tenderness'—a great expansion and improvement, for with all these, rarity was retained, though not enumerated.)

At the risk of repetition it is thought well to summarize under one head, and freed from the text and the confusion of the interpretive clauses, a brief résumé of the very complicated ideas and expressions, which in the suggestions an effort has been made to clarify.

The ideas attempted to be expressed cannot be expressed, because they are in themselves a contradiction, and an impossibility. Shakespeare's conception of the relation between his physical mind and his genius, and which he conceives to be one of union and disunion, existing at the same time; they are dependent, and yet independent; distinct, but undivided; one and yet two; far apart and yet together; mutually loving, and yet each is the other; each bears a distinct name, and yet they are called the same, but are called neither one nor two; reason is confounded by a division that grows together; to themselves they are either, and at the same time neither; they exist as simples, elements, and yet are well compounded, blended; reason cries, How true a twain, is this concordant one; love has reason, but there is no reason, if what parts can still remain; reason made the funeral song to the phœnix and the dove, two joint supremes, and separate stars of love.

Underlying these contradictions, and implied, but not expressed, is the further anomaly, that Shakespeare's self, his will, the dove, is set to resist the appetite for wine, even to the extent of the destruction of the phœnix, his genius, whilst his genius, and his love, cannot exist without it.

The impossible conception, if it were conceivable, is like that contained in the suggestion of the meeting of an irresistible force, and an immovable object. There is no such force or object, and consequently there can be no result. Here Shakespeare imagined the result to be annihilation—death. But later in the Sonnets he found that his immovable object, his will and determination gave way, and his irresistible appetite prevailed.

THE PASSIONATE PILGRIM

THE PASSIONATE PILGRIM.

A book of miscellaneous verse, with the title of *The Passionate Pilgrim* was printed in 1599 by W. Jaggard. It contained a miscellaneous lot of poems by different authors, that had probably been surreptitiously pirated from other publications. Among the number of these were Sonnets 138 and 144 (numbered respectively I and II), varying slightly, but not materially from the text of the Sonnets. There were also included extracts from *Love's Labor's Lost*. These were the only inclusions that are positively known to be Shakespeare's. But students are quite well agreed that certain others of them were his productions. Several of these, which are undoubtedly Shakespeare's, are marked by evident allusions to the theme that so possessed him,—that theme it is hardly necessary to repeat is, Wine and its effects.

The date of these poems is unknown, as indeed are the dates of all Shakespeare's works. It is here assumed that they were written subsequent to the *Phoenix and the Turtle*. It appears from their character and tone, that they were written at about the same period as were the Sonnets,—after the first, and before the last of them. If the construction given to them is correct, then Shakespeare at the time they were written was indulging —over-indulging—in the use of Wine.

The Sonnets taken from *Love's Labor's Lost* do not refer certainly to the effects of Wine. However, they have been included here, as have some of the other parts of the play, and all commented upon in their relation to the subject. The reason for this will appear when they come more directly under review.

The Roman numerals, inserted with the sub-heads, and included in parentheses, designate the number assigned to the poem quoted, as it was designated in the *Passionate Pilgrim*.

FIRST. (VII)

1.

Fair is my love, but not so fair as fickle,
Mild as a dove, but neither true nor trusty,
Brighter than glass and yet, as glass is, brittle,
Softer than wax and yet as iron rusty:
    A lily pale, with damask dye to grace her,
    None fairer, nor none falser to deface her.

(Brittle, in the third line should be defined, fragile, or unreliable.
In the 4th line Wine is softer than wax,—yielding, soothing—yet hard
as iron,—rusty—coarse and ugly. In the 5th line it is lily pale, but dyed
with damask,—its true color.)

2.

Her lips to mine how often hath she joined,
Between each kiss her oaths of true love swearing!
How many tales to please me hath she coined,
Dreading my love, the loss thereof still fearing!
    Yet in the midst of all her pure protestings,
    Her faith, her oaths, her tears, and all were jestings.

(In this stanza Wine is drawn as a lover. This is Wine as Shake-
speare thought of it, and first believed it to be: full of love and help-
fulness. Colloquially we hear the expression, that food that agrees with
one loves him, or if it doesn't agree with him, that it doesn't love him.
It is in this sense that Shakespeare speaks of Wine. In this stanza he
doubts wine's love, and wonders if she isn't jesting.)

3.

She burn'd with love, as straw with fire flameth;
She burn'd out love, as soon as straw out-burneth;
She framed the love, and yet she foil'd the framing;
She bade love last, and yet she fell a-turning.
    Was this a lover, or a lecher whether?
    Bad in the best, though excellent in neither.

SECOND. (XIV)

1.

Good night, good rest. Ah, neither be my share:
She bade good night that kept my rest away;
And daff'd me to a cabin hang'd with care,
To descant on the doubts of my decay.
   'Farewell,' quoth she, 'and come again tomorrow:'
   Fare well I could not, for I supp'd with sorrow.

2.

Yet at my parting sweetly did she smile,
In scorn or friendship, nill I construe whether:
'T may be, she joy'd to jest at my exile,
'T may be, again to make me wander thither:
'Wander,' a word for shadows like myself,
As take the pain, but cannot pluck the pelf.

THIRD. (XV)

1.

Lord, how mine eyes throw gazes to the east!
My heart doth charge the watch; the morning rise
Doth cite each moving sense from idle rest.
Not daring trust the office of mine eyes,
   While Philomela sits and sings, I sit and mark,
   And wish her lays were tuned like the lark;

2.

For she doth welcome daylight with her ditty,
And drives away dark dreaming night;
The night so pack'd, I post unto my pretty;
Heart hath his hope and eyes their wished sight;
   Sorrow changed to solace and solace mix'd with sorrow;
   For why, she sigh'd, and bade me come to-morrow.

3.

Were I with her, the night would post too soon;
But now are minutes added to the hours;
To spite me now, each minute seems a moon;
Yet not for me, shine sun to succour flowers!
    Pack night, peep day; good day, of night now borrow;
    Short, night, to-night, and length thyself to-morrow.

(In both of the last two poems, the poet describes his nights, when drinking. Whether the law forbade the dispensing of liquors during the hours of night, or resorts where it was sold were closed, Shakespeare here, as in the Sonnets, describes long hours of anxious watching and waiting for the dawn. How vividly in the 2d. stanza of the last poem does he portray his cravings, and his relief:
  "The night so packed (gone) I post unto my pretty (wine),
    Heart hath his hope, and eyes their wished for sight;
    Sorrow changed to solace, and solace mixed with sorrow:"
Every drunkard will understand.)

FOURTH.

Under this head will be treated the extracts from *Love's Labour's Lost,* found in *The Passionate Pilgrim,* and also some other parts of the play not found therein. In the collection there appeared two sonnets from the play. While these sonnets are not altogether consistent with the theme when Wine is taken as the subject, they are even more inconsistent as delicate love-making to a beautiful woman, as they are supposed to be in the play. They are so nearly apt as describing the poet's feelings towards Wine, as in the early Sonnets, that they will be included in this review.

There is something so suspicious about these sonnets, as there is about other parts of the text of Act 4 Scenes 2 and 3, of the play, that they deserve some investigation.

In the play the King of Navarre, and three of his attending lords, Biron, Longaville and Dumain enter into an oath-bound obligation to devote three years to uninterrupted study; that during this time they will not converse with a woman, and no woman shall be permitted to come within a mile of the court. Scarcely had this obligation been sealed when the princess of France, with three lady attendants, Rosaline, Maria and Katherine arrived. The Princess had been dispatched by her father, the King of France, as an embassadress, to conduct certain negotiations with the King of Navarre. This, of course, required that she and her lady attendants should be received, as they were, and instantly the king fell in love with the princess, and each of the attending lords fell in love with one of the attending ladies. After the first meeting each of the attending lords addressed to his love a love-letter in poetical form. Three of these love-letters were in sonnet form, and it is two of these that appear in *The Passionate Pilgrim,* each with some slight verbal differences from those found in the play.

When the lovers by accident stand revealed among themselves for the betrayal of their oaths, which betrayal till then each had kept secret from his fellows, Biron begins openly to boast of his love, and to extol his lady in the most extravagant fashion, while the others banter him about her, and the King calls Rosaline, Biron's love, 'black as ebony,' and then Biron defends her by declaring, that no face is fair that is not so black, and in his defence resorts to a character of praise that is very suggestive of expressions contained in Sonnets 127, 130, 131 and 132. These sonnets give to the last group of the Sonnets the name of 'dark woman sonnets.'

The sonnet from Biron to Rosaline as found in *The Passionate Pilgrim* is as follows:

1. (V)

If love make me forsworn, how shall I swear to love?
O never faith could hold, if not to beauty vowed:
Though to myself forsworn, to thee I'll constant prove;
Those thoughts, to me like oaks, to thee like osiers bowed.
Study his bias leaves, and make his book thine eyes,
Where all those pleasures live that art can comprehend.
If knowledge be the mark, to know thee shall suffice;
Well learned is that tongue that well can thee commend:
All ignorant that soul that sees thee without wonder;
Which is to me some praise, that I thy parts admire:
Thine eye Jove's lightning seems, thy voice his dreadful
    thunder,
Which, not to anger bent, is music and sweet fire.
    Celestial as thou art, O do not love that wrong,
    To sing heaven's praise with such an earthly tongue.

If this sonnet be read as addressed to Wine, considering what we have learned of Shakespeare's feelings and expressions in that respect, its praises can be readily applied and understood. But considering its source, it is necessary to read it as a love-song or appeal from a young man to a maiden. As such it would hardly seem fair to charge Shakespeare with it. Biron had just met Rosaline and become enamoured, and had not seen her again before addressing her with this sonnet. How unnatural and inappropriate are its expressions! It is declared if knowledge be one's aim, to know Rosaline will suffice; the tongue is well learned that can commend her and it is ignorance to look on her without wonder; her eyes are like Jove's lightning, and her voice like his dreadful thunder, but these when not in anger, are music and sweet fire; as she is celestial she is implored not to take it as wrong to have her heavenly praises sung by an earthly tongue.

Is it conceivable that a maiden could be flattered by such praises? Or that a lover could see in one of whom he is enamoured, such attributes as are here described? What has knowledge to do with love? Or how can one's love impart knowledge. Or why should it be ignorance to look upon her without wonder? Or why should it require learning to commend her?

On the contrary, if Wine the divine inspirer, be taken as the subject, these apotheoses would have some appropriateness.

The other sonnet is a poetical address by Longaville to his love Maria written under identically the same conditions as the one just discussed. It is as follows:

2.   (III)

Did not the heavenly rhetoric of thine eye,
'Gainst whom the world could not hold argument,
Persuade my heart to this false perjury?
Vows for thee broke deserve not punishment.
A woman I forswore; but I will prove,
Thou being a goddess, I forswore not thee:
My vow was earthly, thou a heavenly love;
Thy grace being gain'd cures all disgrace in me.
My vow was breath, and breath a vapour is;
Then, thou fair sun, that on this earth doth shine,
Exhale this vapour vow; in thee it is:
If broken, then it is no fault of mine.
    If by me broke, what fool is not so wise
    To break an oath, to win a paradise?

This sonnet is not so exaggerated in strain as the former one, but is inappropriate enough, as a love-offering. It is said in this one, that the world could not hold argument against the rhetoric of this girl'd eye, which had persuaded the lover to his perjury; he says he had foresworn a woman,—the very thing a young man in love could not be induced to foreswear—and then claims his love is a goddess, and he had not foresworn goddesses; his vow was earthly—as all love vows should be—but here his love is a heavenly one, whose grace can cure his disgrace; his vow to avoid women was vapor, but her love is the fair sun, that can evaporate vapors, etc.

Now again read this sonnet with Wine as the adored, and all the exaggerations are resolved, or at the least made understandable. Its consistency however when so read is marred by the sentences, 'A woman I foreswore', for this would have no place in a sonnet to Wine.

It is therefore probably a substitution, made to avoid a positive incongruity, in the use to which the sonnet was put in the play.

The other sonnet in *Love's Labour's Lost,* but not in *The Passionate Pilgrim,* is addressed by the King to the Princess and was written under like conditions, as were the other two. It is as follows:

3.

So sweet a kiss the golden sun gives not
To those fresh morning drops upon the rose,
As thy eye-beams, when their fresh rays have smote
The night of dew that on my cheeks down flows:
Nor shines the silver moon one half so bright
Through the transparent bosom of the deep,
As doth thy face through tears of mine give light;
Thou shin'st in every tear that I do weep:
No drop but as a coach doth carry thee;
So ridest thou triumphing in my woe.
Do but behold the tears that swell in me,
And they thy glory through my grief will show:
But do not love thyself; then thou wilt keep
My tears for glasses, and still make me weep.
O queen of queens! how far dost thou excel,
No thought can think, nor tongue of mortal tell.

In the first place: no reason appears why the king should be in tears. We should rather expect rejoicing in a new lover; nor does it appear how or why his loves face should give light through his tears; he says his lady-love shines in every tear he weeps, and like a coach each drop carries her, and she so riding triumphs in his woe; (presumably as a conqueror in his chariot triumphs over his captive and slave); he bids her behold his tears, which show her glory through his grief; he asks her not to love herself, then she will keep his tears for glasses, and make him weep.

Altogether it seems not too much to say, that there is nothing whatever in the sonnet that makes it appropriate as a love epistle. It can be read however as an expression of the grief of him who has been brought to tears and misery by a mistress, whom he worships, in spite of the sorrow she inflicts, and whose triumph is in his tears,—Wine.

Observe also, that the poem contains 16 lines, two lines more than are permissible for a sonnet. Until the last two lines were added it was symmetrically regular, and poetically complete. The last two lines add nothing to the thought of the sonnet, but have apparently been added to aid in applying the sonnet to the use that is here made of it. They are undoubtedly an addition and an afterthought.

The dialogue in Act 4, Scene 3, of *Love's Labor's Lost,* where Biron extols the blackness of his lady-love is as follows:

4.

Biron.   Who sees the heavenly Rosaline,
            That, like a rude and savage man of Inde,
            At the first opening of the gorgeous east,
            Bows not his vassal head, and strucken blind
            Kisses the base ground with obedient breast?
            What peremptory eagle-sighted eye
            Dares look upon the heaven of her brow,
            That is not blinded by her majesty?

King.   What zeal, what fury hath inspired thee now?
            My love, her mistress, is a gracious moon:
            She an attending star, scarce seen a light.

Biron. My eyes are then no eyes, nor I Biron.
O, but for my love, day would turn to night!
Of all complexions the culled sovereignty
Do meet, as at a fair, in her fair cheek,
Where several worthies make one dignity,
Where nothing wants that want itself doth seek.
Lend me the flourish of all gentle tongues,—
Fie, painted rhetoric! O, she needs it not:
To things of sale a sellers praise belongs,
She passes praise; then praise too short doth blot.
A withered hermit, five-score winters worn,
Might shake off fifty, looking in her eye;
Beauty doth varnish age, as if new born,
And gives the crutch the cradle's infancy.
O, 't is the sun that maketh all things shine.

King. By heaven, thy love is black as ebony.

Biron. Is ebony like her? O wood divine!
A wife of such wood were felicity.
O, who can give an oath? where is a book?
That I may swear beauty doth beauty lack,
If that she learn not of her eye to look;
No face is fair that is not full so black.

King. O, paradox! Black is the badge of hell,
The hue of dungeons, and the shade of night;
And beauty's crest become the heavens well.

Biron. Devils soonest tempt, resembling spirits of light.
O, if in black my lady's brows be decked,
It mourns that painting and usurping hair
Should ravish doters with a false aspect;
And therefore is she born to make black fair.
Her favour turns the fashion of the days;
For native blood is counted painting now,
And therefore red, that would avoid dispraise,
Paints itself black to imitate her brow.

Throughout, none of Biron's speech rings true as that of a
lover. The qualities he ascribes to Rosaline are not womanly
or seductive. She is pictured as majestic and awe-inspiring;
no man could look on her without being struck blind, and like
the East Indian, before the rising sun, he would be impelled to

prostrate himself on the earth before her; what eagle-sighted eye would dare to look upon her brow, lest it be blinded by her majesty; but for her, day would turn to night; the sovereignties of all complexions meet in her fair cheek, and several worthies unite to make her dignity,—not loveliness and beauty—but majesty and dignity! a withered hermit, an hundred years old, by looking in her eye might shake off fifty years, and her beauty would give the crutch the cradle's infancy. All of this might, in exaggeration, be said of Wine if it had the virtues that our poet has elsewhere attributed to it. But who would attribute, or want to attribute, such unearthly majesty and dominancy, to a sweetheart?

Beginning, 'O but for my love! etc., on line 13, and ending with, 'O 'tis the sun that makes all things shine' on line 26, we have a complete sonnet, lacking only a line to rhyme with the last one.

The purpose of this investigation is to show that the three sonnets which have been quoted, were written originally as a part of the main body of the sonnets, and that Wine was their subject. These may have been, and probably have been, slightly altered from the originals. Biron's speech as quoted is also composed of like compositions. It is made up either of incomplete sonnets, or parts of dismembered sonnets, after eliminating such parts as would be too noticeably inappropriate for the uses to which they were put in the play.

The very abrupt suggestion by the king in line 27, that Rosaline is black as ebony is undramatic, and certainly not literally true. The praise of her complexion by Biron, is inartistic and far-fetched, as indeed are all other parts of his speech. It must all have been brought about, in a very strained way, in order to use the material already at hand in sonnet form, or in course of composition. In the case of the black woman sonnets, so little of the material was used, that the original sonnets were allowed to hold their places in the body of the sonnets.

It is therefore guessed, with some probability to support it, that these sonnets in praise of wine had been completed, or nearly so, and that Shakespeare in writing the play, or possibly in revising it, rather than take the pains to compose poems to fit the occasion, concluded that those on hand could be made to serve the purpose, and by slight adaptations so made use of them.

Students of Shakespeare have generally concluded that *Love's*

Labour's Lost was the first of his dramatic works. If this be so, his conception of character may not have yet developed to that excellence shown in subsequent plays, and as a novice, the unfitness of his prepared verse would not occur to him, or impress him. It evidently did not, whatever may have been the origin of the poems.

THE LOVER'S COMPLAINT

THE LOVER'S COMPLAINT

This poem consists of 47 stanzas of 7 lines each. It was, so far as is known, published for the first time with the sonnets in 1609. It is not referred to in the dedication, or the title page of the volume, and there is nothing to indicate why it should have been so published.

The lover who makes the complaint is a pale maiden who is seen tearing papers and breaking rings, and 'Storming her world with sorrow's wind and rain'. Upon her head is a platted hive of straw; her appearance gives the impression of beauty spent and done; time had not destroyed her youth altogether, and some beauty peeped through the lattice of seared age. She is further described, but the poem can best speak for itself. A reverend man drew near and solicited her confidence as to the cause of her woe, and thereafter the poem consists of her narrative, detailing how she had attended the suit of a youth just budding into manhood, and how through his beauty, charms and passionate appeals she had been seduced. Her complaint is centered principally upon the fact that after he had accomplished his purpose, 'He preached pure maid and praised cold chastity'.

The construction or interpretation which is proposed to be put upon this poem will identify the maiden as Wine, but not wine generically and as a whole, but some specific alcoholic liquor, which is not named, and is indefinitely described. The youth, of course, is Shakespeare, himself, who is sufficiently described to justify the identification. Here is given the color of his hair, approximately his age when first he began the use of intoxicating liquors, something concerning his character and qualities, the esteem in which he was held, and a very beautiful definition or description of his poetry, quite in consonance with that which time has awarded to it.

It will be found that the qualities ascribed to the maiden are such as belong to wine, and are not, on the whole, such as a maiden could possess, for they are not human. Nor will the loves of the youth, the seducer, be found to correspond with sexual love,—they are the appetite and craving for wine. The descriptions of the youth, and the qualities of his mind, on the contrary, are such as might well befit Shakespeare, and the description of his poetical powers would not be appropriate to any other than Shakespeare, for in this poem he is said to have the power,

> "To make the weeper laugh, the laugher weep,
> He had the dialect and different skill,
> Catching all passions in his craft of will."

Of whom but of Shakespeare could this be said?

1.

From off a hill whose concave womb re-worded
A plaintful story from a sistering vale,
My spirits to attend this double voice accorded,
And down I laid to list the sad-tuned tale;
Ere long espied a fickle maid full pale,
Tearing of papers, breaking rings a-twain,
Storming her world with sorrow's wind and rain.

The poet begins at once to depict the character of the maid: she is Wine, fickle and full pale, tearing of papers (destroying obligations), breaking rings a-twain (disrupting marital ties) and storming the world with sorrow.

2.

Upon her head a platted hive of straw,
Which fortified her visage from the sun,
Whereon the thought might think sometime it saw
The carcass of a beauty spent and done:
Time had not scythed all that youth begun,
Nor youth all quit; but, spite of heaven's fell rage,
Some beauty peep'd through lattice of sear'd age.

The platted hive of straw, may be suggestive of the vessel in which wine is stored and kept,—a demijohn incased in platted straw protecting the contents from the sun. Sometimes it might be thought spent and done (empty), or the carcass of a beauty (wine), but it was not so for time had not scythed (exhausted, restricted) all on which youth had begun, and in spite of heaven's fell rage (the outrage to morals) some beauty peeped through the lattice of age (it was not all spent or exhausted).

3.

Oft did she heave her napkin to her eyne,
Which on it had conceited characters,
Laundering the silken figures in the brine
That season'd woe had pelleted in tears,
And often reading what contents it bears;
As often shrieking undistinguish'd woe,
In clamours of all size, both high and low.

Her napkin, on which were conceited characters (fanciful imagin-
ings, such as Shakespeare himself indulges in), she often raised to
her eye, laundering (wetting) these silken characters in tears of woe,
and reading the contents it bears (reminiscent memories) and often
shrieking the woe of all, both high and low.

4.

Sometimes her levell'd eyes their carriage ride,
As they did battery to the spheres intend;
Sometime diverted their poor balls are tied
To the orbed earth; sometimes they do extend
Their view right on; anon their gazes lend
To every place at once, and nowhere fix'd
The mind and sight distractedly commix'd.

Sometimes her eyes (in exhilaration) seemed to threaten battery to
the spheres; sometimes diverted (sobered) they are tied to the earth;
sometimes they look right on, and anon they are not fixed but look on
every place at once, as when the mind and sight are distracted (in
delirium).

5.

Her hair, nor loose nor tied in formal plat,
Proclaim'd in her a careless hand of pride;
For some, untuck'd, descended her sheaved hat,
Hanging her pale and pined cheek beside;
Some in her threaden fillet still did bide,
And, true to bondage, would not break from thence,
Though slackly braided in loose negligence.

Her hair, neither loose nor tied, proclaimed in her a careless hand
of pride (a sloven); some hung by her pale and pined cheek; some
stayed in its threaded fillet, though slackly braided in loose negligence
(a very characteristic description of a drunken woman).

6.

A thousand favours from a maund she drew
Of amber, crystal, and of beaded jet,
Which one by one she in a river threw,
Upon whose weeping margent she was set;
Like usury, applying wet to wet,
Or monarch's hands that lets not bounty fall
Where want cries some, but where excess begs all.

A thousand favors (fortunes, character) from her maund (hand-basket) she drew, of amber, crystal, jet, which she threw one by one, into a river on whose banks she sat (the river of time) applying wet to wet (adding waste to waste), or like monarch's hands that let not bounty fall where want cries for some, but gives where excess begs all. (Wine yields not to those who drink in moderation, but is bountiful to those who use it to excess, and beg for all.)

7.

Of folded schedules had she many a one,
Which she perused, sigh'd, tore, and gave the flood;
Crack'd many a ring of posied gold and bone,
Bidding them find their sepulchres in mud;
Found yet moe letters sadly penn'd in blood,
With sleided silk feat and affectedly
Enswathed, and seal'd to curious secrecy.

Of folded schedules (plans, ambitions) she had many which she perused, sighed, tore and gave to the flood (all blasted); cracked many a ring of gold and bone (wedded promises) and threw them in the mud; found more letters penned in blood, enswathed in silk and sealed in secrecy (letters vowing love and constancy).

8.

These often bathed she in her fluxive eyes,
And often kiss'd, and often 'gan to tear;
Cried 'O false blood, thou register of lies,
What unapproved witness dost thou bear!
Ink would have seem'd more black and damned here!
This said, in top of rage the lines she rents,
Big discontent so breaking their contents.

These she often bathed with her tears, and kissed and began to tear; cried 'false blood, thou register of lies, what unapproved witness do you bear (how discredited a witness have you proved)! Ink would have seemed more black and damned here!' This said in rage she rends the lines, destroying the letters in her discontent.

9.

A reverend man that grazed his cattle nigh—
Sometime a blusterer, that the ruffle knew
Of court, of city, and had let go by
The swiftest hours, observed as they flew—
Towards this afflicted fancy fastly drew;
And, privileged by age, desires to know
In brief the grounds and motives of her woe.

A reverend man that grazed his cattle (congregation) nigh (was friendly and tolerant of Wine)—sometimes a blusterer that the ruffle knew (does it mean he knew the noise, or the ruffle of court raiment) of court, of city and had let go by the swiftest hours (hours of enjoyment), observed as they flew (by participating), towards this afflicted fancy (wine) fastly drew (evidently in sympathy), and privileged by age, desires to know the cause of her woe.

10.

So slides he down upon his grained bat,
And comely-distant sits he by her side;
When he again desires her, being sat,
Her grievance with his hearing to divide:
If that from him there may be aught applied
Which may her suffering ecstasy assuage,
'Tis promised in the charity of age.

So he sits down upon his staff, by her side at a comely distance, and asks her to tell him of her grievance, and promises in the charity of age to do what he could to assuage her suffering ecstasy.

11.

'Father,' she says, 'though in me you behold
The injury of many a blasting hour,
Let it not tell your judgement I am old;
Not age, but sorrow, over me hath power:
I might as yet have been a spreading flower,
Fresh to myself, if I had self-applied
Love to myself, and to no love beside.

She said: Father though you behold in me the injury of many a blasting hour (the results of many hours of dissipation) do not conclude I am old; it is not age but sorrow that has power over me; I might yet have been a spreading flower (still in my time of bloom) if I had loved myself and no one else beside (but for the injury my love had caused to others).

12.

'But, woe is me! too early I attended
A youthful suit—it was to gain my grace—
Of one by nature's outwards so commended,
That maidens' eyes stuck over all his face:
Love lack'd a dwelling and made him her place;
And when in his fair parts she did abide,
She was new lodged and newly deified.

But woe is me! too early I attended a youthful suit (was sued by a youth) who was by nature in appearance so commended, that maidens eyes stuck over all his face (that his face attracted the worship of maidens): love made him her dwelling place, and in his fair parts she was newly lodged and defied. (The youth, the suitor, is Shakespeare himself.)

13.

'His browny locks did hang in crooked curls;
And every light occasion of the wind
Upon his lips their silken parcels hurls.
What's sweet to do, to do will aptly find:
Each eye that saw him did enchant the mind;
For on his visage was in little drawn
What largeness thinks in Paradise was sawn.

His browny locks hung in curls, and winds blew their parcels on his lips. What's sweet to do, to do will aptly find (we find an opportunity to do that which we are inclined to do): each eye that saw him did enchant the (owners) mind, and on his visage was in little drawn what largeness thinks in Paradise was sawn (in his visage shown the beauty of Paradise).

(This last is probably a reference to Shakespeare's talents, rather than to his physical beauty. The browny locks however cannot be given other than a physical meaning.)

14.

'Small show of man was yet upon his chin;
His phœnix down began but to appear,
Like unshorn velvet, on that termless skin,
Whose bare out-bragg'd the web it seem'd to wear:
Yet show'd his visage by that cost more dear;
And nice affections wavering stood in doubt
If best were as it was, or best without.

Small show of man was yet upon his chin; his phoenix down (his genius) began but to appear like unshorn velvet (raw unfinished work) on that termless skin (unlimited, universal talent), whose bare out-bragged the web it seemed to wear (the bare intellect surpassed or outshown the primitive productions, or first efforts): yet showed his visage by that cost more dear (yet this proof showed the excellence of his talents); and nice affections wavering stood in doubt (his own best judgment stood in doubt) if best were as it was, or best without (whether he was improved by stimulants, or was best without it).

Here is fixed the beginning of indulgements, at the end of youth, and at the beginning of manhood, at which time Shakespeare was experimenting with his pen, and his work while not commensurate with his native talents, was proving the value of them. In the. construction of this poem it should be borne in mind that the complaining lover is not a personality, but an insensate thing that the poet is endowing with senses and feelings in order that it may express itself as possessing those characteristics and qualities with which the poets imagination would endow it. It should also be constantly before us, that often, but not always, when the poet introduces third parties he is personifying his own feelings and estimates. For instance, in this verse he speaks of nice affections in such a way as to suggest the affections of third parties, and their attachment for the wooing lover of the poem. But such is not the case. He is referring to himself, who is sitting in judgment to determine his own course, or the effects of external matters upon himself. So successful is Shakespeare in his dramatic impersonations, that the reader is often deluded, even when he understands what is being enacted,—and sometimes it seems probable that Shakespeare himself is deluded.)

15.

'His qualities were beauteous as his form,
For maiden-tongued he was, and thereof free;
Yet, if men moved him, was he such a storm
As oft 'twixt May and April is to see,
When winds breathe sweet, unruly though they be.
His rudeness so with his authorized youth
Did livery falseness in a pride of truth.

His (social) qualities were beateous as his form (talents), for maiden-tongued (gentle of speech) he was, and thereof free (ready in conversation), yet if men moved him, was he such a storm as oft tween May and April is to see, when winds breathe sweet, unruly though they be (he was gentle yet fearless). His rudeness so with his authorized youth, did livery falseness in a pride of truth (under the guise of truth he dressed falseness to look like truth).

16.

'Well could he ride, and often men would say,
"That horse his mettle from his rider takes:
Proud of subjection, noble by the sway,
What rounds, what bounds, what course, what stop he
    makes!"
And controversy hence a question takes,
Whether the horse by him became his deed,
Or he his manage by the well-doing steed.

Well could he ride (in poetry well poised and confident) and often men would say, "That horse (Pegasus-poetry) his mettle from his rider takes; proud of subjection, noble by the sway (proud of his rider and noble under control) what rounds, what bounds, what course, what stop he makes!" (All very suggestive of the wonders of Shakespeare's poetry). And controversy hence a question takes, whether the horse (poetry) by him became his (the rider's) deed, or by his manage by the well-doing steed (or was the credit due to the well-doing steed, under the rider's manage-control).

Here again is found another case of Shakespeare confounding his genius with wine. Undoubtedly the question propounded in this verse is, whether his poetry is his own product under stimulation, or whether the whole credit for it is due to wine, which he here confounds with his genius or poetry, as has been noted so often before.

17.

'But quickly on this side the verdict went:
His real habitude gave life and grace
To appertainings and to ornament,
Accomplish'd in himself, not in his case:
All aids, themselves made fairer by their place,
Came for additions; yet their purposed trim
Pierced not his grace, but were all graced by him.

But quickly on this side the verdict went: His real habitude (his natural qualities) gave life and grace to appertainings and to ornament (to details and to beauty) accomplished in himself, not in his case (dress, accompaniments—his condition when under the influence of wine). All aids, themselves made fairer by their place (because of the uses Shakespeare would put them to), came for additions, yet their purposed trim (their adaptability) pierced (aided) not his grace, but were all graced by him.

18.

'So on the tip of his subduing tongue
All kinds of arguments and question deep,
All replication prompt and reason strong,
For his advantage still did wake and sleep:
To make the weeper laugh, the laugher weep,
He had the dialect and different skill,
Catching all passions in his craft of will;

So, on the tip of his subduing tongue (analyzing speech) all kinds of arguments, and deep questions, all prompt replies, and strong reasons, for his advantage still did wake and sleep (were ready to his purpose both to act or wait): To make the weeper laugh, the laugher weep, he had the dialect and different (other) skill catching all passions in his craft of will.

19.

'That he did in the general bosom reign
Of young, of old, and sexes both enchanted,
To dwell with him in thoughts, or to remain
In personal duty, following where he haunted:
Consents bewitch'd, ere he desire, have granted,
And dialogued for him what he would say,
Ask'd their own wills and made their wills obey.

That he did in the general bosom reign (that he was supreme in the general esteem) of young, of old, and enchanted both sexes to dwell with him in thoughts, or to remain in personal duty following where he haunted: consents (minds) bewitched, ere he desire, have granted (yielded), and dialogued for him what he would say, asked their own wills and made their wills obey.

(The last three lines are difficult of construction. They seem to mean that among his admirers, when he was merely a listener, and without knowing himself what he desired, that these minds bewitched, would respond to his needs, suggesting dialogues and ideas.)

20.

'Many there were that did his picture get,
To serve their eyes, and in it put their mind;
Like fools that in the imagination set
The goodly objects which abroad they find
Of lands and mansions, theirs in thought assign'd:
And labouring in moe pleasures to bestow them
Than the true gouty landlord which doth owe them:

Many there were that did his picture get (that appropriated his thoughts) to serve their eyes and in it put their mind (by imitation and plagiarism), like fools who imagine the ownership of lands and mansions which they see abroad, and derive more pleasure from imagining what they would do with them, than does the gouty landlord who owns them.

21.

'So many have, that never touch'd his hand,
Sweetly supposed them mistress of his heart.
My woeful self, that did in freedom stand,
And was my own fee-simple, not in part,
What with his art in youth and youth in art,
Threw my affections in his charmed power,
Reserved the stalk and gave him all my flower.

So many have that never touched his hand believed themselves the mistress (inspirer) of his heart. (See the suggestions under the next verse.)

My woeful self that stood free and was my own fee simple (absolutely), not in part (but wholly) because of his combined youth and art, gave him my affections.

22.

'Yet did I not, as some my equals did,
Demand of him, nor being desired yielded;
Finding myself in honour so forbid,
With safest distance I mine honour shielded:
Experience for me many bulwarks builded
Of proofs new-bleeding, which remain'd the foil
Of this false jewel, and his amorous spoil.

Yet, I did not as some of my equals did, demand of him, nor yield to his desire; finding myself in honor so forbid, I shielded my honor with safest distance: experience had built for me many bulwarks, of proof new-bleeding (repeated or renewed) which remained the foil (background or setting) of this false jewel and his amorous spoil.

(The first two lines of stanza 21, and the first line of this stanza indicate that this forlorn lover, so loudly complaining, is not wine in its general sense, when all intoxicants are called wine, but is a particular kind or brand. This will develop more clearly as we proceed.)

23.

'But, ah, who ever shunn'd by precedent
The destined ill she must herself assay?
Or forced examples, 'gainst her own content,
To put the by-past perils in her way?
Counsel may stop awhile what will not stay;
For when we rage, advice is often seen
By blunting us to make our wits more keen.

But, whoever shunned by precedent (who was ever taught by precedent to shun) the destined ill she must herself assay? Or forced examples 'gainst her own content to put the by-past perils in her way? (Who ever by forced or unwelcome examples, which she was not content to consider, would permit past perils to stand in her way as warnings?) Counsel may stop awhile, but will not stay; for when we rage (crave) advice is often seen by blunting (opposing) us to make our wits (desires) more keen.

24.

'Nor gives it satisfaction to our blood,
That we must curb it upon others' proof;
To be forbod the sweets that seem so good,
For fear of harms that preach in our behoof.
O appetite, from judgement stand aloof!
The one a palate hath that needs will taste,
Though Reason weep, and cry "It is thy last."

(This stanza requires no comment in its construction. The last two lines indicate how futile is reason as against appetite, and how irresistible the appetite for wine.)

25.

'For further I could say "This man's untrue,"
And knew the patterns of his foul beguiling;
Heard where his plants in others' orchards grew,
Saw how deceits were gilded in his smiling;
Knew vows were ever brokers to defiling;
Thought characters and words merely but art,
And bastards of his foul adulterate heart.

And further I could say, "This man's untrue," and (I) knew the pattern (method) of his foul beguiling: (I had) heard where his plants in other orchards grew (where he had practiced his deceits on others), saw how deceits were gilded (disguised) in his smiling, knew vows were ever brokers (inducements) to defiling, thought characters and words were merely but arts (pretenses) and bastards (lies) of his adulterate heart.

26.

'And long upon these terms I held my city,
Till thus he 'gan besiege me: "Gentle maid,
Have of my suffering youth some feeling pity,
And be not of my holy vows afraid:
That's to ye sworn to none was ever said;
For feasts of love I have been call'd unto,
Till now did ne'er invite, nor never woo.

And long upon these terms I held my city (realizing this I long resisted his attack), till thus he began to besiege me: "Gentle maid have of my suffering youth (appetite) some pity, and be not of my holy vows (marriage vows—for life) afraid: That's to you sworn to none (no other) was ever said; for feasts of love I have been called unto (I have often been induced to indulge), till now did ne'er invite, nor never woo (till now I have acquiesced, but have never wooed).

(From this to the conclusion of the 40th stanza, it must be kept in mind that the complaining lover is repeating what the seducer said and vowed to her, in order to win her love and consent.)

27.

‘ “All my offences that abroad you see
Are errors of the blood, none of the mind;
Love made them not: with acture they may be,
Where neither party is nor true nor kind:
They sought their shame that so their shame did find;
And so much less of shame in me remains
By how much of me their reproach contains.

All my offences that abroad you see (all my dissipations) are errors of the blood (the taste and physical appetite), none of the mind (not cravings); love made them not; with acture that may be, when neither party is nor true nor kind (commerce without love). They sought their shame that so their shame did find (they who sought their shame found what they sought) and so much less of shame in me remains by how much of me their reproach contains (and so the more the guilty reproach me, the less my shame?).

28.

‘ “Among the many that mine eyes have seen,
Not one whose flame my heart so much as warmed,
Or my offection put to the smallest teen,
Or any of my leisures ever charmed:
Harm have I done to them, but ne’er was harmed;
Kept hearts in liveries, but mine own was free,
And reign’d, commanding in his monarchy.

Among the many that mine eyes have seen, (there was) not one whose flame my heart so much as warmed, or my affections put to the smallest teen (grief), or any of my leisures ever charm (nor did I give my time to making love to them); I have harmed them, but was not harmed; kept (their) hearts in liveries (servitude), but mine was free and reigned, commanding in his monarchy (supremacy).

29.

' "Look here, what tributes wounded fancies sent me,
Of paled pearls and rubies red as blood;
Figuring that they their passions likewise lent me
Of grief and blushes, aptly understood
In bloodless white and the encrimson'd mood;
Effects of terror and dear modesty,
Encamp'd in hearts, but fighting outwardly.

Look, here, what tributes wounded fancies (rejected lovers) sent me, of paled pearls and rubies red as blood (the character, probably colors, of other wines) figuring (assuming) that their passions likewise lent me of grief and blushes, aptly understood in bloodless white and the incrimsoned mood (aptly expressed in their own colors); effects of terror and dear modesty, encamped in hearts but fighting outwardly (while united in their efforts to win his love, each opposing the other).

The seducer in his efforts to win the maiden, whether she be wine, brandy, whiskey, liqueur, or some particular type of one of these, shows her how he has indulged in all, but none of them has ever won his heart. Nor has he ever vowed love to any of them, but now he appeals to this particular one to take pity on him, and pledges himself to her for life, and as will be seen, through his fervent plea wins her. This is the experience of every confirmed drinker; each one comes finally to restrict himself to one drink, eschewing all light wines and beverages. The drink selected as a standby is always one of high alcoholic contents, and the addict will have no other if his favorite can be obtained. It is not plain what particular liquor the beseecher adopted. Probably in his time, as now, the list of available intoxicants was large, and it is not evident what particular one was adopted, or which ones were rejected. It is probable however that the colors employed in this and the following stanzas, indicate the appearance or colors of the wines.

30.

' "And, lo, behold these talents of their hair,
With twisted metal amorously impleach'd,
I have received from many a several fair,
Their kind acceptance weepingly beseech'd,
With the annexions of fair gems enrich'd,
And deep-brain'd sonnets that did amplify
Each stone's dear nature, worth and quality.

(If this stanza could be correctly read, it might be found to have a more definite application than the one here given it. The following are suggested, but not without some doubt as to the correctness of the interpretation which identifies the 'twisted metal' with metal type:
And lo, behold the talents of their hair (the poetry inspired by each particular wine) with twisted metal amorously impleached (as it

appears in metal type), I have received from many a several fair (I have been inspired by the several kinds of wine) their kind acceptance weepingly beseeched (as each appealed to me), with annexations of fair gems enriched (with additions of sober gems of poetry) and deep-brained sonnets (his own) that did amplify each stone's (wine's) dear nature, worth and quality.

Further suggestions are: That the 'twisted metal' refers to the very confused face of metal type, when set into the forms. With, or into this, the poet's sentiments are lovingly, or amorously impleached or woven.

Each wine has its particular inspiration, of which character the poetry produced under its influence partakes, as is clearly shown in the next stanza; and to this was added (annexions) the poet's natural power of thought and expression. These natural qualities are the 'fair gems' with which the inspirations were enriched. There was also added his deep-brained or philosophical sonnets, altogether amplifying and reinforcing the inspirations received from wines.

Incidentally, here is a concession from the poet himself, that his wine-inspired poetry lacked of the depth and substance of his sober work. He calls some of his sonnets deep-brained, which is equivalent to sober. As was noted in the review of the Sonnets, it is possible to distinguish between the sober, beautiful and thoughtful sonnets and those written under, and usually descriptive of, the influence of wine.)

31.

 '"The diamond, why, 'twas beautiful and hard,
Whereto his invised properties did tend;
The deep-green emerald, in whose fresh regard
Weak sights their sickly radiance do amend;
The heaven-hued sapphire and the opal blend
With objects manifold: each several stone,
With wit well blazon'd, smiled or made some moan.

(This stanza is also interpreted with some, but not much misgiving, as follows:

The diamond (what wine?), why, 'twas beautiful and hard (dry? as is said of champagne) whereto his invised properties (the inspiration imparted) did tend; the deep-green emerald (absinthe) in whose fresh regard (renewing quality) weak sights their sickly radiance do amend; the heaven-hued sapphire and the opal blend (what wines?) with objects manifold (highly inspiring): each several stone (wine) with wit well blazoned, smiled or made some moan (resulting in exhilaration or depression).

32.

' "Lo, all these trophies of affections hot,
Of pensived and subdued desires the tender,
Nature hath charged me that I hoard them not,
But yield them up where I myself must render,
That is, to you, my origin and ender;
For these, of force, must your oblations be,
Since I their altar, you enpatron me.

Lo, all these trophies of affection hot (cravings) of pensive and subdued desires the tender (tendering less than the inspiration required), nature hath charged me that I hoard them not (my natural taste and inclination reject them), but yield them up where I myself must render (must yield or worship), that is to you, my origin and ender (my first and last love); for these, of force, must your oblations be (for these must be offered up to you), since I (am) their altar, you enpatron me (you are my patron saint).

33.

' "O, then, advance of yours that phraseless hand,
Whose white weighs down the airy scale of praise;
Take all these similes to your own command,
Hallow'd with sighs that burning lungs did raise;
What me your minister, for you obeys,
Works under you; and to your audit comes
Their distract parcels in combined sums.

Oh, then, advance of yours that phraseless (indescribable) hand (help), whose white weighs down the airy scale of praise; take all their (wines) similes to your own command, hallowed with sighs that burning lungs did raise (sighs of desires and cravings): What me, your minister, for you obeys (what obeys me, your minister) works under (obeys) you; and to your audit comes their distract (separate) parcels in combined sums (as one).

(White, as used in the second line, as being descriptive of the maiden, must be more than a complimentary adjective. It is very probable it is the color of the liquor personified.)

34.

' "Lo, this device was sent me from a nun,
Or sister sanctified, of holiest note;
Which late her noble suit in court did shun,
Whose rarest havings made the blossoms dote;
For she was sought by spirits of richest coat,
But kept cold distance, and did thence remove,
To spend her living in eternal love.

Lo, this device (a specially compounded liqueur or wine) was sent me from a nun, or sister, sanctified of holiest note (distinction); which late her noble suit in court did shun, whose rarest havings (qualities) made the blossoms (young courtiers?) dote; for she was sought by spirits of richest coat (highest rank) but kept cold distance, and did thence remove to spend her living in eternal love (in her nunnery).

(Stanzas 34, 35, 36 and 38 are all devoted to a nun whom the seducer in the poem relates he had captivated. If all of these stanzas refer to wine, as they evidently do, then all must receive a like construction, and none of them should be read as having reference to sexual infatuation. It is believed that the solution is, that all of the stanzas refer to a cordial or liqueur prepared in a monastery. Possibly, and probably, the particular liqueuer is Benedictine which was at first prepared by monks by a secret process. It may have been popular at court for a time, but if it is the liqueuer referred to in the poem, it evidently fell into disuse, as the poem says it removed to spend a life of eternal love. If the theory here advanced is correct, evidently Shakespeare continued its use after it had lost its favor at court.

The construction of the poem requires that any intoxicant referred to should be feminine in character, because the appetite for wine is disguised as sexual love. It therefore became necessary to designate the wine as a nun, and not as a monk.

To have given the whole poem a proper sequence these stanzas should have all preceded stanza 32. As they stand they are strikingly separated from those describing other wines, and as now arranged they follow when they should precede 32 and 33, in which latter stanzas all of the wines are gathered together, and offered as a combined whole to the supreme and all including love.)

It should also be observed, that stanzas 34, 35 and 36 are separated from 38, while all deal with the same subject. 38 seems to take up a subject which had been finished in the former stanzas, and comes in unexpectedly, not to say, confusingly. Further 38 would appear to be an experiment to express in another way, what had already been expressed in the preceding stanzas, for it is obviously a repetition of ideas.)

35.

' "But, O my sweet, what labour is't to leave
The thing we have not, mastering what not strives,
Playing the place which did no form receive,
Playing patient sports in unconstrained gyves?
She that her fame so to herself contrives,
The scars of battle 'scapeth by the flight,
And makes her absence valiant, not her might.

But, O my sweet (wine), what labor is't (it is no achievement) to leave the thing we have not, mastering what not strives, playing (leaving?) the place which did no form receive, playing patient sports in unconstrained gyves? She that her fame so to herself contrives, the scars of battle scapeth by the flight, and makes her absence valiant (her defense), not her might.

(The third line as found in the original is unmeaning, and evidently the first word, 'playing' is a misprint. It is suggested that 'leaving' be substituted therefor, and the line then becomes a reference to her 'remove' as set forth in the preceding stanza. While this emendation somewhat helps it does not altogether solve the difficulty. The line obviously means, that it is no sacrifice to leave the place which has no attractions.)

36.

' "O, pardon me, in that my boast is true:
The accident which brought me to her eye
Upon the moment did her force subdue,
And now she would the caged cloister fly:
Religious love put out Religion's eye:
Not to be tempted, would she be immured,
And now, to tempt, all liberty procured.

(The 5th line is not lucid. The following emendation and construction are suggested with some hesitation:
Religious love put out, Religion's *aye:* The construction then would be: Religious love (having been) put out, Religion is aye (even so).

This construction, it is admitted, is far fetched, but not much more strained than is often necessary to find an meaning for some of Shakespeare's verbal adaptations. As the stanza has always been printed the triple rhyme is, 'eye'—'fly'—'eye,' using the same word twice, which is not permissible, even to Shakespeare. This emendation would at least cure that fault.)

37.

' "How mighty then you are, O, hear me tell!
The broken bosoms that to me belong
Have emptied all their fountains in my well,
And mine I pour your ocean all among:
I strong o'er them, and you o'er me being strong,
Must for your victory us all congest,
As compound love to physic your cold breast.

How mighty, then you are ('Wine) O, hear me tell! The broken
bosoms (the wines whose loves are unrequited) that to me belong, have
emptied all their fountains in my well (they are all mine), and mine I
pour your ocean all among (I give to you): I strong o'er them, and
you o'er me being strong, must for your victory us all congest (must
take us all together), as compound love to physic (excite) your cold
breast.

38.

' "My parts had power to charm a sacred nun,
Who disciplined, ay, dieted in grace,
Believed her eyes when they to assail begun,
All vows and consecrations giving place:
O most potential love! vow, bond, nor space,
In thee hath neither sting, knot, nor confine,
For thou art all, and all things else are thine.

My parts (qualities) had power to charm a sacred nun, who dis-
ciplined, ay, dieted in grace (who lived in the seclusion of a convent),
believed her eyes when they to assail begun, all vows and consecrations
giving place: O, (Wine) most potential love! vow, bond nor space in
thee hath neither sting, knot nor confine (none of these are operative
against thy power), for thou art all, and all things else are thine.

(As before stated, it is believed this stanza is an alternative reading
of verses 84, 85 and 86, and probably was not intentionally incorporated
in the poem, or its inclusion was an oversight.)

39.

' "When thou impressest, what are precepts worth
Of stale example? When thou wilt inflame,
How boldly those impediments stand forth
Of wealth, of filial fear, law, kindred fame!
Love's arms are peace, 'gainst rule, 'gainst sense, 'gainst
      shame;
And sweetens, in the suffering pangs it bears,
The aloes of all forces, shocks and fears.

When thou, Wine impresseth (intoxicates), what are precepts worth
of stale example? When thou wilt inflame, how coldly those impedi-
ments stand forth, of wealth, of filial fear, law, kindred, fame! Love's
(Wine's) arms are peace 'gainst rule, 'gainst sense, 'gainst shame; and
sweetens in the suffering pangs it bears, the aloes (bitterness) of all
forces, shocks and fears.

(Let it be noted here that 'filial fear,' 'law,' and 'kindred,' are among
the great obstacles that stand forth to menace the poet in the consum-
mation of his love. Filial fear could hardly arise from any source,
except as fear of his father. The reference to law could hardly be taken
to indicate a fear of legal punishment, but it is more likely to refer to
the probability of his failure in the pursuit of the law as a profession,
if indeed he was so fitting himself to that end. Probably there will be
occasion to revert to this later on.)

40.

' "Now all these hearts that do on mine depend,
Feeling it break, with bleeding groans they pine;
And supplicant their sighs to you extend,
To leave the battery that you make 'gainst mine,
Lending soft audience to my sweet design,
And credent soul to that strong-bonded oath
That shall prefer and undertake my troth."

Now all these hearts (of various wines) that do on mine depend, feel-
ing it (my heart) break, with bleeding groans they pine; and supplicant
their sighs to you extend, to leave the battery (opposition) that you
make 'gainst mine, lending soft audience to my sweet design, and (lend-
ing) credent (confiding) soul to that strong-bonded oath (an oath of
wedded constancy) that shall prefer (make) and undertake my troth.

(With this stanza the plea of the seducing lover, who is taken to be
Shakespeare himself, ends. As before noted it began with 26th and
ends with the 40th verse. The complaining lover, Wine, now resumes
and continues her narrative to the end.)

41.

'This said, his watery eyes he did dismount,
Whose sights till then were levell'd on my face;
Each cheek a river running from a fount
With brinish current downward flow'd apace:
O, how the channel to the stream gave grace!
Who glazed with crystal gate the glowing roses
That flame through water which their hue encloses.

This said his watery eyes he did dismount (divert) whose sights till then were levelled on my face; each cheek a river running from a fount, with brinish currents downward flowed: O, how the channel (his cheek) to the stream gave grace! Who (the stream) glazed with crystal gate the glowing roses (on his cheek), that flame through water which their hue incloses (which shown through his tears).

(The seducer, it should be considered, is a beautiful youth, just entering manhood, and it is therefore permissible to describe his cheeks as glowing roses.)

42.

'O father, what a hell of witchcraft lies
In the small orb of one particular tear!
But with the inundation of the eyes
What rocky heart to water will not wear?
What breast so cold that is not warmed here?
O cleft effect! cold modesty, hot wrath,
Both fire from hence and chill extincture hath.

O cleft (divided effect! cold modesty, hot wrath, both fire from hence and chill extincture hath (both modesty and wrath are fired by his tears, and are extinguished by them).

43.

'For, lo, his passion, but an art of craft,
Even there resolved my reason into tears;
There my white stole of chastity I daff'd,
Shook off my sober guards and civil fears;
Appear to him, as he to me appears,
All melting; though our drops this difference bore,
His poison'd me, and mine did him restore.

Though our drops this difference bore, his poisoned me, and mine did him restore (Wine through his debasement was brought into ill repute, whilst it restored or comforted him in his nervous extremity).

44.

'In him a plentitude of subtle matter,
Applied to cautels, all strange forms receives,
Of burning blushes, or of weeping water,
Or swounding paleness; and he takes and leaves,
In either's aptness, as it best deceives,
To blush at speeches rank, to weep at woes,
Or to turn white and swound at tragic shows:

In him a plentitude of subtle matter, applied to cautels (deceitfully applied), all strange forms receives, of burning blushes, or of weeping water, or swounding paleness (he could simulate blushes, tears or dismay); and he takes and leaves, in either's aptness, as it best deceives (and he uses either method best calculated to deceive), to blush at speeches rank, to weep at woes, or turn white and swound at tragic shows:

45.

'That not a heart which in his level came
Could 'scape the hail of his all-hurting aim,
Showing fair nature is both kind and tame;
And, veil'd in them, did win whom he would maim:
Against the thing he sought he would exclaim;
When he most burn'd in heart-wish'd luxury,
He preach'd pure maid and praised cold chastity.

That not a heart which in his level (sight or range) came could 'scape the hail (harm) of his all-hurting aim, showing fair nature is both kind and tame; and veiled in them (through his deceits he) did win whom he would maim (he won Wine and then discredited it): against the thing he sought he would exclaim (denounce it); when he most burned in heart-wished luxury (when he most indulged in what he most desired—Wine) he preached pure maid and praised cold chastity (he preached and praised abstinence).

(Here is summed up the lover's complaint: She was not abandoned and cast off for another, but only condemned, and her evil influence exposed. This condemnation so denounced, is probably that contained in the last series of the Sonnets.)

46.

'Thus merely with the garment of a Grace
The naked and concealed fiend he cover'd;
That the unexperient gave the tempter place,
Which, like a cherubin, above them hover'd.
Who, young and simple, would not be so lover'd?
Ay me! I fell, and yet do question make
What I should do again for such a sake.

Thus merely with the garment of a Grace (under a disguise, and not practicing what he taught) the naked and concealed fiend he covered; that the unexperient (inexperienced and deceived Wine) gave the tempter place, which (the tempter) like a cherubin above them (wines) hovered. Who, young and simple (like wine) would not be so lovered? Ay me! I fell, and yet do question make what I should do again for such a sake.

47.

'O, that infected moisture of his eye,
O, that false fire which in his cheek so glow'd,
O, that forced thunder from his heart did fly,
O, that sad breath his spongy lungs bestow'd,
O, all that borrow'd motion seeming owed,
Would yet again betray the fore-betray'd,
And new pervert a reconciled maid!'

The indications are that *The Lover's Complaint* was intended as a supplement to the Sonnets, with which, and following them, it was published. In the poem Shakespeare assumes for himself the guise of a tempter and seducer. This is in accordance with the character he portrayed for himself throughout the first 126 sonnets. He was always the aggressor and blameable for all that had happened. Wine was the innocent helpmate, yielding beneficial aid, whilst he abused its uses.

In the last 28 sonnets however he turns the attack upon wine, and denounces it bitterly, but nevertheless does not divorce himself from its use, and so far as is shown he never did. It is permissible then to conclude, that the condemnation by Wine, the complaining lover in this poem, is founded, not upon his desertion, but upon his denunciation of it which is contained in the last sonnets. For it is in his denunciation that Wine finds his offense.

SHAKESPEARE AND BEN JONSON

SHAKESPEARE AND BEN JONSON.

Shakespeare was born in 1564, and as far as is now known, gained his first literary fame in 1593, when *Venus and Adonis* was published, and when he was 29 years old. Ben Jonson was born in 1573, and his first fame as a dramatist came from his play of *Every Man in his Humor,* which was acted in 1596, when Jonson was 23 years old. Although Shakespeare was 9 years older than Jonson, they may be said to have been in every way contemporaneous. It would not be possible at this time to determine which, as poet, was held in the higher esteem. They were then considered the most important dramatists of the day, and that estimation has continued to the present time. Both were reputed to be actors, and both were writers for the stage. But it is doubtful if either followed the profession of acting very persistently, though both may have appeared upon the stage intermittently, for several years.

Jonson for some reason, which does not clearly appear, incurred the antagonism of several playwrights of the time, particularly of Dekker and Marston. This resulted in much bitterness on both sides, and several plays produced and acted at the time were made the vehicles for the conduct of this stage conflict. As to whether Shakespeare was a party to this controversy, either actively or passively, has become a matter of much dispute. Many modern critics have come to the conclusion that although he was not an aggressor or participant, that he was unjustly and viciously assailed by Jonson, the reason assigned for this feeling on Jonson's part being his jealousy of Shakespeare's superior literary qualities.

Nothing that Jonson wrote, which can be said certainly to apply to Shakespeare, can justify this judgment. It is true that he criticised Shakespeare's art, but in his severest criticism he concludes, "There was ever more in him to be praised than to be condemned." No writer of that day has left so much concerning Shakespeare as has Jonson, and most of what he has left is of the very highest praise, some criticism (mostly just), and nothing abusive or that can be construed into a feeling of enmity. On the contrary everything that Jonson wrote of or about Shakespeare would indicate that Shakespeare held rather a high place in his (Jonson's) affections. So far as is known Shakespeare never expressed himself openly concerning Jonson, and certainly not in such a way as to make the allusion definite.

The Poetaster.

Jonson's controversy with the theatrical fraternity, and particularly with the poets who were writing for the stage, was a very bitter one. As Shakespeare is supposed to have been closely associated with the players, against whom the war was being waged by Jonson, many imagine that some of the thrusts that are found in Jonson's writings were aimed at Shakespeare. On Jonson's side the principal production relating to this controversy, was a play called *The Poetaster,* written and produced in 1601. There is not much, if anything, said in this play at which Shakespeare or his friends could take offense. There were two prologue speeches, one by Envy, and one by Prologue in Armor, that showed much personal feeling, which was undoubtedly heart-felt. The production of the play brought Jonson into trouble, and he then attached to the play what he called *'An Apologetical Dialogue,'* giving his reasons for writing the play, and disclaiming much that was charged against him, and defending himself for his attacks upon the players. He insisted that the attack was only on some of them, and then as to the others offers an apology as follows:

> "Only amongst them, I am sorry for
> Some better natures, by the rest so drawn
> To run in that vile line."

By many it is imagined that Shakespeare was included in these 'better natures,' which of course must imply that Shakespeare felt offended at the play.

The object of discussing this matter at this time, is to suggest that Shakespeare may have been in fact represented in the play, and that thereby considerable light may be thrown upon his habits, his studies, his association with the theatre, and that much mooted question, his study of the law. If this be true, what is attributed to Shakespeare is free from viciousness, and on the contrary may be said to be inoffensive, if not considerate. But that is not to say that it might not have excited some feeling of anger in Shakespeare, for it probably did. But of this the evidence is not positive, but only the inferences which may be indirectly drawn.

In connection with this (and that is the principal reason for the review and examination of the Poetaster), it will be suggested that Shakespeare's sonnets, devoted to the rival poet, refer to Jonson, for the reasons hereafter to be given.

The scene of the Poetaster is laid in Rome, at the time of the rule of Augustus Caesar. Augustus Caesar, Virgil, Horace, Ovid, Propertius and many others are represented as characters. Marston and Dekker, the playwrights against whom the play was principally aimed, are caricatured under the names of Crispinus and Demetrius. It is generally assumed that Jonson drew himself in the character of Horace, and it is now suggested that Shakespeare was represented in the character of Ovid, the poet. In the first part of the play he is designated as junior, for the reason that his father is represented as Ovid Senior. Under this designation there is a probability that Shakespeare's father was disguised.

Although the scene of the play is laid in Rome at about the beginning of the Christian Era, and the characters all bear Roman names, the subjects and matters treated, and which give to the play its interest, are the local affairs and controversies existing in London at the time of the production of the play. In the prologue speeches and in the Apologetical Dialogue, Jonson admits this to be the case.

The play opens discovering Ovid, the poet, in his study. He is reading from what he was in the act of composing, and as the scene draws, reads aloud:

> "Then, when this body falls in funeral fire,
> My name shall live and my best part aspire."

This expresses (not in Shakespeare's art, but in fact), the burden of the sonnets, as has been seen, and at once suggests the character of Shakespeare. This difference, however, exists: In the Sonnets as we have seen the promise of a living fame was made often, but not always to the addressee of the Sonnets, and Shakespeare rarely claimed the fame for himself, but when not for Wine it was for his verse. But in the changed construction which this review has given to the Sonnets, these opening lines at once arouse a suspicion that they may have a reference to Shakespeare.

At once Luscus enters with a gown and cap, and admonishes Ovid to be done with his songs and sonnets, and to be on with his gown and cap (indicative of the study of the law), as his, Ovid's, father would soon be there.   Luscus expresses a great contempt for poetry, but as Ovid persists in his fancy, Luscus leaves him in irritation, and Ovid proceeds to read his elegy, which has just been completed, as follows:

> "Envy, why twit'st thou me my time's spent ill,
> And call'st my verse, fruits of an idle quill?
> Or that, unlike the line from whence I sprung,
> War's dusty honors I pursue not young?
> Or that I study not the tedious laws,
> And prostitute my voice in every cause?
> Thy scope is mortal; mine eternal fame,
> Which through the world shall ever chaunt my name."

Then follows, in Jonson's usual strain, a long discourse on classical authors and subjects.   The elegy then concludes:

> "Frost-fearing myrtle shall impale my head,
> And of sad lovers I be often read.
> Envy the living, not the dead, doth bite!
> For after death all men receive their right.
> Then, when this body falls in funeral fire,
> My name shall live, and my best part aspire."

As Ovid concludes the reading of his poem, his father and others enter, and his father at once begins to berate him, for neglecting the study of the law, and devoting himself to poetry and play-making, and asks, if this is the fruit of all his travail and expenses, and complains that his son, whom he had hoped to see a pleader had become a play-maker.   He exclaims, "What, shall I have my son a stager now? an enghle for players? a gull, a rook, a shot-clog, to make suppers and be laughed at?"   He then threatens to withdraw his support, and to disclaim his son, if he persists in his course.

The only reply of consequence that Ovid makes to his father is as follows:

> "They wrong me, sir, and do abuse you more,
> That blow your ears with these untrue reports.
> I am not known upon the open stage,
> Nor do I traffic in their theatres:
> Indeed, I do acknowledge, at request
> Of some near friends, and honorable Romans,
> I have begun a poem of that nature."

The last is in answer to his father's charge that he had heard that Ovid was writing a tragedy, called Medea.

As the father continues his protests, Lupus intercedes for the son and says: "Come, do not misprize him." To which the father replies, "*Misprise!* ay, marry, I would have him use some such words, now; they have some touch and taste of the law." Lupus, supporting the father, says: "Why the law makes a man happy, without respecting any other merit; a simple scholar, or none at all, may be a lawyer." As the father is about to leave, he promises his son that if he will pursue his law studies dutifully, he will allow him what will suit the rank of a gentleman, and maintain him in society with the best. Ovid is then left alone, and soliloquizes, as follows:

"O, sacred, Poesy, thou spirit of arts,
The soul of science, and the queen of souls;
What profane violence, almost sacrilege,
Hath here been offered thy divinities!
That thine own guiltless poverty should arm
Prodigious ignorance to wound thee thus!
For thence is all their force of argument
Drawn forth against thee; or, from the abuse
Of thy great powers in adulterate brains:
When, would men learn but to distinguish spirits,
And set true difference 'twixt those jaded wits
That run a broken pace for common hire,
And the high raptures of a happy muse,
Borne on the wings of her immortal thought,
That kicks at earth with a disdainful heel,
And beats at heaven's gates with her bright hoofs;
They would not then, with such distorted faces,
And desperate censures, stab at Poesy.
They would admire bright knowledge, and their minds
Should ne'er descend on so unworthy objects
As gold, or titles; they would dread far more
To be thought ignorant, than be known poor.
The time was once, when wit drowned wealth; but now,
Your only barbarism is t'have wit, and want.
No matter now in virtue who excels,
He that hath coin, hath all perfection else."

Tibullus then enters and delivers a note to Ovid from Julia, and Ovid at once in raptures, calls Julia his gem and the jewel of his soul, from whose eyes beauty takes all its lustre, and declares she is his heaven, praised in herself, above all praise.

In Act 4 of the play, the players by agreement assume the characters of gods and goddesses, and disguise themselves accordingly. Ovid takes the part of the supreme god Jupiter, Julia of Juno, and the other inferior gods and goddesses are represented by other players and poets. The following announcement is made:

> "Jupiter, of his licentious goodness, willing to make this feast no fast, from any manner of pleasure, nor to bind any god or goddess to be anything the more god or goddess for their names: he gives them all fair license, to speak no wiser than persons of base titles; and to be nothing better than common men, or women. And therefore no god shall need to keep himself more strictly to his goddess than any man does to his wife: nor any goddess shall need to keep herself more strictly to her god, than any woman does to her husband. But since it is no part of wisdom, in these days, to come into bonds; it shall be lawful for every lover to break loving oaths, to change their lovers, and make love to others, as the heat of every one's blood, and the spirit of our nectar, shall inspire."

The banquet was given over to light mocking and jesting, and was suddenly interrupted by the entrance of Augustus Caesar with others. Caesar denounces the company, and especially Ovid and his (Caesar's) daughter Julia, for their irreverence and profanity, and banishes Ovid, whom he calls by his sirname Naso, from the presence of the court, and commits Julia to prison.

Scene 7 of Act 4, is a scene between Ovid and Julia. Ovid is an open space before the palace, and Julia appears at her chamber window above. It is a fervent love scene, and a very close imitation of the balcony scene from *Romeo and Juliet*.

The foregoing is a very incomplete synopsis of the play, and touches only those scenes in which Ovid appears.

Several of the incidents relating to Ovid in the play have a foundation in fact. His father did desire him to become a lawyer, but he declined to follow the profession, and like Shakespeare became a poet instead. He wrote one play, Medea, which has not been preserved. He had a mistress Corinna, and Jonson in the Poetaster makes him say that his true love was Julia, the Emperor's daughter, a reckless and wanton woman, and that she was disguised under the name of Corinna. Both Ovid and Julia were in fact banished from Rome, not from the court. The reasons for the banishment of Ovid are not known, but in the play the reason assigned is, for 'soothing the declined affections of our base daughter.'

The grounds upon which it is suggested, that Shakespeare was disguised as Ovid, in the Poetaster, are as follows:

First. The inordinate longing of Shakespeare for the immortality of his verse, as is so often expresed in the Sonnets, and a like expression in the play, put into Ovid's lines, and which we may imagine were suggested by the Sonnets. This desire may be said to be the burden of the Sonnets, and it is the sole theme of the elegy attributed to Ovid in the opening of the play.

Second. The very clear imitation, in the setting at least, in the *Poetaster,* of the balcony scene from *Romeo and Juliet.* Besides the setting, there is even a clearer allusion to the loves of Romeo and Juliet, where, in Ovid's composition, he says:

"And of sad lovers I be often read."

Notice that it is not *by,* but *of* sad lovers, that he is to be often read. Shakespeare's sad lovers have become a commonplace. But it could hardly be appropriate to say that Ovid's lovers are *sad* ones.

In Julia's speech in Scene 6, Act 4, he says:

"Here! and not here! O, how the word doth play
With both our fortunes, differing, like ourselves,
Both one; and yet divided as opposed!"

How plainly is this suggestive of Sonnets 36 and 39, as well as of the *Phenix and the Turtle.*

Also notice the emphasis, by italics, put upon the word *'misprise,'* when Ovid's father hears the word, and is pleased at its use, because it has some touch and taste of the law. In Sonnet 87 Shakespeare uses the word, 'misprision,' with an unmistakable legal application, and it is probably to the use of such a word in poetry that Jonson was calling attention. It being altogether technical, and unusual, impressed Jonson, as it does most of readers, and points with exactness to Shakespeare.

Third. It is noticeable that Jonson should have gone so fully, and with so much detail, into the objections of Ovid's father, to the son's neglect of the law, and to his devotion to poetry. It is a fact that Ovid's father desired him to study and practice law, and that the son failed to comply with his wishes. But here, in the *Poetaster* we have much more than that. The father not only desires and advises it, but protests against the son's failure to follow the course. And also against the son's association with players, and against his devotion to poetry, and to play writing, threatening to withdraw his support unless reformation should take place. At the same time he offers to maintain his son as a gentleman, if he will but persist in the law. This is going far beyond anything to be found in the life of Ovid, and if referring to Ovid, they are not matters of interest. When we stop to consider that the whole interest in the play was centered in what was transpiring in London, and not as to what had transpired in Rome, sixteen hundred years before, it becomes at once suggestive that these were not the incidents in Ovid's life, but London incidents in the life of someone represented in the play, and such incidents as would be understood and appreciated by a London audience. As we have assumed that Ovid was Shakespeare in disguise, we must therefore look into the life of Shakespeare to find if these incidents might, by any chance, be a part of his life.

We know that Shakespeare had a father who lived until 1601, the year of the production on the stage of the *Poetaster*. He had been formerly an official and prosperous citizen of Stratford. The records tend to show that prior to 1590 he had met with some adversity, and it has generally been assumed, but not shown, that the last part of his life was spent in poverty. But it is not certain that this assumption is correct.

The records show that in 1596 John Shakespeare, the father, made application to the College of Heralds for a coat-of-arms, and on October 20th, 1596, the application was granted, and it was certified that he was of "good reputation and credit." The grant for some reason, not stated, was not completely executed at that time, but was afterwards, in 1599 awarded, and in the award it was stated that John Shakespeare had "borne magistracy, and was Justice of Peace at Stratford-on-Avon; he married the daughter and heir of Arderne, and was able to maintain that estate." The investigators have generally assumed that these proceedings were instituted and prosecuted by the son, William Shakespeare, the poet, who through his prosperity had brought relief to the bankrupt father and family. These assumptions are without proof, and may or may not have been the case.

If it were conceded that the conditions as shown in the *Poetaster,* actually refer to Shakespeare's father, a very different face would be put upon the matter.

It has generally been conceded by the critics, that the poet Shakespeare was possessed of a considerable legal knowledge, but just to what extent, or by what means it was acquired, have remained unsolved questions. In none of his writings has his legal knowledge been more evident than in the Sonnets. There the instances and application of legal terms and principles are very frequent. They are not however such displays as might be expected from a trained and practiced lawyer, but rather the uses of terms and principles as might be impressed upon a novice or student. If the statements contained in the *Poetaster* can be taken as having a reference to Shakespeare and his study of the law, they would very well corroborate the suspicion that is aroused by the legal learning shown in the Sonnets. Conceding that such is the case, then it would appear that his father was maintaining him in London as a law student, and whilst he, the son, was so engaged he was giving much more attention to poetry and play writing than to his studies, and as a playwright was associated with the players, and interested in the theatres. So far as the writer has been able to ascertain, Ovid was never in any way connected with players or the theatre. If not, references to that effect in the *Poetaster* would be wholly inapplicable to him, and are at least suggestive that under his name some other poet is disguised.

In the dialogue that has been quoted, Lupus assures Ovid that a "simple scholar, or none at all, may be a lawyer." This serves also, quite strongly to point to Shakespeare, and to Jonson's estimate of his learning. Jonson knew Shakespeare very well, and regarded him as an uneducated man, for he has said of him, that he had "small Latin, and less Greek." On the contrary Ovid was a man of quality and education, and this statement coming from Lupus would have no fitness in the dialogue, if it were addressed to Ovid.

In several instances in the dialogue Ovid the father suggests that his son is too poor to follow the life of a poet, and in one instance speaking of Homer, he says: "You'll tell me his name shall live; and that now being dead, his works have eternized him, and made him divine: but could this divinity feed him while he lived? Could his name feast him?" After the departure of the father, Ovid in the monologue which has been quoted, comments upon this. Is it probable that all of this should have been discussed by Jonson, in a play, with so much minuteness, and so fully, unless it had a local application? Considering the situation, this whole matter would have been dull and unendurable to the audience, if this was really a part of Roman history, or of Ovid's biography. It is true that Jonson utilized the incidents in Horace's "The Literary Bore," but this was not for the purpose of showing incidents in Horace's life, but to cast ridicule upon Crispinus, who was thereby shown as the bore.

Again, as has been shown in the quotations, Ovid declares to his father that he is not known unto the open stage, nor does he traffic in the theatres. This may have pertinence as to Shakespeare, but would lack altogether of interest as applied to Ovid. If it were true as to Shakespeare, it would at the time have identified him clearly. To this, our age, it is rather a stratling disclosure. It has always been assumed that Shakespeare, sometime in his life, had been an actor. Upon what this positive assumption has been based, it would be difficult to say. That there have been traditions to that effect, is not to be denied, but direct evidence of the fact can hardly be said to exist. Notwithstanding this declaration, if it be intended as Shakespeare's, it may still be probable that at sometime he may have appeared on the stage, in subordinate parts, or as a makeshift, without really being identified as an actor. But if he had followed acting as a profession, there should be some evidence showing the time, place, and the part taken. Jonson knew about these things, and if he so represented Shakespeare, it would wellnigh demolish the whole theory of Shakespeare being an actor.

In Ovid's soliloquy, in the first act, he condemns the times for the lack of learning, and for its want of sympathy with art and poetry, and for its contempt for poverty, and says, "He that hath coin, hath all perfection else." None of this could be true of Ovid. He thought the time in which he lived the most ideal of all the ages, and was well contented with his own station and condition. He would never have thought of philosophising as Jonson makes his Ovid do. This soliloquy, however, is in some respects an echo of some of Shakespeare's Sonnets, where he bewails his outcast state, his poverty and his loneliness, and yet finds consolation in that which he loves. (See Sonnets 25, 29, 37.)

It is a marked coincidence, that Jonson in his *Poetaster* should show Ovid, the son, under the domination of his father, who was protesting against the neglect of the study of the law, and insisting that the son was thereby inviting poverty and the father's displeasure, and the statement by Shakespeare in the 39th stanza of *The Lover's Complaint*, that these same objections were confronting him in his course of indulgence. There he says:

> "When thou wilt inflame,
> How boldly these impediments stand forth
> Of wealth, of filial fear, law, kindred, fame!"

As noted under that stanza, Shakespeare felt that he was menaced by poverty, by the fear of his parent, or parents (for they were both living in 1601), by his failure in the law, by his kindred (probably referring to his wife and children) and by the loss of his fame. Observe that Shakespeare himself suggests the existence of conditions which Jonson in the play attributed to Ovid, and are therefore confirmatory of the possibility of Shakespeare being the Ovid of the play.

Fourth. In Shakespeare's time, probably no poet, modern or ancient, was more read and admired than was Ovid. It was from his *Metamorphosis* that Shakespeare obtained the stories of *Venus and Adonis* and of *The Rape of Lucrece,* his first two important productions that brought him fame. Modern criticism has shown that no other author exerted so much influence over Shakespeare as did Ovid. This could not have escaped Ben Jonson, who took rather an excessive pride in his learning, and particularly in his proficiency in Latin, and in Roman history and literature. Nor is there any doubt but that he highly appreciated the quality of Shakespeare's poetry.

It is reasonable then to conclude, that if Jonson intended to have Shakespeare represented in the *Poetaster* that no Roman character would be so suitable to him, as would that of Ovid. If therefore, any person of the time is veiled under the name of Ovid, we may expect it to be Shakespeare. And, e converso, considering the plan and purpose of the play, and Shakespeare's great prominence among the players, his omission from the *Poetaster* would have been a most notable absence, and this is evidenced by the fact that every interested reader of the play expects to find him concealed in some hiding place therein.

Fifth. If it should be considered possible that Shakespeare was represented as Ovid, then the question arises: Who was Julia? and what is the significance of his banishment from the court? Now, in fact, Ovid was not banished from the presence of the court, as stated in the play, but was exiled to Tomi, on the Black Sea, where he spent the last years of his life. Had Jonson not modified the severity of this sentence of exile, as is done in the play, it would not have conformed to the penalty, which in all probability was actually inflicted on Shakespeare.

From what has been learned in these reviews of Shakespeare, it does not seem probable that he was ever brought into disgrace through illicit relations with any woman, high or low, and it is not necessary to consider the statement that he was actually banished from the presence of the court. Now, that Shakespeare's weakness is known, it is not at all unlikely that this made him a very willing exile, not only from the court, but from all social functions, and in fact from nearly all social intercourse. His history, or rather the lack of any history, justifies this conclusion. That Jonson knew of his weakness, is not to be doubted, and if he purposely veiled Shakespeare under Ovid's name, only one solution of this reference to banishment is tenable, and that is, that the reference is to the ostracism that was the necessary result of his dissipation. To this, and to this only, is the sentence limited.

As to Julia, that too is but a name and a disguise. This is so, whether Ovid be Ovid, or Shakespeare. If he be Shakespeare, then Julia is Wine. There is much in the *Poetaster* dialogue to support the supposition that Ovid's love for Julia was not a sexual passion, but an appetite. Ovid in history was not in love with Julia, either Julia the daughter, or granddaughter of Augustus. The mistress whom he celebrates in his poetry is Corinna, but in the *Poetaster* Jonson has him say:

> "I would not for all Rome, it should be thought
> I veil bright Julia underneath that name."

Whoever then was being referred to, Ovid or Shakespeare, there was a veiling or hiding of the object of his love.

In the play Ovid's first exclamation regarding Julia is "O my life, my heaven!" Then he says:

> "Julia the gem and jewel of my soul,
> That takes her honors from the golden sky,
> As beauty does all lustre from her eye.
> The air respires the pure Elysian sweets
> In which she breathes, and from her looks descend
> The glories of the summer. Heaven she is,
> Praised in her self above all praise; and he
> Which hears her speak, would swear the tuneful orbs,
> Turned in his zenith only."

How like this is to the sonnets taken from *Love's Labour's Lost*.
And again Ovid says:

> "Hence law, and welcome Muses, though not rich,
> Yet are you pleasing; let's be reconciled,
> And new made one. Henceforth I promise faith,
> And all my serious hours to spend with you:
> With you whose music striketh on my heart,
> And with bewitching tones steals forth my spirit,
> In Julia's name; fair Julia: Julia's love
> Shall be a law, and that sweet law I'll study,
> The law and art of sacred Julia's love:
> All other objects will but abjects prove."

All of this is from the last part of Act 1.

These quotations are far from the genuine frenzy of love.
Ovid (Shakespeare) is henceforth to devote his serious hours
to the Muses, and is to be inspired and comforted by Julia, who
is to be his law and his art. Though the manner is not that of
Shakespeare, it would seem to be a crude attempt to imitate the
spirit of some of the Sonnets.

Jonson, the Rival Poet.

In all attempts that have been made to identify the rival poet
of the Sonnets, the search has been confined to those poets con-
temporaneous with Shakespeare and who could be shown to have
been a rival of his in seeking the favor of the same high person-
age whom Shakespeare had made his patron, and to whom he
has been supposed to have addressed the Sonnets. As Jonson
could not be shown to have conformed to these requirements, his
name has not been suggested as the rival. But, if the present
exposition has shown that the Sonnets in fact were not addressed
to any individual, but to Wine, the scope of the inquiry becomes
changed and much broadened, and if every devotee and pane-
gyrist of wine becomes a qualified competitor in the list of rivals,
to no one will the qualification be more fitting than to Ben
Jonson. Unlike Shakespeare he openly avowed his love for
wine, and was not unlike him in that he became wine's devoted
slave.

Dekker responded to Jonson's *Poetaster* with the *Satiromastix*.
While this play lacked of Jonson's literary art, it surpassed
Jonson's play in abuse, and undoubtedly Jonson felt quite out-
done by it. Dekker took up the fight like an angry man and was
not at all careful as to how or where he struck.

About this time there was produced at St. John's College,
Cambridge, several plays by an unknown author. One of these
was called *"The Return from Parnassus."* In this play Richard
Burbage and William Kempe, real persons and actors associated
with Shakespeare, were made characters, and in the course of
the dialogue Kempe says to Burbage:

> "Few of the university pen plaies well, they smell
> too much of that writer Ovid, and that writer Metamor-
> phosis, and talk too much of Proserpina and Juppiter.
> Why, here's our fellow Shakespeare puts them all
> down, I and Ben Jonson too. O, that Ben Jonson is a
> pestilent fellow, he brought up Horace giving the poets
> a pill, but our fellow Shakespeare hath given him a
> purge that made him beray his credit."

This is about the only evidence that has been produced showing that Shakespeare had any part in the stage controversy. But that it concerned him is evident from what is here said. What purge Shakespeare administered to Jonson, as here alleged, has remained unknown. The reference to a purge undoubtedly refers to the *Poetaster,* where Horace administers an emetic to Crispinus to vomit him of his offenses. Now it is said that Shakespeare administered a like purge to Jonson. This intimates that Jonson had been guilty of some offense towards Shakespeare, and the inference is that such offense arose out of the *Poetaster.*

Conceding that Shakespeare was represented as Ovid there is very little that is put into his mouth, or that is said to or about him, that in itself could give serious offense. But when the general effect of the play is considered it is otherwise. Virgil and Horace (supposedly Jonson) and others are represented as men of refinement and of artistic tastes, and are readily received by Augustus as men of quality, and are admitted to the court where their judgments are appealed to and relied upon. In short, they are men of high station, and the whole company is above the low and vulgar.

On the other hand Ovid is aligned with the players and although a poet of high standing, is portrayed as one of low associations, indulging in an orgy with men and women of a disreputable kind, where virtue is discarded, and all respect for morals and piety are abandoned. Not only is he one of such, but he is shown as Jupiter, the head and leader of the company of immoral characters. As a consequence of his arch offense he is denounced by Augustus above all others, and he and his illicit love, Julia, are convicted and severely sentenced, while the faults of their companions are condoned, and they are forgiven and reinstated in favor.

Admitting that it was not intended to be as represented, and that Ovid (Shakespeare) was not really banished, and that his love for Julia was not to be taken literally, and that it was symbolical of his love for Wine only, yet would it be a coarse and very unkind allusion, and one that would be keenly felt and resented by a kindly and sensitive man, such as we are compelled to believe Shakespeare was.

It is suggested that under the smart of this affront Shakespeare responded with Sonnets 67, 68, 69 and 70, and this is the "purge that made him (Jonson) beray his credit."

The first four lines of Sonnet 67,

> "Ah! wherefore with infection should he (I) live
> And with his presence grace impiety,
> That sin by him advantage should achieve,
> And lace itself with his society."

are all but a confession of the truth of what Jonson sets forth in the *Poetaster*, and shows how deeply chagrined Shakespeare felt over the exposure.

Then in the next two lines,

> "Why should false painting imitate his cheek
> And steal dead seeing of his living hue?"

is a charge of imitation against Jonson, which will be noticed farther on.

Sonnet 68 is as follows:

> "Thus is his cheek the map of days outworn,
> When beauty lived and died as flowers do now,
> Before those bastard signs of fair were born,
> Or durst inhabit on a living brow;
> Before the golden tresses of the dead,
> The right of sepulchures, were shorn away,
> To live a second life on second head;
> Ere beauty's dead fleece made another gay:
> In him those holy antique hours are seen,
> Without all ornament, itself and true,
> Making no summer of another's green,
> Robbing no old to dress his beauty new;
> And him as for a map doth Nature store,
> To show false Art what beauty was of yore."

This is as severe and telling an arraignment of the plagiarist as could be found in any language. If its charges are true, and they were in fact aimed at Jonson, they may well be said to beray, or soil, his credit as a poet.

69.

"The parts of thee that the world's eye doth view
Want nothing that the thoughts of hearts can mend;
All tongues, the voice of souls, give thee that due,
Uttering bare truth, even so as foes commend.
Thy outward thus with outward praise is crowned;
But those same tongues that gave thee so thine own
In other accents do this praise confound
By seeing further than the eye hath shown.
They look into the beauty of thy mind,
And that, in guess, they measure by thy deeds;
Then, churls, their thoughts, although their eyes were kind,
To thy fair flower add the rank smell of weeds:
    But why thy odour matcheth not thy show,
    The soil is this, that thou dost common grow.

Here Shakespeare refers to the fact that his foes (probably referring to Jonson, whom he in fact knows is not a foe) commend his verse and praise its quality, but confound that praise by calling attention to his weakness, by adding "the rank smell of weeds." In other words the sonnets depict very lucidly what is shown in the play as to the character of Ovid.

70.

"That thou art blamed shall not be thy defect,
For slander's mark was ever yet the fair;
The ornament of beauty is suspect,
A crow that flies in heaven's sweetest air.
So thou be good, slander doth but approve
Thy worth the greater, being woo'd of time;
For canker vice the sweetest buds doth love,
And thou present'st a pure unstained prime.
Thou hast pass'd by the ambush of young days,
Either not assailed or victor being charged;
Yet this thy praise cannot be so thy praise
To tie up envy ever more enlarg'd;
If some suspect of ill mask'd not thy show
Then thou alone kingdoms of hearts shouldst owe.

In this sonnet Shakespeare pretends to believe that Jonson was actuated by envy, and that he had been intentionally slandered. It is not probable that Shakespeare really believed such to be the case, and yet, like any man feeling an injury, it was quite natural that he should so attribute it. As will be shown hereafter Shakespeare was inclined to repent of what he had said in these sonnets, and upon a sober consideration overlooked what in his temper he imagined was an affront.

All this, of course, is based upon the assumption that these sonnets were directed at Jonson, and that they were instigated by the sting contained in the *Poetaster*. It is evident there was some actuating cause, and that the sonnets were directed against some individual. Except as has here been shown, in the literature of the times nothing has survived to show that Shakespeare was ever assailed in a manner to justify the complait made in these sonnets, nor has any other reason been shown why he should have felt offended at any other poet of his time.

As to the charge of imitation: It is difficult to say with certainty what specific imitations Shakespeare had in mind. That Jonson was influenced by Shakespeare seems evident, and it can hardly be denied that he appropriated some of Shakespeare's ideas, and that if other likenesses are not sheer appropriations, they probably had their origin in suggestions arising from what Shakespeare had written.

Attention has already been called to likenesses in some of Jonson's expressions to ideas which are to be found in the Sonnets. These could hardly be accidental, but their uses might very well be held to be legitimate, if they were used to identify Shakespeare as Ovid. The same may be said of the imitation of the balcony scene from *Romeo and Juliet*, and the reference to 'sad lovers,' and also to the very obvious emphasis placed on the word 'misprise,' which word Jonson had before used in *The Case is Altered*. If therefore it is to be urged that Ovid was really Shakespeare, none of these appropriations should be branded as plagiarisms, although in his anger Shakespeare might not have looked upon the matter so reasonably and leniently.

In *The Case is Altered* the character of Jacques, and his frenzied devotion to his gold, and the leaving of his daughter Rachel, as guardian over it, and her elopement, are all too reminiscent of Shylock and Jessica to leave any doubt that they were creations purloined from *The Merchant of Venice*.

But to the writer the greatest and most daring plagairism, and possibly the one that awakened the most feeling in Shakespeare, was the attempt in the *Poetaster*, to imitate, if not altogether appropriate, Shakespeare's greatest characterization, Falstaff, in the character of Captain Tucca. With all the other imitations Shakespeare might well be content to leave his characters to their own defence, for in an artistic sense they were not approached. But in the character of Tucca Jonson displayed a real creative talent, lacking in the greatest merit, only because it is a copy and not the original. That it is a copy after Falstaff is too evident to be mistaken.

There is but one defect in the character of Tucca, as compared with Falstaff, and that is not in the spoken word or action, but in the inexpressible atmosphere that surrounds them. We have not that toleration and sympathy for Tucca that we have for Falstaff. Towards one goes out our unjustifiable sympathy and cordiality, while towards the other we are more inclined to feel contemptuous. What makes this difference is a something that lies beyond our judgment, and is also beyond our control. It is born of something so small that it is indistinguishable to our eyes, but Shakespeare saw it, and either added or extracted it, as was necessary. It is a shade that only the true artist can discriminate. Shakespeare expresses it himself when he says:

> "Why should poor beauty indirectly seek
> Roses of shadow, since his (my) rose is true?"

Jonson was a learned man, and almost a great poet, and though impetuous and sometimes nearly brutal, he was in the aggregate of all his qualities a kindly and loveable man, without lasting malice, and ultimately just. It is therefore not in a spirit of maligning him to suggest that his capacity for drawing Tucca was innate, he and Tucca being of the same type, and characteristically alike. With all his brusqueness, coarseness, domineering manner and egotism, he had a kind heart, and could not hate beyond the hour. Yet no man, especially in early manhood, had more implacable enemies. Like Tucca, and unlike Falstaff, he left a swollen memory whenever he stung.

Would it be permissible to wonder, if Jonson himself might not have been the fleshly embodiment of Shakespeare's Falstaff?

It is believed that Shakespeare and Jonson were in reality friends as long as Shakespeare lived. Jonson attested as much in his writings whenever Shakespeare is referred to, and Jonson's sincerity is unquestionable. For a time the *Poetaster,* we may imagine, interrupted their cordiality, and during the heat of the controversy that the play produced, Shakespeare wrote the four sonnets as his defence against the imputations of the play. Thereafter their old-time relations were restored, and Shakespeare magnanimously atoned for what he had said, by writing Sonnets 78, 79, 80, 82, 83, 84, 85 and 86. These sonnets, unlike the four charging imitation and envy, express a friendly admiration for the rival, and have none of the display of temper shown in the former ones. If they all refer to the same poet, and it is difficult to conclude otherwise, it is evident Shakespeare had buried his resentment and returned to his former friendship, and was willing to make amends for the offence he had given.

Possibly Sonnets 81 and 84 should be included as a part of these last apologetical sonnets. They fit well in tone with the others, but in themselves there is no direct reference to the rival.

In Sonnet 78 Shakespeare defines himself as dumb, and of heavy and rude ignorance, and yet notwithstanding these impediments through wine's "fair assistance" he had been taught "on high to sing" and "aloft to fly," and had been advanced as high as the learned. Wine, he also claims, has "added feathers to the learned's wing," and has given to its "grace a double majesty." All of this serves, rather indefinitely to be sure, to identify Jonson as the rival. He was universally recognized as a man of high learning, and never himself hesitated to claim the distinction, and was most diligent in displaying his erudition. While the same might be shown to apply to others, there can be no doubt that it certainly applied to Jonson.

In 79 Shakespeare states that while he alone called upon Wine's aid, his verse had all of its gentle graces, but now his "numbers are decayed," and his "sick Muse doth give another place." Here again Jonson is identified as a younger rival, and one who had supplanted, or was supplanting, Shakespeare. All of which was true in fact.

In 80 Shakespeare speaks of a "better spirit" using Wine's name,

> "And in the praise thereof spends all his might,
> To make me tongue-tied, speaking of your fame."

Again this well befits Jonson, who as will be shown later, never speaks of wine but in the most exaggerated praise. The twelfth line of the sonnet describes the rival as,

> "He of tall building, and of goodly pride."

which well summed up Jonson's increasing social and intellectual status.

The first four lines of sonnet 82,

> "I grant thou wert not married to my Muse,
> And therefore mayst without attaint o'erlook
> The dedicated words which writers use
> Of their fair subject, blessing every book."

refer very appropriately to the introductions, dedications and prologues which Jonson used so frequently as a preface to his plays. Most of these are extremely egotistical, being full of praise of himself, his subject, and his literary achievement.

In the foregoing quotation Shakespeare probably means that while Wine is not married to his Muse, i.e., his is not the only Muse entitled to claim Wine's inspiration, she wine, may therefore overlook, or excuse these dedications. Which of course would mean that Shakespeare considered that some of these dedications had a personal reference to himself. This may have a particular reference to the dedicatory words accompanying *Every Man in his Humor* and *The Poetaster,* both the prologue and Apologetical Dialogue. It has often been assumed that parts of these had reference to Shakespeare.

In this same sonnet, too, reference is made to the rival poet's "strained touches" of rhetoric, and to his "gross painting." In 83 Shakespeare says that he never saw that the subject, Wine, "did painting need," and that he had to its "fair no painting set." In 84 he protests against exaggerations, "making worse what nature made so clear." In 85 he refers to the rival using "precious phrase by all the Muses fil'd," etc.

As has been noticed in the discussion of the Sonnets, Shakespeare always adheres to the practice of never calling wine by its name, and of never using descriptives, superlatives or exalted phrases to identify it, or to enhance its qualities. On the contrary Jonson rarely refers to wine without an effort to exalt it, either in its effects or quality. In *The Poetaster* (and it is probable that this play was principally in Shakespeare's mind in his criticisms) Jonson uses the word "nectar" as almost synonomous with wine. The following are taken almost at random from the play: "feast of sense," "ambroiac odours," "delicious nectar," "bowl of nectar," "wine and good livers, make good lovers," "He has filled nectar so long till his brain swims in it," "the spirit of our nectar," and others. In the introductory dialogue to *Every Man out of his Humor,* he calls Canary, "the elixir and spirit of wine," and says "a cup of wine sparkles like a diamond," and in Act V Scene 4, he calls wine, "nectar the very soul of the grape." Such expressions could be continued, were it necessary. It is to these Shakespeare evidently refers, when he says:

> "Then others for the breath of words respect,
> Me for my dumb thoughts speaking in effect."

In 83 the last two lines of the sonnet are:

> "There lives more life in one of your fair eyes,
> Than both your poets can in praise devise."

Here Shakespeare plainly shows, that he felt there were only two poets who could be considered as songsters of wine. Besides himself, to whom could he refer, but to Jonson? In that category Jonson could certainly not be excluded.

The only insuperable difficulty that has been found in applying these sonnets to Jonson, as the rival, is in the construction of Sonnet 86, where Shakespeare says he has no fear of the rival,

> "He nor that affable familiar ghost
> Which nightly gulls him with intelligence."

So far as the writer knows, there is nothing in Jonson's writings to justify this allusion. But that fact does not preclude the possibility that he may have held such ideas, notwithstanding. This sonnet has been the subject of much research and discussion, but no certain conclusion has been arrived at, as to who is the poet referred to. Probably the best opinion has fixed on Chapman, but he has not been identified with that certainty that precludes all further speculation, for many investigators have declined to accept the conclusiveness of the evidence on which the judgment is based.

Should the theory that wine is the subject of the Sonnets be the true solution of them, and should it be that the rival of the Sonnets is a rival for wine's graces, Chapman would perforce of his religious and temperate life and habits be excluded from all further consideration. Considering the views that have been expressed, and have been sought to be maintained, it is not possible to concede that Chapman may be the rival. If what this review has attempted to do has, in fact, been done, there is but little room left for doubt of Jonson's complete identification as the rival. And this despite of the failure to relate him with the curious conception found in this 86th sonnet. Possibly time and further investigation may bring a satisfactory solution of that,

PART II

AN ELIZABETHAN MANIA

II.

AN ELIZABETHAN MANIA.

FOLLOWING the lead of the meaning found in the Shakespearean Sonnets, a most curious, if not startling development arises out of the study of the voluminous sonnets that were the products of that part of the Elizabethan age, and which were published subsequent to 1590.

Sir Philip Sidney, the foremost of these sonneteers, both in time, and in social and intellectual standing, was the first of the company to indulge in this form of poetry. He died in 1586 without having published any of his literary works. In 1591 his sonnets were published, and soon after this, in 1593, a veritable flood of sonnets, by numerous authors were published in London. It is most likely that these were all inspired by Sidney's effort.

Many of these sonnets were in the strain of most of the Shakespearean sonnets which have been reviewed. They are very enigmatical, and while often of high literary merit, they have remained most puzzling to those seeking their meaning. Sidney gave to his sonnets the title of *Astrophel and Stella*. Astrophel is himself, and Stella is his Love, of his sonnets. She is just as indistinct and indefinite as is the object of Shakespeare's Love (the she or it) that is limned in his sonnets. Each of the other sonneteers gave to his passion or love a feminine designation, and in each case she is as incapable of being defined or understood, as are Shakespeare's or Sidney's pseudo creations. (This however does not apply to all of the sonneteers of that age, as will be seen.) In all of the cases, now being reviewed, the author represents himself as deeply infatuated, and at the same time these mystical objects of love, continually inspires the author with unspeakable sorrow, grief, horror and disgrace. If she indulges her would-be lover, the author, she multiplies his sufferings, and if she withholds her indulgence from him, she leaves him in the most pitiable condition, in floods of tears and anguish.

273

It would be a waste of effort to undertake a detailed analysis of the ever changing passion of these sonnets. It is enough to know that they all run the gamut of extremes of both love and grief. Just as has been seen in Shakespeare's sonnets. It is therefore needless to delay the announcement of the conclusion that these sonnets, like the Shakespearean, are the expressions of the exaltations and depressions of drunken poets. This announcement is not made with any degree of pleasure, nor has the discovery been welcome because, perhaps, it may be corroborative of the construction which has been given the Shakespearean sonnets. That construction will stand without support, and may be considered as established. This further unfolding may be considered rather as a hindrance to the acceptance of what has been shown. For it is understood that it would be a task more easily accomplished, to brand one poet with so great a weakness, than to bring many (nearly all) of the great poets of an enlightened age within the same class. And yet the evidence is quite as conclusive against the many of them, as against the greatest of them all.

A remarkable feature, too, is the fact that this character of sonnet, where the writers were truly actuated by an appetite or lust for wine, ceased with Shakespeare, and there has been no product of the kind since. (Drayton published the last of his sonnets in 1619, but much the greater part of his sonnets were published before Shakespeare's.) It is therefore asserted that Shakespeare concluded this character of sonnet construction, and since it has become a lost art.

It is a striking peculiarity of English sonnet literature of the kind here under discussion, that all are similar in form and structure, and in the methods of the subject's treatment. While in many cases it rises to the highest poetical plane, it cannot be said of it, that there is any very great originality in it. Whether it was done purposely, or through the blindness of saturation in sonnet literature, each sonneteer becomes a marauder, appropriating without shame the product of his fellows. So like are they that the sonnets of any writer might be mingled with those of another author and not appear discordant, either in the workmanship or the plan and scheme of treatment. This is so true, that in the light of to-day it is impossible to determine whether any poet was an exploiter, or had been exploited. Even Shakespeare is not above suspicion. The only fair judgment that can now be formed is, that the English sonnets of the period and character mentioned is a composite mass. The ideas throughout are built up with standardized parts, and the only credit that can be safely awarded to any individual is for the manner in which he has fitted them together.

What can all this mean? and how came it about? It would overtax one's imagination to conclude that five or six or seven brilliant men and poets, all living at the same time, could have had like experiences with the one seducing woman. It would also discredit womanhood to think there could exist in one generation, and within so limited a space, women enough, of such character as the sonnets depict, to pair one with each of these poets. Truly imagination completely fails when it is sought, through it, to create one such woman. But waiving that, and conceding the being of such a creature, the serious problem still remains unsolved, as to how each of these writers, writing independently of the others, should treat his subject identically as all the others do, with so many features in common as to render one, nearly, if not altogether indistinguishable from the others. Furthermore if Wine be accepted as the Love of the authors of the sonnets, this independent accord would still remain unexplained.

The solution of this must be, that none of the authors were writing or acting independently of the others. They were each and all treating the same subject, and knowing it to be the same. Each had gone through the same experiences and had felt the same cravings (not love), and had experienced the same exhilaration (intoxication), and had suffered the same agonies and deliriums, and had thirsted through the same periods of abstinence and reforms, so wracking and wrecking to the drunkard. The mysterious thing of all the sonnets was not a person at all, but an inanimate thing—an intoxicating wine. The author's love was habit and appetite, and his sufferings were the penalties that over-indulgence inflicts.

Furthermore, these sonneteers were not writing independently of each other. Sidney had set the example, and each of the others set out assiduously to copy it, or to copy what Sidney had copied. In those times it was not necessary that writings should be published for sale to be known to the literary classes. The manuscripts of poems particularly, of all forms, were circulated from hand to hand, and within bounds, were quite as well known as if they had been published. Each poet therefore, may have been aware of the works of others, and as the sonnet was then the most prized form of verse, there was a rivalry to occupy the field, and each was appropriating the ideas of others, and at the same time his own may have been purloined. In this way the numerous comparisons, similes and conceits that appear promiscuously in the sonnets may be accounted for. Or possibly all were getting their inspirations from the same source or sources. The same characteristics that permeate all the sonnets, now under review, are such as may be attributable to Wine. True, it was treated by all as a sensate thing, with human as well as inhuman feelings, sentiments, purposes and wills. If the sonnet's cryptic character was understood or suspected by readers, no instance has been discovered where the secret has been betrayed. It is therefore assumed, that only the initiated—the addicts—divined the true meaning, and among them the knowledge was held inviolable.

From the facts, as thus stated, it should not be assumed that these anomalous sonnet compositions were of English origins, or that they were indigenous to the times in which they were born, flourished and died on English soil. For many years prior to this period the English had been ardent admirers of the sonnets of both Italy and France, in both of which countries this form of verse was much in vogue, and had reached a high degree of perfection. It had been employed sparingly by a few English writers prior to the time of Sidney, but its use was not general. The inquiry therefore cannot be confined to English literature, for as will appear the cryptic sonnet was certainly a derivative.

For those desiring to pursue the history of the subject, attention is called to the fact that Sir Sidney Lee has issued a valuable work in two volumes, under the title of *The Elizabethan Sonnets*. In it are collected many, if not all, of the sonnets of value, excepting Shakespeare's, that were published during the sonneteering craze of the period noted. Many of the sonnets are not otherwise available, and to one investigating the subject the work is invaluable. Among the sonnets is other poetry, some of which bears the same meaning as the sonnets do. The work is prefaced by a valuable discussion, showing the relation between the Italian, French and English sonnet literature. There are numerous demonstrations of how much of the English product is dependent on the foreign. One omission therefrom, and an important one, is *Willobie His Avisa,* which is not in sonnet form, and therefore not within the purview of the book. The Avisa will be noticed further on.

While it is permissible in the writer to draw the conclusions being advanced, as to the cryptic meaning of the English sonnets, he cannot assert with equal positiveness that the continental Europeans, subsequent to Petrarch, are in the same class with the English, and that their sonnets are amenable to the same construction. A translation of the sonnets of some of these later poets are not at hand, if any exist, and therefore any suggestions that may be made with reference to them must be considered to be tentative. This much however may be ventured, that such evidence as is at hand supports the assumption that they possessed the same ideas that were in the minds of their English followers and copyists. This appears in Lee's work before referred to. There whole sonnets of Desportes and Ronsard, and extracts from those of others are parallelled with sonnets from Lodge, Daniels and other English poets. From what appears it is permissible to conclude that the French sonnets have been literally plagiarized. If these paraphrases are correct, and they are not to be doubted, the French sonnets are as saturated with the spirit of idolatry for wine, as any to be found in English.

But the investigation should not cease, even here. To discover the common source of all such sonnets it is necessary to go back to Petrarch, and there the fountain head will be revealed. Thus will it be seen that from thence on, the Italian, French and English sonneteers were all copyists after Petrarch and that from him has descended the prevailing Idea (with a capital I) along with the sonnet form. This Idea was the very soul and being of the sonnet, and without which it could not exist with vigour. If those sonnets so inspired be excepted, there will remain in the English language very few of this difficult form of verse, to justify the claim that it is a form of high literary art.

From what has been said the conclusion has been formed that the likeness of expression among the English poets originated not only in their imitation of each other, but that the ideas were borrowed direct from the Italian and French writers, or from those who had borrowed from them. As has been seen this applies especially to Lodge and Daniel. There is further evidence to support the theory, in the fact that Sidney in his sonnet XV arraigns the English writers for their slavish imitation of Petrarch, and declares that he himself is no 'pickpurse.' While it may be that Sidney was not so brazen and ruthless as some of the others, he does not seem to realize that he himself is a very evident borrower, and that his only originality was in the expression of that which he had so appropriated.

PETRARCH THE SOURCE.

It was in Petrarch, then, that the Wine Inspirited sonnet originated. Either directly, or indirectly, from him this remarkable conception, or mania, spread through Italy, France and England, as epidemics do, and for a time afflicted nearly every poet exposed to it. Nor does the similitude end here, for the malady having run its course, just as suddenly and unaccountably disappeared, without leaving a trace of further infection. The identity of the disorder is not to be doubted, for in every case the symptoms are so characteristic that no one need mistake them.

Were it a conceded fact that the Laura of Petrarch's sonnets was but a pretence, and that he was disguising under the name the personality of Wine, there would be no hesitation in recognizing the same identity in the poetry of those who were truly his followers. Likewise, it would be quite as easy to distinguish those attempts by would-be imitators who misconceived the thing disguised for a true personality. If then it be true that Wine has been identified as the subject of the verse of Petrarch's imitators, the conclusion is justified, that through them, the followers, we may unmask the true figure hidden behind Laura's robes. It is one and the same, whatever the figure may prove to be when once revealed. This will appear from the reviews to follow. It is not planned to review the sonnets of Petrarch here. That undertaking would require a volume in itself. There will be found enough in the English poets to demonstrate that they were imitators of Petrarch, and that they had discovered Laura's identity to be Wine.

To read the present day commentators on the literature of the sonnets, it could but be inferred that the personalities disguised as Petrarch's Laura, Sidney's Stella and Spenser's Amoretti were all known real persons, and that no question remains as to who they were. This is a distortion of the facts. Their realities are myths, and their identities are unsupported assumptions. It is but an attempt to construct embodied souls out of the mysteries that envelop the sonnets. In each case a unique plan has been adopted of assuming the existence of some woman love, and then finding her character and history in the sonnets. These details are then set forth and speculated upon as if they were true biographical sketches. The logic of such a proceeding is, that given a sonnet, a woman may be created out of it, and yet not be the material of which the sonnet is made. None of the sonneteers asserts that his love is a definite human entity. There is no more to support the theories that the sonnets of any of the poets were written to, or of, or concerning a real living being, than there is to that curious and unsupported impression that Shakespeare's sonnets were addressed to his patron, and that a mistress lurked in his cryptical Dark Woman sonnets. It is a curious circumstance that no one yet has claimed to have identified Daniel's Delia, Lodge's Phyllis or Drayton's Idea or Willobie's Avisa with any woman then living. And yet they are not less real than the loves of the other poets. Shakespeare used no name to designate her—or it—of whom he was enamoured, and yet some have imagined an identity, and gone so far as to name women with whom it is most likely Shakespeare was never acquainted.

It will be found upon an analysis of Petrarch's sonnets that in character, spirit and meaning they are not distinguishable from the sonnets of Sidney, Drayton, Daniel, Lodge, Spenser, Willobie and Shakespeare. This assertion excludes, of course, literary quality and character. But if Petrarch's meaning be sought and brought out under like developments and tests, as applied to the other above named poets, the result will be found to be the same.

The identity and very existence of Petrarch's Laura were doubted and questioned in his own day, and the name was thought to be ideal and unreal, and so it has been ever since. Petrarch never claimed her to be a reality by any character of identification. He did call her a woman, which is nothing more than is implied in the name he gave. It was his desire and purpose to conceal the true meaning of his sonnets, and he sought very cunningly to perpetuate the prevailing misconception, but not by falsehood, or any positive misrepresentation. His sonnets are divided into two parts, the first being 'Laura in Life,' and the other 'Laura in Death.' This too, was a part of his consummate Italian acting. For her death Petrarch meant only his eschewal of Wine. It was dead to him. After twenty-one years of excessive drinking he reformed his habits, and thereupon announced Laura's *withdrawal,* not death, and thereafter spoke of her generally as being in heaven, and not longer in life. After her death he continued, as did the English poets, after their abstinences, to enshrine Laura in his praises. Curiously enough, after her death she came to relieve him from time to time. To continue the deception he speaks of her visits, some of them, as if they were made in his dreams. But this was not always the case, for there are some instances in which her presence was very real and consoling.

It is not practicable to undertake extensive quotations from Petrarch, but a few will be submitted to support the positions which have been taken. As to his habits: in his *Espistles to Posterity* he says,

> "As for the looser indulgencies of appetite, would indeed that I could say that I was a stranger to them altogether; but if I should say so, I should lie."

In a letter written in 1345, he says,

> "To make me change my purpose, you put before my eyes the errors of my youth, which I ought to forget, a passion whose torments have made me take flight, because I had no other resource, the frivolous attractions of a perishable Beauty, with which I have occupied myself far too much."

This might by a strained construction be applied to a woman, and undoubtedly Petrarch was willing that it should be so construed. But had he been alluding to a woman, would he have spoken of the torments of his passion, and would his passion have made him take flight? would there have been no other resource? would he have disguised her under the description of a 'perishable Beauty'? Call his passion Wine, and how much better it would accord with what is said.

As to Laura he says, she

> "first appeared to my eyes in the days of my youth, in the year of our Lord 1327, and on the 6th day of the month of April, in the Church of Santa Clara at Avignon, in the morning hour; and in the same city, on

the same month of April, on the same 6th day, and at the same first hour, but in the year 1348, that light was *withdrawn* from the light of day, when I by chance was at Verona, ignorant alas! of my fate."

Here is the same suspicious indefiniteness, with an attempt to conceal, and at the same time express a truth, but most adroitly permitting a false impression.

In the dialogue between himself and Saint Augustine, Petrarch discusses his love for Laura, in the same evasive manner but there is nothing said that is not consistent with the theory that Laura is Wine.

In support of the statement that Laura visited with Petrarch after her reported death, sonnet III of *Laura in Death* will be quoted in full.

III (Nott)

That burning toil, in which I once was caught,
While twice ten years and one I counted o'er,
Death has unloosed: like burden I ne'er bore:
That grief ne'er fatal proves I now am taught.
But Love, who to entangle me still sought,
Spread in the treacherous grass his net once more,
So fed the fire with fuel as before,
That my escape I hardly could have wrought.
And, but that my first woes experience gave,
Snared long since and kindled I had been,
And all the more as I'm become less green;
My freedom death again has come to save,
And break my bond; that flame now fades and fails,
'Gainst which nor force nor intellect prevails.

It is not only thus shown that Laura revisited him, but that her visit (his indulgence) came near wrecking his reform, and casting him back into the slough of drunkenness. He says that from his first slavery of 21 years he had been released by death (his abstinence), and then from the new threat of thralldom, but for his former experience, he would again have been enthralled, but that death again (a new abstinence) had come to save him.

Students of the sonnets, being unable to restore Laura to life after her death, have concluded that Petrarch had, after Laura's death fallen in love with another woman, whose timely death, had rescued him from the repetition of his former woe, which had been the greatest burden he had ever borne.

The last line of the sonnet disposes conclusively of any suggestion that his love could have been a woman.

One other sonnet from *Laura in Death* will be quoted in full.

LXXII (Morehead).

To that soft look which now adorns the skies,
The graceful bending of the radiant head,
The face, the sweet angelic accents fled,
That soothed me once, but now awake my sighs
Oh! when to these imagination flies,
I wonder that I am not long since dead!
'T is she supports me, for her heavenly tread
Is round my couch when morning visions rise!
In every attitude how holy, chaste!
How tenderly she seems to hear the tale
Of my long woes, and their relief to seek!
But when day breaks she then appears in haste
The well-known heavenward path again to scale,
With moistened eye, and soft expressive cheek!

Here is seen Laura administering her solace at night, but departing with the daybreak, and leaving the poet for the daytime to his own resources. These nocturnal visits must have been frequent, for the heavenly path which she begins '*again* to scale' has become '*well-known.*'

In the same series, sonnet V (Wrangham), the last two lines are expressive.

"Fatal for us that beauty's torturing view,
Living or dead alike which desolates our peace."

The use of the word 'beauty' is here again significant. It also appears that Laura was quite as efficient in death as in life, in desolating the poet's peace.

The foregoing are but specimens of the Petrarchian strain throughout his sonnets. Others quite as suggestive might be cited, to the limit of the reader's patience. But there must be an end, and here we leave off.

THE ENGLISH PETRARCHISTS

Sir Philip Sidney
Samuel Daniel
Thomas Lodge
Henry Willobie
Michael Drayton
Edmund Spenser

THE ENGLISH PETARCHISTS.

Without continuing the discussion further, it is now proposed to examine briefly the writings of some of the 16th Century English sonneteers, for the purpose of showing that those included in the present review were all expending their efforts in the characterization of an intoxicant, as has been shown of Shakespeare. It will be impracticable to examine the works of any of these authors in such detail. After what has been said and shown it is felt that it is not necessary to go into such fulness, for the same methods apply in each case. It will be the effort to show enough to indicate the truth, and leave it to the interested reader to further pursue the inquiry to his own satisfaction. It is confidently believed that in the case of each poet, to be presently named, that a clear and convincing interpretation of his poetry may be obtained by adopting Wine as the subject.

The following is a list of the poets whose works have been found to so respond:

Sir Philip Sidney	Michael Drayton	Edmund Spenser
Samuel Daniel	Thomas Lodge	Henry Willobie

SIR PHILIP SIDNEY.

The Sonnets of Sir Philip Sidney that were numbered and published in sequence consisted of 107. These were published under the title of *Astrophel and Stella* in 1591. Subsequently other sonnets, unnumbered, and other miscellaneous poems were published. Among the poems were eleven songs, numbered in order, and also a poem under the title of *The Smokes of Melancholy*. This latter poem will be reproduced in full hereafter.

Excepting the 6th and 7th songs, which purport to describe a contest between Beauty and Music, all of Sidney's poetry may be used to demonstrate the theory contended for. Heretofore there has been difficulty encountered in extracting a meaning from all of this poetry, such as was found in the poetry of Shakespeare. The Stella of Sidney's sonnets, it is claimed, has been identified as one of Sidney's youthful sweethearts, and this claim is still persisted in, despite the fact that the sonnet's contents are in the extremest degree unsuited to such a fancy, under any conceivable conditions.

In a discussion of this kind, the temptation to quote with fulness from every part of Sidney's poetry must be resisted, for if all that is pertinent should be reproduced, nothing less than the whole would suffice. It is, therefore, the plan to be restricted to brief and disconnected quotations, which must necessarily fail to convey the full and true effect.

In his first sonnet Sidney discloses how he had tried to induce his Muse to sing, when finally she directed him

"Fool! look in thy heart and write."

He then proceeds in II,

"Not at the first sight, nor with a dribbled shot
Love gave the wound which while I breathe will bleed."

Here is a clear declaration that his drinking has become habitual, and was not a 'dribbled shot,' but was excessive.

In VII, he says Stella's eyes are black, a mourning weed,

"To honor all their deaths, which for her bleed."

Her victims were evidently numerous, and her influence fatal. Truly, a curious description of a sweetheart.

In VIII Love had found a place in his heart, where,

"He burnt un'wares his wings and cannot fly away."

In XV he condemns the imitators of Petrarch. In XVI, describing his condition before his drinking had become habitual, he says he did not find his love the restless flame which, others said made their souls to pine, but

"I thought these babes, of some pin's hurt did whine,"

But when

"Mine eyes (shall I say curst or blest) beheld Stella"

he realized

"As who by being poisoned doth poison know."

In XVIII he finds himself a bankrupt

"Of all those goods which heaven to me hath lent."

In XIX

"When most I glory, then I feel most shame."

In XX

> "Fly! Fly! my friends; I have my death wound, fly!
> See there that boy! that murdering boy, I say!" (Cupid)

In XXI

> "For since mad March great promise made of me:
> If now the May of my years much decline,
> What can be hoped my harvest time will be?"

In XXIII he tells how he has been judged and misjudged, but always misunderstood, for

> "O fools! or overwise! alas, the race
> Of all my thoughts hath neither stop nor start,
> But only Stella's eyes and Stella's heart."

In XXVIII

> "When I say Stella! I do mean the same
> Princess of Beauty; for whose only sake
> The reins of love I love, though never slack;
> And joy therein, though nations count it shame."

Is it possible any nation considers a man's love for woman a shame? What does he mean?

In reciting the public problems confronting the countries of Europe, among which was his father's rule in Ulster, he concludes in XXX

> "These questions busy wits to me do frame:
> I—cumbered with good manner—answer do;
> But know not how, for still I think on you."

In XXXIII a night of delirium is described, and he concludes

> "O punisht eyes!
> That I had been more foolish or more wise!"

In XXXIV the question is presented,

> "Art not ashamed to publish thy disease?"

He answers, "Nay that may breed my fame." The idea was probably borrowed from Petrarch, who while realizing the errors of his habits, was yet thankful that his love had inspired him to write his sonnets, and felt that the experience had been justified.

Sonnets XXXVIII, XXXIX and XL describe nights of privation and torture, which, to get the true effect, should be read entire. XLI describes his winning the prize in a contest of

horsemanship and strength, where, he says, some attributed his
success to skill, some to strength, some to chance and some to his
inheritance on both sides, as a man of arms. But he concludes:

> "How far they shot awry! The true cause is,
> Stella lookt on, and from her heavenly face
> Sent forth the beams which made so fair my race."

He was sustained by the stimulus of Wine. To forestall:
Sonnett LIII describes a like contest, in which his overindul-
gences, and not his opponent, overthrew him. He tells of his
wretched failure as follows:

> "I looked, and Stella spied
> Who, hardby, made a window send forth light:
> My heart then quaked, then dazzled were mine eyes,
> One hand forgot to rule, th' other to fight.
> Nor trumpets' sound I heard; nor friendly cries;
> My foe came on, and beat the air for me:
> Till that her blush taught me my shame to see."

In XLV

> "Stella oft sees the very face of woe
> Painted on my beclouded stormy face;
> But cannot skill to pity my disgrace,
> Not though thereof the cause herself she know:"

The conclusion of XLVII, is as follows:

> "I may, I must, I can, I will, I do
> Leave following that which it is gain to miss.
> Let her do! Soft! but here she comes. Go to!
> Unkind! I love you not! O me! that eye
> Doth make my heart give to my tongue the lie."

For dramatic effect this is unexcelled in all the sonnets. Be-
hold how weak the drunkard's resolution is, when the tempting
cup is offered. His heart loves it, beyond the strength of his
resolution, and gives to his tongue the lie, when it would deny
his love.

In XLVIII, like all over-perplexed Petrarchists, he desires
death.

> "Whose cureless wounds, even now, must freshly bleed:
> Yet since my death wound is already got;
> Dear Killer! spare not thy sweet cruel shot!
> A kind of grace it is, to slay with speed."

In LII he strives to reconcile Virtue and his Love, that he may still retain his Stella. In LV, comes his final resolve to desert his Love, except to call on her name, and thereby preserve his inspiration, without indulgence. So far as is known, in effect, this resolve was kept to the end. The history of his life and his poetry both so indicate. The struggle was a hard and prolonged one. His wounds never wholly healed, and it would appear that his longings never entirely ceased. In LVI, a week without a look (a drink) has passed, and he concludes the sonnet

> "No Patience! If thou wilt my good: then make
> Her come and hear with patience my desire:
> And then with patience bid me bear my fire."

In LX, in the throes of his denied desires, he cries,

> "Then some good body tell me how I do!
> Whose presence, absence; absence, presence is:
> Blessed in my curse, and cursed in my bliss."

In LXIV, his wail is pitiful indeed.

> "No more! My Dear! no more these counsels try!
> I give my passions leave to run their race!
> Let fortune lay on me her worst disgrace!
> Let folk o'ercharged with brain, against me cry!
> Let clouds bedim my face, break in mine eye!
> Let me no step but of lost labor trace!
> Let all the earth in scorn recount my case;
> But do not will me from my love to fly!"

In the heart-breaking strife, none but the staunchest will could have won. All of the sonnets in this group should be read to appreciate the depth of distress expressed by the poet.

In LXVII he says:

> "I am resolved thy error to maintain;
> Rather than by more truth to get more pain."

In LXXI, he cries,

> "But Oh! Desire still cries, 'Give me some food'."

In LXXII

> "But thou Desire! because thou wouldst have all;
> Now banisht art; but yet, alas, how shall?"

From sonnets LXIX to LXXXIII it would seem that he was indulging to a limited extent,—a drink now and then. This was probably under a physician's direction.

In sonnet LXXXII, he says,

> "I will but kiss, I never more will bite."

In LXXXIII,

> "Cannot such grace your silly self content;
> But you must needs, with those lips billing be?
> And though those lips drink nectar from that tongue?
> Leave that, Sir Phip! lest off your neck be wrung!"

From this it is apparent that his reform was a matter of life and death. He must restrain himself, or expect the direst results.

In XC Sidney declares he does not seek the fame of a poet. That Stella's lips are his history.

> "In truth I swear, I wish not there should be
> Graved on my epitaph, a poet's name."

To the end Sidney's lamentations continue, and he finds little consolation in living. Notwithstanding, he continues his fast. Read in CIV,

> "Where rigour's exile locks up all my sense;
> But if I by a happy window pass;
> If I but stars upon mine armour bear;
> Sick, thirsty, glad (though but of empty glass!)
> Your moral notes straight my hid meaning tear
> From out my ribs, and puffing prove that I
> Do Stella love. Fools, who doth it deny?"

Finally in CVII he expresses the desire that his example may not be a cause for Wine's condemnation.

> "O let not fools in me thy works reprove;
> And scorning say, See! what it is to love!"

The other sonnets unnumbered, and not in series, are of like expression, and convey a like meaning. But these must be passed over. His other poetry is also a witness to his passion. Two selections from these will be given. His Fifth Song was probably written before his reform. One stanza therefrom is as follows:

"Yet witches may repent. Thou art far worse than they.
Alas, that I am forced such evil of thee to say.
I say thou art a Devil! though clothed in Angel's shining;
For thy face tempts my soul to leave the heavens for thee,
And thy words of refuse do pour even hell on me.
Who tempt, and tempted plague; are Devils in true defining.

Where, or when, has such a woman ever existed? foul or pure?

Another poem written after his reform, and possibly among
the last, if not the last of his poems, will be quoted in full, and
therewith close the discussion, as to Sidney.

THE SMOKES OF MELANCHOLY.

Who hath ever felt the change of love,
And knows those pangs that the loosers prove,
May paint my face, without seeing me;
And write the state how my fancies be:
The loathesome buds grown on Sorrow's Tree.

But who by hearsay speaks, and hath not fully felt
What kind of fires they be in which those spirits melt,
    Shall guess and fail, what doth displease:
    Feeling my pulse; miss my disease.

O no, O no! trial only shows,
The bitter juice of forsaken woes;
Where former bliss, present evils to stain:
Nay, former bliss adds to present pain;
While remembrance doth both states contain.

Come learners then to me! the model of mishap!
Engulfed in despair! Slid down from fortune's lap!
    And as you like my double lot,
    Tread in my steps, or follow not!

For me, alas, I am full resolved
These bands, alas, shall not be dissolved;
Nor break my word, though reward comes late;
Nor fail my faith in my failing fate;
Nor change in change, though change change my state,

But always one myself, with eagle-eyed truth to fly
Up to the sun; although the sun my wings do fry:
    For if those flames burn my desire,
    Yet shall I die in Phœnix's fire.

Coming from one of the most chivalric and highest minded
men in history, this wail is truly pathetic.

SAMUEL DANIEL.

Samuel Daniel wrote 55 sonnets. Some of these were intermingled with some of Sidney's and published in 1591. Others, along with those mentioned, were published in 1594, under the name of *Delia*. All of Daniel's sonnets are unmistakably Petrarchan, and readily yield their meaning when Wine is taken as their subject.

It is not the purpose to follow his cycle of sonnets throughout, not even to the extent that Sidney's have been reviewed. A few sonnets will be quoted entire, and leave further investigation for the interested.

The following sonnet credited to Daniel, was XXII in the 1591 publication, and IX in the 1594. It is one of the sonnets that Lee sets out in parallel, as taken from Desportes I.XXXIX, where it was published under the title of *L'Amours de Diane*. Thus it will be seen how literally some of the English poets copied from the French, and at the same time exhibit the prevalence and sameness of ideas in all of the Petrarchists.

IX.

> If this be love, to draw a weary breath,
> To paint on floods till the shore cry to the air;
> With prone aspect still treading on the earth.
> Sad horror! pale grief! prostrate despair!
> If this be love, to war against my soul,
> Rise up to wail, lie down to sigh, to grieve me,
> With ceaseless toil Care's restless stones to roll,
> Still to complain and moan, whilst none relieve me.
> If this be love, to languish in such care,
> Loathing the light, the world, myself and all,
> With interrupted sleeps, fresh grief's repair;
> And breathe out horror in perplexed thrall.
> If this be love, to live a living death:
> Lo then love I, and draw this weary breath.

Sonnet XXXVIII in Daniel's sequence, shows that his love is identical with Petrarch's Laura. At least Daniel thought it was, and unquestionably he was right.

XXXVIII.

Thou canst not die, whilst any zeal abound
In feeling hearts, that can conceive these lines:
Though thou a Laura, hast no Petrarch found;
In base attire, yet, clearly, Beauty shines.
And I, though born within a colder clime,
Do feel mine inward heart as great (I know it).
He never had more faith, although more rhyme:
I love as well, though he could better show it.
But I may add one feather to thy fame,
To help her flight throughout the fairest Isle;
And if my pen could more enlarge thy name,
Then shouldst thou live in an immortal style.
For though that Laura better limned be;
Suffice, thou shalt be loved as well as she.

One other sonnet from Daniel should be sufficient to convict him of his weakness.

LV.

Lo here, the impost of a faith unfeigning,
That love hath paid, and her disdain extorted!
Behold the message of my just complaining,
That shews the world how much my grief imported!
These tributary plaints, fraught with desire,
I send those Eyes, the Cabinet of Love!
The Paradise whereto my hopes aspire,
From out this Hell, which mine afflictions prove.
Wherein I thus do live, cast down from mirth;
Pensive, alone, none but despair about me;
My joys abortive, perished at their birth;
My cares long lived, and will not die without me.
This is my state; and Delia's heart is such!
I say no more. I fear, I said too much.

(This last sonnet with some variations was published in the first edition, and was numbered XXV.)

THOMAS LODGE.

Thomas Lodge wrote 40 sonnets (15 and 16 are missing). They were published in 1593 under the title of *Philliis*.

Had Lodge been less a plagiarist, it would be necessary to conclude that he had truly felt Wine's enchantment and enthrallment. But, he copied so literally that it is impossible to say whether his writing were heart-felt, or were but simulations. Only two sonnets will be submitted from his series. Lee shows that one of these, XXXV, was copied from Ronsard's *Amours*, I.XII.

XXXV.

I hope and fear, I pray and hold my peace,
Now freeze my thoughts, and straight they fry again,
I now admire and straight my wonders cease,
I loose my bonds and yet myself restrain;
This likes me most that leaves me discontent,
My courage serves and yet my heart doth fail,
My will doth climb, whereas my hopes are spent,
I laugh at love, yet when he comes I quail;
I would be thanked, and yet I freedom love,
I would redress, yet hourly feed my ill,
I would repine, and dare not once reprove;
And for my love I am bereft of power,
And strengthless strive my weakness to devour.

The following sonnet is probably as much Lodge's as any that are accredited to him. It has not been shown that it is a copy of any other.

XXV.

I wage the combat with two mighty foes,
Which are more strong than I ten thousand fold;
The one is when my pleasure I do lose,
The other when thy person I behold.
In seeing thee a swarm of loves confound me,
And cause my death in spite of my resist,
And if I see thee not, thy want doth wound me,
For in thy sight my comfort doth consist.

The one in me continual care createth,
The other doth occasion my desire;
The one the edge of all my joy rebateth,
The other makes me a phœnix in love's fire.
So that I grieve when I enjoy your presence
And die for grief by reason of your absence.

If in fact this sonnet be Lodge's, then he had a full understanding, and may be considered a well qualified addict.

The case against Lodge will be rested on the two foregoing sonnets, and is considered to be conclusively proven and unimpeachable. Further proof is considered unnecessary.

WILLOBIE HIS AVISA.

This production, consisting of about 450 stanzas of six lines each, was first printed in 1594. The circumstances surrounding the work and its publication are puzzling. If in fact one Willobie was the author, much concerning it is still left obscure. One Hadrian Dorrell—the name is probably fictitious—claims that his friend, Henry Willobie, departing abroad in her Majesty's service had left with him, Dorrell, the key to his study. There he found the manuscript of the poem and proceeded, in his friend's absence and without his consent, to publish it.

Avisa is admittedly a fanciful name, and Dorrell in a preface to the poem discussing it, and particularly the use of the name Avisa, admits that it is a feigned one. He says he also discovered a note of the author stating that the name was derived from the initial letters of five Latin words, *Amans, vxor, inviolata, semper* and *amanda,* which words, being translated mean, *A loving wife, that never violated her faith is always to be loved.* The name, therefore, is intended to be expressive of the maiden's —or wife's—nature and character. But, again in an 'Apology' in the 1596 edition of the poem, he suggests that the word Avisa is compounded of 'A' after the Greek manner, meaning 'non' and of 'visa,' which means 'seen,' so that its true meaning would be, *Such a woman as was never seen.*

These explanations do not seem to be quite sincere, and it may be suspected that *Hadrian Dorrell* is evasive, and is seeking rather to becloud than to clarify the situation. It is not improbable that the author of the poem is also the author of both explanations, and that all the names used are fictitious. This suspicion is supported by a statement made by one Peter Colse, the author of *Penelope's Complaint,* where in the dedication to his book, published in 1596, he assails Avisa, and states that the author is unknown.

In the poem, Avisa is described as having been created by the Graces. Venus framed the 'lurid eye,' the aspect and comely grace; Pallas gave the head, a settled mind—'not fancy-led'—

with blushing cheeks and 'filed tongue': Diana gave 'A quiver full of piercing darts,' and a golden shaft 'To conquer Cupid's creeping craft.' Diana then named her 'Avisa,' and made her her chief attendant. Juno, jealously refused to confer wealth on her, fearing that Jove seeing her might prove untrue. Avisa is then said to be the daughter of the Mayor of the town, and

> There she dwells in public eye,
> Shut up from none that list to see;
> She answers all that list to try,
> Both high and low of each degree:
>> But few that come, but feel her dart,
>> And try her well ere they depart.

It is not expressly declared that she is a bar maid, but the inference seems unavoidable. This is substantiated by the fact Caveleiro, one of her mad suitors, upon his suit failing, says:

> "Well, give me than a cup of wine,
> As thou art his, would thou wert mine."

She replies,

> "Have t'ye good luck, tell them that gave
> You this advice, what speed you have."

All, very suggestive of the barroom.

Elsewhere, in Canto I (the stanzas are unnumbered), Avisa's traits are ennumerated. Two consecutive stanzas are as follows:

> In lieu of Juno's golden part
> Diana gave her double grace;
> A chaste desire, a constant heart,
> Disdain of love in fawning face,
>> A face and eye that should entice,
>> A smile that should deceive the wise.
>
> A sober tongue that should allure,
> And draw great numbers to the field;
> A flinty heart that should endure
> All fierce assaults, and never yield,
>> And seeming oft as though she would;
>> Yet fartherest off when that she should.

After the experiences that we have had in exploring the haunts and guises of Wine, it should require no great acumen, even in this early stage of the present search, to penetrate the gauzy disguise of this maid, and to discover the old familiar Wine, lurking beneath her delegated virtues.

In due course of the poem the simple announcement is made, that Avisa is "now in wedlock tied," "To one that loves her as himself." Who the husband was, or what of his character, is left to conjecture. The husband, if it be assumed that her *marriage* is to be literally construed to have been such, receives no further attention, and throughout the long narratives of her many temptations, is never seen, and is but incidentally spoken of. Avisa maintains her own chastity without his concern or intervention. So far as it appears he was content to attend his own affairs, and to grant a like privilege to his spouse. There is no indication that she needed a protector. Notwithstanding her marriage, she continues throughout to expose herself to all who might desire to approach her with lewd proposals. While all were repulsed and reproved, it was done by an appeal to their moral natures, rather than by an indignant repelling of an insulting proposal. Such proposals came from a Nobleman, ruffians, roisterers, young gentlemen and lusty Captains, a Frenchman, an Anglo-German, and from (the last recorded) Henry Willobie, an Italo-Spaniard.

Much the greater part of the poem is devoted to narrating the proposals of suitors—would-be seducers,—and Avisa's reply to these. Her character, as defined in her answers, is irreproachable. With moderation she attempts to reason with her wooers, and only when they become too importunate, or abusive, does she resort to defiance with warnings against going beyond indecent proposals. She maintains herself throughout as a woman of strictest chastity and temperance, despising lewdness, and fixed in the ways of all moral virtues. So endowed, it would seem at first thought, that this paragon would be an unfitting symbol for Wine. And so indeed she would be, if there be attributed to Wine the woes and evils that a lust for wine produces. But has it not been seen how those who have most cause for hate, can always find good reasons for their loves? The drunkard in his despair will curse it, and yet it is always his dearest and only love. He ever blames himself and never that which begets his woes. In all of those whose verses have been, and are to be, reviewed Wine is a divine inspirer. And many are those, not drunkards, who yet consider it so, if it could be used, and continued in use, in discretion and moderation.

It is in this aspect that Wine is considered in the Avisa. It is a heavenly agency, virtuous and discreet, condemning all excesses and ever counselling its votaries to a sensible moderation. Any indulgence in excess is lewdness, which inevitably will bring its punishment. Wine, then, is not a curse, but a blessing, as is the discreet and virtuous woman; as is the food which we require, and which with intemperate use may entail bad results. As well charge indigestion to food, as drunkenness to wine. The fault is his who eats and drinks to excess, and not to that which is consumed. Wine has its uses, but is, itself, opposed to being misused. Therefore, the evils of drunkenness are not attributable to Wine, but to those who indulge to excess. As Avisa shows, they are the lecherous seducers, who prostitue Wine. From the viewpoint of personified Wine, its over-use is nothing less than a forceful rape. This view may be logical enough to him who is master of himself, and can indulge and also refrain. But it is the veriest irony, when applied to the confirmed inebriate. But the merits of this ever-recurring controversy are not for discussion here. The whole purpose of this inquiry is to identify and analyze Avisa.

It must suffice to say, that the whole of this poem yields its meaning to the touch of Wine. The further quotations to be made, while incidentally helpful to such an exposition, are principally made to show that the initials "W. S." are those of William Shakespeare, and the reference surely applies to him. And here will be found confirmation of what has been shown as to Shakespeare's inebriety. Having discovered through these investigations how many of the 16th Century poets were addicted to the same enslaving habits, more forebearance may be extended to this the most beloved of them all. It is very probable that the references contained in this poem to William Shakespeare, gave to Willobie His Avisa, its greatest importance, and thus rescued it from oblivion.

Beginning with Henry Willobie's court to Avisa, is a prose introductory, as follows:

"H. W. (Henry Willobie) being suddenly affected with the contagion of a fantastical fit, at the first sight of A. (Avisa) pineth awhile in secret grief, at length not able any longer to endure the burning heat of so fervent a humour, bewrayeth the secresy of his disease unto his familiar friend W. S. (William Shakespeare?), *who not long before had tried the curtesy of the like passion, and was now newly recovered of the like infection;* yet finding his friend let blood in the same vein, he took pleasure for a time to see him bleed, and instead of stopping the issue, he enlargeth the wound, with the sharp razor of a willing conceit, persuading him that he thought it a matter very easy to be compassed, and no doubt with pain, diligence and some cost in time to be obtained. Thus this miserable comforter comforting his friend with an impossibility, either for that he now would secretly laugh at his friend's folly, *that had given occasion not long before unto others to laugh at his own,* or because he would see whether another could play his part better than himself, and in viewing a far off the course of this loving Comedy, he determined to see whether it would sort to a happier end for this new actor, than it did for the old player. But at length this Comedy was like to have grown to a Tragedy, by the weak and feeble estate that H. W. was brought unto, by a desperate view of an impossibility of obtaining his purpose, till Time and Necessity, being his best Physicians brought him a plaster, if not to heal, yet in part to ease his malady. In all which discourse is lively represented the unruly rage of unbridled fancy, having the reins to rove at liberty, with the divers and sundry changes of affections and temptations, which Will, set loose from Reason, can devise &c.

H. W.

(The words in parentheses and the Italicizing have been added by the writer.)

The statements in this Introductory require no interpretation. They fully confirm the conclusions set forth in the review of the Shakespearean sonnets, to the effect that Shakespeare had reformed his early habits of insobriety, and that this abstention had continued until the Sonnets were begun. It was during the time of this abstinence that Willobie appealed to him for advice, as above set forth. Evidently Shakespeare in a bantering and humourous spirit attempted to convince him, that he could in time, by continuing his excesses finally harden and accustom himself so that he could drink with impunity. This brought H. W. near to his death.

In the stanzas following the introduction, H. W. finding him-

self enslaved and suffering, bewails his woe, and then seeing his
friend, W. S., approaching flies to him for advice. Then fol-
lows five stanzas attributed to W. S., commenting on the woe-
begone looks of H. W., and enquiring after his health. H. W.
replies in one stanza, as follows:

> Seest yonder house, where hangs the badge
> Of England's Saint, when captains cry
> Victorious land, to conquering rage,
> Lo, there my hopeless help doth lie:
> > And there that friendly foe doth dwell,
> > That makes my heart thus rage and swell.

Then follows seven stanzas by W. S., advising H. W. how to
enforce his suit, and telling him that in time he must succeed.
The first of these is as follows:

> Well, say no more: I know thy grief,
> And face from whence these flames arise,
> It is not hard to find relief
> If thou wilt follow good advice:
> > She is no saint, she is no nun,
> > I think in time she may be won.

H. W. accepts W. S.'s advice, and presumably follows it to
the end. Many stanzas follow. These consist of his supplica-
tions and pleas, and Avisa's unyielding answers. At the end of
Avisa's last reply there is a note, in these words:

> "H. W. was now again stricken so dead, that he has
> not yet any further assayed, nor think I ever will, and
> where be he alive or dead I know not, and therefore I
> leave him."

Then follows the author's conclusions in five stanzas!

In the 1596 edition Hadrian Dorrell announces that the
author is "late gone to God." All in all, there is much mystery
and no certainty as to who the author was.

MICHAEL DRAYTON.

Michael Drayton published 64 sonnets, all under the title of
Ideas. The first publication was made in 1594 of 18 sonnets.
In 1599 twenty-one additional were published, and with these
was a prefatory sonnet addressed "To the Reader." In 1602
eight more were published; in 1605 seven, and in 1619 ten.

The fact that Drayton is to be discussed in the class under
consideration, indicates that the writer construes his sonnets to
be of the Petrarchan type. As such they hold a high rank,
probably second only to Shakespeare's. If read critically much
in them will be found that is suggestive of Shakespeare's. Be-
cause Drayton's were the first published it would seem fairer to
reverse this comparison and say, there are some of Shakespeare's
sonnets that bear a marked likeness to Drayton's. The least that
can be said in this matter is, that one of them has been influenced
by the works of the other, and as the most of Drayton's sonnets
were first accessible through publication, it would only be fair,
in our present state of knowledge, to let Shakespeare stand
charged with the imitation.

The prefatory (unnumbered) sonnet, is as follows:

> Into these Loves, who but for Passion looks;
> At this first sight, here let him lay them by!
> And seek elsewhere in turning other books,
> Which better may his labour satisfy.
> No far-fetched Sigh shall ever wound my breast!
> Love from mine eye, a Tear shall never wring!
> No "Ah me's"! my whining sonnets drest!
> A Libertine! fantasticly I sing!
> My verse is the true image of my mind,
> Ever in motion, still desiring change:
> And as thus to variety inclined;
> So in all humours sportively I range!
> My Muse is rightly of the English strain,
> That cannot long one fashion entertain.

The construction of this sonnet must be, that Drayton
expressly disclaims his Loves to be sexual. Passion, sexual pas-

sion, is not their theme. He will not indulge in Sighs nor Tears nor Ah Mes, nor are his sonnets whining ones. All sonnets are well named 'whining' ones, if in the Petrarchan class, and if they be read as addressed to a woman love. He sings as a Libertine, a drunkard, and as such tells what is in his mind. To construe this sonnet otherwise, would be to find its statements false, for like all others of his class he expresses the same woes and sheds like tears. This will soon appear.

He boasts that his verse is the true image of his mind, and no doubt it is. In this he is neither more nor less than his contemporaries. For it is a fact that each one of the Petrarchan English poets (and this may be applied to Petrarch as well) has displayed a remarkable frankness and honesty in the expressions of his frailties. Nothing has been concealed, however discreditable we may now consider it. In reading the sonnets it cannot but be felt that all of the sonneteers have, in the most ingenuous way bared their very souls in their weaknesses. In each case the sonnets are truly autobiographical sketches, so unevasive as to abash the reader with their unrestrained exposures. Can it be that Wine possesses the quality to inspire a man with such emotions? That it divests him of the artificialties of human pride and self-esteem? and reverts him to his primitive state of unconcern for the regard of others? Possibly. But may it not be true, that it is a more probable theory to attribute this frankness to the times in which they lived? that imparted a kind of gentility to drunkenness, and made the drunkard exult in a weakness of which he might better have been ashamed? Perhaps both considerations had a part in these curious manfestations.

The next sonnet selected for consideration is VII, published in 1599.

VII.

Love in a humour played the prodigal,
And bade my senses to a solemn feast;
Yet more to grace the company withal,
Invites my heart to be the chiefest guest:
No other drink would serve this glutton's turn
But precious tears distilling from mine eyne,
Which with my sighs this epicure doth burn,
Quaffing carouses in this costly wine;
Where, in his cups o'ercome with foul excess,

> Straightways he plays a swaggering ruffian's part,
> And at the banquet in his drunkenness,
> Slew his dear friend, my kind and truest heart:
> A gentle warning (friends) thus may you see,
> What 't is to keep a drunkard company.

In this, as in the sonnet before quoted, Drayton makes no pretense that his love is other than Wine. There is nothing left to conjecture. He allows no excuse for imagining or believing that his condition is the consequence of any other cause than his excessive indulgence in Wine. Here we have both *Sighs* and *Tears,* that he declared in the first sonnet love could never wring from him.

The next sonnet to be quoted is IX, published in 1602. It will also be quoted in full.

IX.

> As other men, so I myself do muse,
> Why in this sort I wrest invention so,
> And why these giddy metaphors I use,
> Leaving the path the greater part to go;
> I will resolve you: I am lunatic,
> And ever this in mad-men you shall find,
> What they last thought of when the brain grew sick,
> In most distraction they keep that in mind.
> Thus talking idly in this bedlam fit,
> Reason and you (you must conceive) are twain,
> 'T is nine years now since first I lost my wit,
> Bear with me then, tho' troubled be my brain:
> With diet and correction men distraught,
> (Not too far past may to their wits be brought.

The date of the publication of this sonnet being in 1602, it becomes apparent that his habit must have been contracted not later than 1593. His appetite was developed, probably, in 1592, for the first sonnets were published in 1594. The intimation here is, that he believes after nine years it is not too late, with 'diet and correction'—abstinence and control—to bring about a reform.

XX. (1599)

> An evil spirit your beauty haunts me still,
> Wherewith (alas!) I have been long possessed,
> Which ceaseth not to tempt me to each ill,

> Nor give me once but one poor minute's rest:
> In me it speaks, whether I sleep or wake,
> And when by means to drive it out I try,
> With greater torments then it me doth take,
> And tortures me in most extremity;
> Before my face it lays down my despairs,
> And hastes me on unto a sudden death;
> Now tempting me to drown myself in tears,
> And then in sighing to give up my breath:
> Thus am I still provoked to every evil,
> By this good wicked spirit, sweet Angel Devil.

Here again are both *Sighs* and *Tears*. This and the prefatory sonnet were first published together. Can any other explanation be offered, than the one that has been suggested? It is difficult to conceive that in a sonnet directly addressed to the reader, offering this and other sonets, that he would have stultified himself by declaring that he would never do, what he was then doing.

Sonnet XXXII (1594) is "To the River Ankor." This river is near the poet's birthplace, and it was there probably that his young manhood was spent, and there contracted his intemperate habits. This is quite clearly stated in the last two lines of the sonnet, which are as follows:

> "Arden's sweet Ankor, let thy glory be,
> That fair *Idea* only lives by thee."

In the same publication, 1594, was another sonnet addressed, "Another to the River Ankor." This sonnet is subsequent editions is numbered LIII, and is as follows:

> Clear Ankor, on whose silver-sanded shore,
> My soul-shrined saint, my fair *Idea* lies,
> O blessed brook, whose milk-white swans adore
> Thy crystal stream refined by her eyes,
> Where sweet myrrh-breathing zephyrs in the spring
> Gently distils his nectar-dropping flowers,
> Where nightengales in Arden sit and sing,
> Amongst the dainty dew-empearled flowers;
> Say thus, fair brook, when thou shalt see thy queen,
> Lo, here thy shepherd spent his wand'ring years,
> And in these shades, dear nymph, he oft had been,
> And here to thee he sacrificed his tears:
> Fair Arden, thou my Tempe art alone,
> And thou, sweet Ankor, art my Helicon.

Sonnet XLI (1594) is entitled "Love's Lunacy." It is quoted in full.

> Why do I speak of joy, or write of love,
> When my heart is the very den of horror,
> And in my soul the pains of hell I prove,
> With all his torments and infernal terror?
> What should I say? what yet remains to do?
> My brain is dry with weeping all too long,
> My sighs be spent in uttering of my woe,
> And I want words, wherewith to tell my wrong?
> But still distracted in love's lunacy,
> And bedlam-like thus raving in my grief,
> Now rail upon her hair, then on her eye;
> Now call her goddess, then I call her thief:
> Now I deny her, then I do confess her,
> Now do I curse her, then again I bless her.

Sonnet LXI (1619) is generally considered to be Drayton's finest achievement in sonnet writing. Had the other sonnets been correctly understood, perhaps this judgment would not have prevailed. There are others that are certainly of deeper feeling and finer expression.

LXI.

> Since thre's no help, come let us kiss and part,
> Nay, I have done, you get no more of me,
> And I am glad, yea glad with all my heart,
> That thus so cleanly I myself can free,
> Shake hands forever, cancel all our vows,
> And when we meet at any time again,
> Be it not seen in either of our brows,
> That we one jot of former love retain;
> Now at the last gasp of love's latest breath,
> When his pulse failing, passion speechless lies,
> When faith is kneeling by his bed of death,
> And innocence is closing up his eyes,
> Now if thou wouldst, when all have given him over,
> From death to life thou might'st him yet recover.

Here, again we arrive at the familiar stage in the life history of the Petrarchist—his reform. If they live long enough they all seem to pass through the same cycles. Drayton was born in

1563, and this sonnet was published when he was 56 years old. He lived to be 68, dying in 1631. Shakespeare did not celebrate his final reform in verse, but he lived seven years after the publication of his sonnets. It is a consoling thought that these years must have been more placid than the turbulent ones of his sonnet times.

Sonnet LXII (1594) although among the first written, is found arranged after the declaration of reform. This place was probably given it by the author himself. It may be assumed that the reason for this was, that it expressed his sufferings while putting his resolution of abstinence into effect, which condition required him to yield sparingly to his desires, until a complete severance of relations had been effected. These periods are necessarily frequent, and the poet considered a former sonnet as effective as any he could write, and adapted it accordingly. During one of these trying spells his feasts were always followed closely by famines. In one he was ravished, while in the other he was in his hell of woe.

LXII.

When first I ended, then I first began,
Then more I travelled further from my rest,
Where most I lost, there most of all I wan,
Pined in hunger, rising from a feast.
Methinks I fly, yet want I legs to go,
Wise in conceit, in act a very sot,
Ravished with joy amidst a hell of woe,
What most I seem, that surest am I not.
I build my hopes a world above the sky,
Yet with the mole I creep into the earth,
In plenty I am starved with penury,
And yet I surfeit in the greatest dearth:
I have, I want, despair, and yet desire,
Burned in a sea of ice, drowned midst a fire.

One more sonnet from Drayton. This is LXIII (1599). It is the closing sonnet of the sequence. We may well believe that the author gave it this place, as showing his determination to end his servitude, even though death threatened his attempt. The sonnet is not given because more evidence is needed to prove the case, but because there is a hesitation about closing the discussion with such clear and convincing evidence unused.

LXIII.

Truce, gentle love, a parley now I crave,
Methinks 't is long snice first these wars begun,
Nor thou, nor I, the better yet can have,
Bad is the match, where neither party won.
I offer free conditions of fair peace,
My heart for hostage that it shall remain,
Discharge our forces, here let malice cease,
So for my pledge thou give me pledge again:
Or if no thing but death will serve thy turn,
Still thirsting for subversion of my state;
Do what thou canst, raze, massacre, and burn,
Let the world see the utmost of thy hate:
I send defiance, since if overthrown,
Thou vanquishing, the conquest is mine own.

The sonnets are but a small part of Drayton's poetry. He wrote prolifically, as did both Shakespeare and Spenser, and it would therefore appear that his drinking must have been of the same character as Shakespeare's. That is to say, it was probably intermittent. The greater mass of his work was done in soberness, while his sonnets, most of them, were the products of his sobering times. It was then that his desires and cravings were the greatest, and being deprived of a full measure of his comforter, and curse, he was in a condition to realize his nervous frenzy, and yet capable of expressing it. This he did, principally, in the sonnets.

But his wine-songs were not confined wholly to the sonnets. He wrote several elegies, some of which are quite as pregnant with *Ideas,* as are the sonnets. One of his elegies, in this respect, is not doubtful. It is entitled "To the noble Lady, the Lady I. S. of Worldly Crosses." Three others are suspicious. One is entitled, "Of His Lady not Coming to London," another, "An Elegy Upon the Death of Lady Penelope Clifton," and another "Upon the Noble Lady Aston's Departure for Spain." Two of these purport to relate to specifically named persons, and (if there were such persons) one must hesitate to dispute the sincerity of the titles. A reading of all will show that if they were actually intended to refer to either living or dead ladies, they are far-fetched, and lacking in such quality as might be expected from Drayton's facile pen. It is felt that none of these are necessary to support the contention that is being urged, and these will therefore be passed without a detailed examination.

The poem called "The Quest of Cynthia," is but the quest of Wine. This is not doubtful.

"The Shepherd's Sirena" is without hesitation put in the same class. A brief analysis of this poem will be submitted.

"Dorilus" is Drayton himself. Other shepherds—poets of the day—are referred to under fanciful names, in much the same manner in which Spenser referred to contemporaneous poets in *Colin Clout's Come Home Again*. The names used by Drayton in the Sirena are as follows, "Nimble Tom sirnamed the Tup," "Ralph," "Rock," "Rollo," "Gill" and "Collin." The last is probably Spenser, the others have not been identified.

Dorilus (Drayton) in a state of distress, undertaking a reform, brings forth a letter from his Sirena (Wine) in which is recalled their former pleasures, and expressing her love for him, and sympathizing with him in his misery. He muses on his state, and after a soliloquy concludes,

> "Hard the choice I have to choose;
> To myself, if friend I be
> I must my Sirena lose,
> If not so, she loseth me."

The other shepherds having learned a song which Dorilus had written to Sirena, their presence being concealed, sing the song to him. At its conclusion Dorilus upbraids them, and calls down on them the same miseries and woes that afflict him. Whereupon, one of the shepherds merrily (?) commands him, "Get thee up, thou arrant beast," and demands that he take his sheep-hook and his dog, Cut-tail, and stand for battle in a contest with "Rogueish Swineherds" (the protestants against the evils of wine?) who threaten to bring their swine, and root up all the shepherd's downs (their rights to indulge?). He tells Dorilus,

> "Angry Olcon sets them on,
> And against us part doth take,
> Ever since he was out-gone
> Off'ring rhymes with us to make."

Evidently Olcon, was a former shepherd with them, who had 'out-gone' (left) them, and was now urging on the restrictionists, in their efforts to root out the evils of wine. We are left curious as to who Olcon is. If the date of the composition of the *Sirena* could be ascertained, his identity might be, at least, surmised.

The appeal to Dorilus was successful,

> "When as Dorilus arose,
> Whistles Cut-tail from his play,
> And along with them he goes."

There may be others of Drayton's poems of like tenor. Much of his poetry is inaccessible, and as to such nothing can be ventured.

EDMUND SPENSER.

The works of the sonneteers, including Shakespeare, which
have been discussed, have been found to yield their interpreta-
tion to the same test, and by its application they can be fully
understood, leaving nothing to conjecture. But now we come to
a poet, Edmund Spenser, whose sonnets may also be said to be
amenable to the same test, but not just in the same strain as
the others. There is a difference in the tone and spirit. He
does not, in some of the sonnets, cover the same ground as do
the others, but is evidently more restricted. Like the others his
light is also a reflected one, yet he does not always show the
same phases, and never reaches a fullness.

This difference may be accounted for when the conditions
under which Spenser wrote are taken into consideration. In
Sonnet LX he says, that since the 'winged god,' which is con-
strued to mean the inspiration of wine, began in him to move,
one year is spent, and that year appears to him to have been
longer than the forty years which his life 'out-went.' This is
because the year had been wasted in "long languishment," which
seemed the longer for his "great pains." It is well to quote this
sonnet in full, for it is the key to the construction of the Spenser
sonnets.

LX.

They, that in course of heavenly spheres are skilled,
To every planet point his sundry year:
In which her circle's voyage is fulfilled.
As Mars in threescore years doth run his sphere.
So, since the winged god his planet clear
Began in me to move, one year is spent:
The which doth longer unto me appear,
Than all those forty which my life out-went.
Then by that count, which lover's books invent,
The sphere of Cupid forty years contains,
Which I have wasted in long languishment,
That seemed the longer for my greater pains.
But let my love's fair planet short her ways,
This year ensuing, or else short my days.

From this it may be believed that the year past was one well filled with grief and pains, and that the poet would rather die than go through the like for another year. This certainly seems to dispose of the current, but unfounded theory, that these sonnets were written to extol the woman who in 1594 became the wife of Spenser. The sonnets were all published in 1595 with the statement that they had been "written not long since." They were entered in the Stationer's Register November 19, 1594. The sonnets themselves fix their date of composition, the most of them, at least, between the first and last of the year. The prevailing calendar at that time fixed the beginning of the year on March 25th. Consequently they could not have been begun later than March 25th, 1593, and were completed within about one year from thence. This is the time to which they are generally assigned by the critics. Accepting the statement in the sonnets as facts, Spenser was 40 years old when the sonnets were begun.

These assumptions are so well supported as to be all but indisputable. They also accord well with the evidence to be adduced hereafter. Thus there is presented a strange and unwholesome attempt on the part of a man of sense and high standing, to distort his own life, and render himself abject. This consisted of a man of the age of 40 years attempting to induce in himself a state of chronic alcoholism, that he might be so circumstanced as to realize the unquenchable thrist of the Petrarchists sonneteers, in order to express himself in the veins of their sonnets.

Taking Spenser at his word, that is just what he did, and his sonnets are the chronicles of his experiences. He understood the meaning of the sonnets of the Petrarchists, and could interpret them, but had never felt what they felt, and consequently could not write soulfully as they had written. For three years England had been sonnet-mad, and every poet in England, if Ben Jonson be excepted, was exerting himself in the art of writing sonnets. Spenser knew that such poetry as it was his desire to write, must come from the heart, and that was impossible unless the writer should know and feel the pangs that must be portrayed. So he deliberately set about to make of himself a dipsomaniac, that he might join in this chorus of depravity. This is the story he tells himself. He came near to death in his attempt to establish a lust, and he was long in qualifying himself as a

Petrarchist, and in learning to sing as they sang. His endeavor
is the burden of his sonnets, and when the goal was reached, if
it ever was, he was compelled to desist and to abandon the
unholy attempt. It was at the end of the year, that he had set
apart to qualify himself, that he wrote this sixtieth sonnet, and
herein he tells how he had suffered forty years in one, and that
he would prefer death to a repetition of his experiences.

The first few of Spenser's sonnets are not particularly char-
acteristic of the subject. They might as well be considered as
having a relation to Queen Elizabeth as to wine. Read by them-
selves one would not dare to construe them as having any specific
meaning. They were in fact but preparatory, having been writ-
ten in contemplation of a step to be taken.

In IV, he says:

> "New Year forth looking out of Janus' gate
> Doth seem to promise hope of new delight."

Clearly a looking forwards to a hoped for result. Then to
himself he say,

> "Prepare yourself new love to entertain."

In VI, we read,

> "Be nought dismayed that her unmoved mind
> Does still persist in her rebellious pride:
> Such love, not like to lusts of baser kind,
> The harder won, the firmer will abide."
>
> *   *   *
>
> "Then think not long in taking little pain
> To knit the knot that ever shall remain."

He thus early discovered that such a habit as he coveted,
requires time for establishment, and that the path to his ideal
was not at all times a rosy one. But contemplating in the future
a perfect and enduring elysium, he considered it worth the pain
and toil necessary to its acquirement.

Henceforth the Roman numerals indicate the sonnet from
which quotations, usually partial, are taken.

VIII.

> "Dark is the world where your light shined never;
> Well is he born who may behold you ever."

He imagines that when he shall be able to drink without stint, that he will have proved himself well-born. In this he was but voicing a prevailing sentiment of the times, that a man's capacity for indulgence was one of the indications of his quality. Daniel expresses the same sentiment in his sonnet XXXIX, where he says his love's eyes have redeemed him from the vulgar. Spenser in his Sonnet LXI says:

> "Such heavenly forms ought rather worshipped be,
> Than dare be loved by men of mean degree."

Though Spenser was himself a man of 'mean degree' it was ever a nightmare to his sycophantic soul.

XI.

> "Daily when I do seek and sue for peace,
> And hostages do offer for my truth
> She, cruel warrior, doth herself address
> To battle, and the weary war reneweth."
>   *   *   *
> "But then she seeks with torment and turmoil
> To force me live, and will not let me die."

XII.

In this sonnet he sought to make a truce with his Love, but was ambushed, and was

> "Too feeble to abide the brunt so strong,
> Was forced to yield myself into their hands:
> Who me captiving straight with rigourous wrong,
> Have ever since me kept in cruel bands."

This was simply a breakdown, and one of the pains described in LX.

XIII.

> "Yet lowly still vouchsafe to look on me;
> Such lowliness shall make you lofty be."

As in other sonnets he is pleading with Wine, and promising to immortalize her in his verse, if she will only adopt and inspire him.

XIV.

Return again, my forces late dismayed,
Unto the siege by you abandoned quite.
Great shame it is to leave, like one afraid,
So fair a piece for one repulse so light.
'Gainst such strong castles needeth greater might
Than those small forts which ye were wont belay:
Such haughty minds, inured to hardy fight,
Disdain to yield unto the first assay.
Bring therefore all the forces that you may,
And lay incessant battery to her heart;
Plaints, prayers, vows, ruth, sorrow and dismay;
Those engines can the proudest love convert.
And if those fail, fall down and die before her;
So dying live, and living do adore her.

We have seen high-minded men, seriously inviting death, as a
release from a degrading and enslaving appetite. But here is a
man purposely and forcefully, and against his natural inclina-
tions, seeking to win such an appetite, even at the risk of his
life, and this, that he might thereby prove his quality.

XVI.

One day he observed, when waiting on his love,

"Legions of loves with little wings did fly
Darting their deadly arrows, fiery bright,"

One of these darts was aimed at him, but a damsel broke the
dart, which otherwise would have splain him, and he says,

"Yet as it was, I hardly scaped with pain."

This was another serious collapse, with delirium, that nearly
ended fatally.

XVIII.

His love remains unyielding to his appeals,
"So do I weep, and wail and plead in vain,
While she as steel and flint doth still remain."

XIX.

At this stage of his new experience he has heard the cuckoo
three time, and concludes,

> "Therefore, O Love, unless she turns to thee
> Eere cuckoo end, let her a rebel be."

He has concluded that unless a change soon comes about, that he will have to abandon his attempt.

XX.

> "In vain I seek and sue to her for grace,
> And do mine humbled heart before her pour:
> The whiles her foot she on my neck does place,
> And tread my life down in the lowly floor."

XXI.

> "With such strange terms her eyes she doth enure,
> That with one look she doth my life dismay,
> And with another doth it straight recure:
> Her smile me draws, her frown me drives way."

XXII.

At the holy season, he pledges,

> "There I to her, as the author of my bliss,
> Will build an altar to appease her ire;
> And on the same my heart will sacrifice,
> Burning in flames of pure and chaste desire:"

From feeling expressed in such as the foregoing quotations, it is difficult not to conclude that this great poet had deluded himself into believing in the miraculous character of the fetish he is worshipping and relying upon, and that he really expected that it would ultimately hear and grant his supplications, and that it would in the end reward his sufferings.

XXIII.

> "For all that I in many days do weave
> In one short hour, I find by her undone.
> So when I think to end that I begun,
> I must begin and never bring to end:
> For with one look she spills that long I spun,
> And with one word my whole year's work doth rend!"

XXIV.

> "But when I feel the bitter baleful smart
> Which her fair eyes unwares do work in me,
> That death out of their shiny beams do dart,
> I think that I a new Pandora see;"

XXV.

How long shall this like dying life endure,
And know no end of her own misery,
But waste and wear in terms unsure
Twixt fear and hope depending doubtfully?
Yet better were at once to let me die,
And show the last ensample of your pride,
Than to torment me with this cruelty,
To prove your power, which I too well have tried.
But yet if in your hardened breast ye hide
A close intent at last to show me grace,
Then all the woes and wrecks which I abide
As means of bliss I gladly will embrace,
And wish that more and greater they might be,
That greater meed at last may turn to me.

These extracts are made, primarily, to show that Spenser's sonnets are not of the same range as are those of the other Petrarchists. Their's are wails in bondage, while he complains that the same mistress will not accept his enslavement; their woes are the penalties of an unfeigned love, his are passionless and coldly designing; their's are the offsprings of an irresistible impulse, his of a premeditated purpose; their appetites are insatiable, his unattainable; they wail in agony, he blusters in regrets. To summarize: they were honest, and he insincere.

All intervening sonnets until the 33rd are apposite, but for obvious reasons cannot be quoted. They are all repetitions of the same thoughts.

XXXIII.

In this sonnet the poet admits wrongdoing in not pursuing and finishing the Faerie Queene. But how can he work on it in his present state,

> "Since that this one is tossed with troublous fit
> Of a proud love, that doth my spirit spoil?"

XXXIV.

Like a ship, that through the ocean wide
By conduct of some star doth make her way,
When as a storm hath dimmed her trusty guide,
Out of her course doth wander far astray;
So I, whose star, that wont with her bright ray

Me to direct, with clouds is overcast,
Do wander now in darkness and dismay,
Through hidden perils round about me placed.
Yet hope I well, that when this storm is past,
My Helice, the loadstar of my life,
Will shine again, and look on me at last,
With lovely light to clear my cloudy grief.
Till then I wander care-full comfortless,
In secret sorrow and sad pensiveness.

In the light of circumstances this sonnet defines the conditions surrounding Spenser, since he has undertaken the writing of the sonnets. Heretofore he has been industriously engaged in literary work of the highest order. But now, with that work unfinished, he is out of his course and wandering far astray; overcast with clouds, and in darkness and dismay. Yet, he is hoping that when the storm is past, that his cloudy grief will clear. All of this is within the year that he has set aside for a turbulent experiment, upon the expiration of which he hopes that his loadstar will shine again. See the next sonnet for a continuation of the discussion.

XXXV.

My hungry eyes through greedy covetize
Still to behold the object of their pain,
With no contentment can themselves suffice,
But having pine, and having not complain.
For lacking it they cannot life sustain,
And having it they gaze on it the more:
In their amazement like Narcissus vain,
Whose eyes him starved: so plenty makes me poor.
Yet are mine eyes so filled with the store
Of that fair sight, that nothing else they brook,
But loathe the things that they did like before,
And can no more endure on them to look.
All this world's glory seemeth vain to me,
And all their shows but shadows, saving she.

XXXVII.

The poet describes his mistress with golden hair in a golden net, and says,

> "Take heed therefore, mine eyes, how ye do stare
> Henceforth too rashly on that guileful net,
> In which if ever ye entrapped are,
> Out of her bands ye by no means shall get."

It is plain that Spenser realizes that he has never yet been entrapped, and reasons as to the consequences, if he should be. Clearly he is not, and never has been, a true Petrarchist.

Sonnets XXXVIII to XLVI are all in Spenser's best vein, and are all confirmatory of the theory that is being advanced as to their cryptic meaning. So apt are they that it is most difficult to select parts for quotation, by any character of elimination. Besides it is felt that the limits of quotation are being exceeded.

XLVI.

This sonnet announces the expiration of Spenser's year of indulgement. It must be heard.

> When my abodes prefixed time is spent,
> My cruel fair straight bids me wend my way:
> But then from heaven most hideous storms are sent,
> As willing me against her will to stay.
> Whom then shall I, or heaven or her, obey?
> The heavens know best what is the best for me:
> But as she will, whose will my life doth sway,
> My lower heaven, so it perforce must be.
> But ye high heavens, that all this sorrow see,
> Since all your tempests cannot hold me back,
> Assuage your storms, or else both you and she
> Will both together me too sorely wrack.
> Enough it is for one man to sustain
> The storms which she alone on me doth rain.

The construction of this sonnet would seem to be, that severe storms prevailed on March 25th. On that day, his time of experiment having expired, Spenser was willing enough to surrender the battle with Wine, and stop the strife. His condition however was such that there must be a spell of easing off before complete abstinence. He interpreted the weather storm to be the decree of the heavens that he should delay his reform. He was glad enough, however, to conclude, that as Wine, his lower heaven, had willed that he should cease his excesses, that he would abide by her decision. Consequently he acquiesced, and enters a complaint against the weather, that it was adding to his wrack, when he had enough otherwise to bear. When he says that his love, Wine, had straight bid him wend his way, to soberness, he simply means that she is no longer inviting to him, and that his desires no longer urge him to continue his indulgements with her.

Thus ended the year that Spenser had set apart for his conversion to drunkenness. But he was not constituted for a drunkard, and could not be fashioned into one. Like all, who are so blessed, he could drink himself to drunkenness, but then his physical body revolted against a continuance of the fare, which, to one so constituted becomes unbearably repulsive. The physical ills that ensue result in great suffering. Spenser evidently thought that it was only a matter of enuring himself, and with that end in view persistently renewed the indulgements, as detailed in the sonnets, expecting—even hoping—that he could become a true devotee. Under such conditions it may well be believed, that at the end of his allotted period he was glad enough to abandon the essay. It may well be believed that it was without regret that he abandoned his excesses, and except for those stimulations which become necessary to bridge the drunken subject over to an established sobriety, he took a welcome leave of that which he had so painfully sought to make his love and mistress.

Many sonnets following the 46th tell of the intermediate stage between drunkenness and established sobriety. Those written in this interim include all those up to the 60th, which is the sonnet with which the discussion was begun. As will be seen, he was not fully restored until the 63rd sonnet.

Extracts from some of these sonnets may be found of interest. Some curious developments will be exhibited.

XLVII.

> "Trust not the treason of those smiling looks,
> Until you have their guileful trains well tried:
> For they are like but unto golden hooks,
> That from the foolish fish their baits do hide:
> So she with flattering smiles weak hearts doth guile
> Unto her love, and tempt to their decay;
> Whom being caught, she kills with cruel pride,
> And feeds at pleasure on the wretched prey."

Note how the sufferer, in the process of being released, has no kind word for his tormentor, but views her only as such while yet his wounds are unhealed. But when she becomes a memory only, he will forget his pains and also forget to hate her.

L.

> "Long languishing on double malady,
> Of my heart's wound and of my body's grief,
> There came to me a leech, that would apply
> Fit medicines for my body's best relief."

He is passing through the curative stage.

LIV.

> "Yet she beholding me with constant eye,
> Delights not in my mirth, nor rues my smart:
> But when I laugh she mocks, and when I cry
> She laughs, and hardens ever more her heart.
> What then can move her If not mirth nor moan,
> She is no woman, but a senseless stone."

It would not seem necessary that the poet should declare the fact as above, when hundreds of sonnets tell it just as plainly. Yet, no doubt, there will be some to believe that the love of this and many other sonnets, by this and other Petrarchists, is a woman.

LVII.

> Sweet warrior, when shall I have peace with you?
> High time it is this war now ended were:
> Which I no longer can endure to sue,
> Ne you incessant battery more to bear.
> So weak my powers, so sore my wounds appear,
> That wonder is how I should live a jot,
> Seeing my heart through launched every where
> With thousand arrows which your eyes have shot:
> Yet shoot ye sharply still, and spare me not,
> But glory think to make these cruel stoures.
> Ye cruel one! What glory can be got,
> In slaying him that would live gladly yours?
> Make peace therefore and grant me timely grace,
> That all my wounds will heal in little space.

LXII.

"The weary year, his race now having run,
The new begins his compassed course anew:
With show of morning mild he hath begun,
Betokening peace and plenty to ensue,
So let us, which this change of weather view,
Change eke our minds, and former loves amend;
The old year's sins forepast let us eschew,
And fly the faults with which we did offend."

LXIII.

"After long storms and tempests sad essay,
which hardly I endured heretofore,
In dread of death and dangerous dismay,
With which my silly bark was tossed sore,
I do at length descry the happy shore,
In which I hope ere long for to arrive:"

Thus, we now arrive at the completion of the year of *silly* experimenting. One might well hesitate to use so disrespectful a term, were there not such high authority to sustain it. But having ventured so far, the writer feels that an apology is due to the reader, for having used a word of such inadequate significance for describing so colossal a misadventure.

Henceforth to the end of the sonnets quotations are unnecessary to enforce the conclusions which have been so frequently announced and verified. The poet's normal condition having been fully restored, he seems quite content to let it remain so. There are indications that he may have indulged in an occasional drink, which a man constituted as Spenser was might do, and not endanger himself. It is wholy unlikely that he ever again adventured with his 'silly bark' into deep flows.

In the subsequent sonnets there are two statements expressly confirming the conclusions that have been stated to the effect that Spenser was constitutionally incapable of excessive alcoholic indulgements. In LXXVI, he says

"Sweet thought, I envy you so happy rest,
Which oft I wished, yet never was so blest."

Also in LXXXIII he advises his friends to use wine even to excess, as follows,

"Go visit her in her chaste bower of rest
Accompanied with angelic delights.
There fill yourself with those most joyous sights,
The which myself could never yet attain:"

The remaining sonnets to the end, are little less than an apotheosis of wine. Having regained his health, except as his hurts may have become incurable, Spenser undertook to make amends for all the evil things he had said of it. This, he carries to extremes, so far, indeed, as to arouse the suspicion that his praises are spiced with insincerity. He was certainly imbued with the thought that it was a mark of distinction to be able to bear one's full share in carousals, and that no true gentleman would shrink from such a test. Not only should he drink like a gentleman, but he should ever stand ready to extol and defend the virtues of this recognized god of inspiration and song. In it was the spirit of chivalry, and it was the heart of courage and of all manly deeds.

Realizing his lack of capacity as a votary, he is deeply troubled lest this great defect should mark him as one of lowly origin and of vulgar tastes. That such a conception might not gain currency, he seems to imagine that it could be counteracted by him assuming vehemently to champion the virtues of that which had refused to lend itself to his use. As in all such cases, the advocate of an unfriendly cause, strives to hide his lack of sincerity under a profusion of partisan expressions, which generally exceed the limits of honest zeal. Not only does he exceed good taste in his avowals of love and devotion, but he also enlisted as an enemy of those whom he deemed to be wine's traducers. It is not known what called forth his bitter denunciation of, and curses upon, those who had assailed wine's character or use. Whatever the onslaught may have been, it must have been particularly effective, to have called forth from Spenser one of the bitterest maledictions to be found in the English language. Here it is.

LXXXV.

Venomus tongue, tipped with vile adder's sting,
Of that self kind with which the furies fell
Their snaky heads do comb, from which a spring
Of poisoned words and spiteful speeches well,
Let all the plagues and horrid pains of hell

> Upon thee fall for thine accursed hire,
> That with false forged lies, which thou dost tell,
> In my true love did stir up coals of ire;
> The sparks whereof let kindle thine own fire,
> And catching hold on thine own wicked head,
> Consume thee quite, that didst with guile conspire
> In my sweet peace such breaches to have bred.
> Shame be thy meed, and mischief thy reward,
> Due to thyself, that it for me prepared.

It is probable that this sonnet was called forth by some attack made on the prevalence of drunkenness in England, and which may have involved Spenser, as one of the advocates of the virtues of wine. Here then, we may witness, at its very source, the origin of the contest waged for the restriction of the liquor traffic, and which has been waged so unceasingly ever since. The issue has grown and broadened far beyond any proposals made at this early date. Out of this development comes the present day prohibition, with controversies of no less bitterness than those of the Elizabethan period. But it is not imaginable that anything more vindictive than this sonnet has found expression.

Spenser was inclined to be intemperate both in expression and feeling. Several things in his writings and in his history stand to his discredit. It is generally noticeable that towards those in high station, and in authority, he was obsequious and inclined to fulsome praise (which was a prevalent failing of the times), while towards opponents, enemies and those of low stations, he was rudely intolerant and exhibited little of consideration, tolerance or fairness. As in the sonnet just quoted his denunciations are never keen, thrusting or satirical, but coarsely and dully abusive. An instance of the kind is strikingly noticeable in his elegy on Sir Philip Sidney, that was written five years after Sidney's death, which occurred from a wound received at the battle of Flushing. In the heat of the battle he was struck in the thigh by a bullet. It was never known by whom the bullet was fired. No doubt it came from Sidney's foes in battle, and it is not probable that he who fired it knew that it had found its mark in Sidney. It is very certain that Spenser did not know who fired it. He thus describes him,

> So as he raged amongst that beastly rout,
> A cruel beast of most accursed brood
> Upon him turned (despair makes cowards stout)

> And with fell tooth accustomed to blood,
> Launched his thigh with so mischievous might,
> That it both bone and muscles rived quite.

Much of the latter part of Spenser's life was spent in Ireland. There he had gone in the service of the English authorities, and finally took up a permanent residence, having received a crown grant of a large tract of forfeited lands. His life in Ireland was far from peaceful, and he and his neighbors seemed to live on very bad terms. He wrote a book entitled, *View of the State of Ireland*. These views and proposals set forth well support what has been heretofore said as to his character. The proposals urged were, in brief, that the Irish be given twenty days in which to come in, and that after the lapse of this time they be given no quarter, but that they be hunted down like wild animals in the winter when covert was thin, and after one such winter, he predicted, there would be little more to be done, and that in eighteen months the ground would be completely cleared for English colonists.

One can hardly realize that such proposals could come from an Englishman. It may seem needless to say, that they were not adopted.

THE PSEUDO-PETRARCHISTS

Thomas Watson

Giles Fletcher

Barnabe Barnes

R. Lincke

William Smith

Robert Tofte

THE PSEUDO PETRARCHISTS.

Not all of the Elizabethan poets who imagined themselves to be Petrarchists were in fact such. A number of those who had read the great master's impassioned sonnets, or those of his followers, did not discern the essential thing that animated them. Some of them—a few—realized that there was an overcasting shadow that blurred the subject, and left it not quite distinct. But they could not penetrate the mystery nor solve the riddle. To them the only course remaining was to accept at the full face value the spurious designation, and let it pass current for what in fact it was not—a woman.

Out of this perplexity of mind came a furious poetical mania in which every poet, who imagined he could write a sonnet, engaged in a quantitive production of this then popular form of poetry. Unless he was an initiate his subject—his love— was a woman, definitely and substantially of flesh and blood, and singularly, just one of such. It would not be true to assert this passion was real, however specific. For no lucid man truly in love would consent to malign his passion by defining it in the terms employed by the Petrarchists. Those who essayed to do this, had no real conception of the subject they were attempting to treat, but were simply and blindly following a pattern suitable to the subject which the Petrarchists had in mind, but ludicrously inappropriate when applied to the joys, griefs and disappointments of a man infatuated with one of the opposite sex.

The number of those who attempted, through raw imitations, to match the frenzy (as they imagined it) of those whom they would imitate, were greater than those who knew the subject and wrote feelingly. These latter, so far as they are known have all been reviewed. In volume the poetry of the pseudo-Petrarchists also exceeds that of those who knew whereof they were writing. The following list of the former is made up from the *Elizabethan Sonnets*. In each case the date of publication and the title of the sonnets are given.

> Thomas Watson, 1593—The Tears of Fancy, or, Love Disdained.
>
> Giles Fletcher, 1593—Licia.
>
> Barnabe Barnes, 1593—Parthenophil and Partenophe.
>
> H. Constable, 1594—Diana.
>
> W. Percy, 1594—Coelia.
>
>   ?   , 1594—Zephira.
>
> B. Griffin, 1596—Fidessa.
>
> R. Linche, 1596—Diella.
>
> W. Smith, 1596—Chloris.
>
> R. Tofte, 1597—Laura.

Some, but not all, of these will be briefly discussed.

Not mentioned in *Elizabethan Sonnets* is another sonneteer, William Drummond of Hawthornden, a Scotchman, deeply learned in Petrarchan literature, but unenlightened as to the nature of its mystery. His sonnets were first published in 1616, and are, therefore, not strictly of the Elizabethan period, which probably accounts for their omission from Lee's treatise. These sonnets are divided into parts one and two. The first division is devoted to his love (unnamed) in life, and the second to her in death, thus following literally the plan of Petrarch. Of these sonnets it may be said, that they are quite as worthy as are those of any of the pseudo-Petrarchists, and are likewise, soulless, as such a mistaken treatment must be.

THOMAS WATSON.

Watson was among the earliest of the English sonneteers. He very frankly sought to imitate Petrarch, and comes wonderfully near to succeeding in his attempt. But he mistook the malady with which all Petrarchists are afflicted. His imitations, however, are so close that at times it seems as if he had caught the meaning. But he never quite masters it. Sidney said that those who would read his sonnets understandingly must first learn how to spell. Watson never progressed quite so far in his bibulous education. He did not divine that Wine was the spirit of the sonnets he would imitate, but thought, as most of the world had thought, that the love of Woman was the agonizing passion that drove his predecessors mad. With that idea (not Idea) he plunged into the mystery, and appropriated every note of his masters, but never accomplished the expression of their theme. He did not understand what they were singing about, but he thought he did, and he wildly exaggerated as he thought they had done, and as he thought, therefore, must be permissible. The result is a mass of discords—sound and fury, meaning nothing. He undertook to sing of the pangs of unrequited love, and forged such passions as sanity cannot feel.

Spenser, in *Colin Clout's Come Home Again* refers to many of the contemporaneous poets under sobriquets. Among the others he mentions *Alcon*. By some this has been taken to mean Watson, and this assumption is probably correct. He says of him,

> "And there is pleasing Alcon, could he raise
> His tunes from lays to matter of more skill."

If *skill* here be interpreted to mean *understanding,* which is the only interpretation that would seem to be lucid, then the couplet well expresses the character of Watson's poetry. It is tuneful enough, but shows a lack of understanding of the subject being treated.

GILES FLETCHER.

Giles Fletcher did not attempt to disguise the fact, that he was wandering in a maze. It did not occur to him that Petrarch, and his cognizant followers were guided on their way by the sign posts which Wine establishes. He realized that they, through some mysterious acquirement were in possession of a key which he could not master. He sought through the range of his knowledge and experience to find the object that would conform to the bewildering attributes with which the initiates had endowed it. Failing to fathom the mystery he, like the others of his class, undertook with lifeless phrases to match the cryptical sonnets, and so far as lifeless words could do so he accomplished his purpose. Yet, he was not deceived, for he realized that he lacked in understanding. He wrote 52 sonnets, which he dedicated to Lady Mollineux, and also prefaced them with an address, *To the Reader*. This address is so enlightening, and so well analyzes the inconsistencies of the expressions contained in the sonnets, when read as applying to the love of a man for a woman, that a part of it may well be quoted.

"But the love wherewith Venus' son hath injuriously made spoil of thousands, is a cruel tyrant: occasion of sighs, oracles of lies, enemy of pity, way of error, shape of inconstancy, temple of treason, faith without assurance, monarch of tears, murderer of ease, prison of hearts, monster of nature, poisoned honey, impudent courtezan, furious bastard: and in one word, not Love.

Thus Reader, take heed thou err not! Esteem Love as thou ought.

If thou muse, what my Licia is? Take her to be some Diana, at the least chaste; or some Minerva: no Venus, fairer far. It may be she is Learning's Image, or some heavenly wonder: which the Precisist may not mislike. Perhaps under that name I have shadowed (The Holy) Discipline. It may be I mean that kind courtesy which I found at the Patronness of these Poems, it may be some College. It may be my conceit, and pretend nothing."

Thus does Fletcher put the facts before his readers. The Love of the sonnets is a monstrosity. A tangled mass of inconsistencies. In short, it is not love at all, and his readers are warned and beseeched not to accept it as a true passion.

Yet, Fletcher, imbued with the mania of the times, set about to imitate the phrases in which this apparent hallucination had been set forth. And when he was done, he realized that he had created a nondescript pattern that he could not mentally grasp, and that in all the world of his imaginings there was nothing like it. Not in mythology, nor imagery, nor idealisim, nor religion nor nature could he select a prototype to which he could fit the formless vestments which he had woven. Had it then dawned on him that Wine was the Circe of the sonnets, which metamorphosed its votaries into swine, he might have realized how blindly he had spun.

BARNABE BARNES.

Neither did Barnabe Barnes know his subject. Either he was blindly imitating the Petrarchan manner, and was wholy in the dark, or had conceived the true meaning and was trying to express it, but being unlettered, knew nothing of Wine's despotism. Failing, as he realized he had failed, to impress his lines with vitality, he sought to gain effect by a multiplication of words. He wrote tiresomely, and nearly endlessly. There are 104 sonnets, 26 madrigals, 5 sestines, 3 canzons, 21 elegies and 20 odes.

Several of the poets in this classification will be passed without further notice. There is little in their sonets that it notable, except, that their Loves are palpably women. With their perceptions they could be nothing else. But the treatment used, as applied to a woman, is necessarily exaggerated, and usually stilted and unappealing.

There are, however, a few, undoubtedly young men, who found nothing to daunt them in construing the Petrarchan sonnets as genuine love-making, and these unrestrainedly bellowed forth bare passions. They are frank, grotesquely so. Yet this but emphasizes their honesty. They were, or thought they were, true disciples of Petrarch, and being faithful to his teachings, as they construed them, they pursued them to legitimate ends, and so applied them as to produce realistic and denuded effects, with scant artistry. They went little further than the Petrarchists, however, if one will but shut his eyes and in blind faith discern the figure of a woman obscured in the Petrarchists' maze of words. Are their tears, groans, wails, despairs, beseechings and languishings less extravagant than those of their misguided imitators, when judged from the same viewpoint? A little more of art, and a little less of truth, are about all that divide them.

Let us see a few of the sonnets of three of these unsophisticated Elizabethans.

R. LINCHE.

Thirty-eight sonnets under the title *Diella* are attributed to R. Linche. In Sonnet XIX this poet interprets the pains and frenzy of a night, through which the Petrarchists endure such nervous tensions, as has been seen. Linche imagines they are like this.

XIX.

When Night returns back to his ugly Mansion,
And clear-faced Morning makes her bright upraise;
In sorrow's depth, I murmur out his cantion
(Salt tears distilling from my dewey eyes),
"O thou deceitful Somnus, god of dreams!
Cease to afflict my over-pained sprite

With vain illusions, and idle themes!
Thy spells are false! thou canst not charm aright!
For when, in bed, I think t' embrace my Love
(Enchanted by thy magic so to think),
Vain are my thoughts! 'tis empty air, I prove!
That still I wail, till watching make me wink:
And when I wink, I wish I ne'er might wake,
But sleeping, carried to the Stygian lake."

The true Petrarchists in their hopeless and unstimulated delusions often invite death to relieve them of their tortures. Linche imagined that these aberrations were caused by such conditions as he sets out in sonnet

XXXVII.

Did I not love her as a lover ought,
With purest zeal and faithfulness of heart,
Then she had cause to set my love at naught,
And I had well deserved to feel this smart!
But holding her so dearly as I do,
As a rare jewel of most high esteem;
She most unkindly wounds and kills me, so,
My ne'er-stained troth most causeless to misdeem!
Never did one account of woman more
Than I of her! nor ever woman yet
Respected less, or held in lesser store
Her lover's vows, than She by mine doth set!
What resteth then? but I despair and die!
That so my death may glut her ruthless eye.

WILLIAM SMITH.

William Smith wrote 49 sonnets under the title of *Chloris*. These he dedicated to *Colin Clout* (Edmund Spenser), with apologies for their crudeness, which he begged might be attributed to his youth. There is no lack of directness in Smith's sonnets, nor does he leave any doubt as to the cause of his complaints and miseries. Apparently it never occurred to him that there was anything he could love, except a woman. His expressions are so earnest, direct and simple as to leave not a suspicion of concealment or double meaning. The first line of Sonnet XV is a repetition of the last line of Sonnet XIV. *Corin* is Smith's own adopted sobriquet.

XV.

These weeping Truce-men shew I living languish;
My woeful wailings tell my discontent:
Yet Chloris nought esteemeth of mine anguish;
My thrilling throbs, her heart connot relent.
My kids to hear the rhymes and roundelays,
Which I, on wasteful hills, was wont to sing,
Did more delight than lark in summer days:
While echo made the neighbor groves to ring.
But now my flock, all drooping, bleats and cries:
Because my Pipe, the author of their sport,
All rent, and torn, and unrespected lies:
Their lamentations do my cares consort.
They cease to feed, and listen to the plaint;
Which I pour forth unto a cruel Saint.

XXVI.

Though you be fair and beautiful withal;
And I am black, for which you me despise:
Know that your beauty subject is to fall!
Though you esteem it at so high a price.
And time may come when that whereof you boast,
Which is your youth's chief wealth and ornament,
Shall withered be by winter's raging frost;
When beauty's pride and flowering years are spent.
Then wilt thou mourn! when none shall thee respect.
Then wilt thou think how thou hast scorned my tears!
Then, pitiless, each one will thee neglect;
When hoary grey shall dye thy yellow hairs.
Then wilt thou think upon poor Corin's case!
Who loved thee dear, yet lived in thy disgrace.

XLVII.

But of thy heart too cruel I thee tell,
Which hath tormented my young budding age;
And doth (unless your mildness, passions quell)
My utter ruin, near at hand presage.
Instead of blood, which wont was to display
His ruddy red upon my hairless face;
By over-grieving, that is fled away:
Pale dying colour there hath taken place.
Those curled locks, which thou wast wont to twist,
Unkempt, unshorn, and out of order been;

Since my disgrace, I had of them no list,
Since when, these eyes no joyful day have seen:
Nor never shall, till you renew again
The mutual love which did possess us twain.

ROBERT TOFTE.

The sonnets of Robert Tofte are in three parts of 40 sonnets each.　In form they are not true sonnets, but alternate with twelve and ten lines.　The odd numbers all have twelve lines, while the even numbers have ten lines throughout.　The title is *Laura,* the same as Petrarch's.

Part 1.

X.

If, Laura, thou dost turn 'gainst me in hate;
Then me, such busses sweet why dost thou give?
Why checkst thou not the cheeks which give the mate?
The vital cause whereby I breathe and live?
Perhaps it is, because through too much joy,
As in sweet swound, I might away depart:
If so thou do, and think me so to 'noy;.
Kiss hardly! and with kissing, breed my smart!
Content am I to lose this life of mine;
Whilst I do kiss that lovely lip of thine.

This sonnet as compared with those of Petrarchists which are in the same vein, sounds quite boorish.　And yet, if the Petrarchists intended theirs to apply to a woman's love, there is in meaning no difference between the two.　How often is the reader required to wonder why a lover being granted indulgence should, threfore, be cast down into despair? or as Tofte expresses it, why should kissing breed his smart? and make him content to lose his life?　Any less expression of substance than is contained in the foregoing sonnet, would not be a true paraphrase of that which was sought to be imitated.　So, it is evident, that in a homely way Tofte has faithfully expressed the meaning of the sonnet or sonnets which it was his purpose to imitate.

XVII.

Rocked in a cradle, like as infants be,
When I was young, a little wanton child,

Two dainty dugs did nourish life in me;
Whilst oft on them, with teat in mouth, I smiled.
Ah, happy I! thrice happy, might I say;
Whilst in that harmless state I then did stay.
But now that I am come to man's estate;
Such dugs as nursed me in delight and joy,
Do seek my death, by poisoned sugared bait;
Whose sight, without possession, breeds me 'noy.
So what, in childhood, caused me to live;
Now, in my youth, doth death unto me give.

Here, again, the two expressions are strictly parallel, and yet apparently incongruous. That which should nourish (and no reason given why it should not) proves to be a "poisoned sugared bait." This anomaly is met throughout the Petrarchists' sonnets. Tofte's error, if he was in error, lies in taking their words at their face value, when in fact they were spurious.

Part 2.

XVIII.

My Laura wonders that, in visage pale,
I bear of death itself, the lively show:
But if she muse at this, her musing's stale;
For this sad colour had I long ago.
The fire, close burning in my veins, doth make
That outward ashes in my face you view:
But if that she would on me pity take,
Who is the cause of this my palish hue,
This kindled heart shall die, which now doth burn;
And my first colour shall again return.

WILLIAM SHAKESPEARE AGAIN

WILLIAM SHAKESPEARE, AGAIN.

In closing the discussion of the Elizabethan Sonneteers, the writer feels that some explanation should be added concerning the order the whole discussion has taken. Particularly, as to why the last of these sonneteers, Shakespeare, should have been discussed before all the others, while, in an orderly way that discussion should have followed what has, in fact, followed it.

The reason for this is, that until about the close of the treatment of *The Shakespearean Enigma* the writer was not aware of the disclosures that awaited an examination of the works of those other poets that have since been reviewed. Until then no doubts had obtruded themselves into the writer's mind of the entire originality of the Shakespearean sonnets. It had not occurred to him that any one before or after Shakespeare had utilized sonnets in a like fashion. The first enlightenment came from a study of Drayton's sonnets, and from these the suggestion arose that Shakespeare must have to some extent imitated Drayton, nor has that suspicion been entirely allayed. Next was *Willobie His Avisa,* and it soon became evident that a like cryptical meaning was inherent in this poem. Thereupon a suspicion was aroused, that perhaps this curious adaptation of the sonnet might have extended still further. A further research led to Lee's *Elizabethan Sonnets,* which proved to be a veritable storehouse of all pertaining to the subject. Beyond this it is not likely that there is much, if any, English literature that would justify further research.

This development requires a few brief observations concerning Shakespeare's relation to this pervading mania that seems to have obsessed so many of the poets of his day.

In the first place, the conclusion would seem to be justified, that Shakespeare at the beginning of his sonnets, was not aware of the true nature of the sonnets that were then so much the vogue. If he was so aware, it is very certain that he did not, in the beginning, imitate them. That he knew of such sonnets, and was even familiar with them cannot be doubted. But that is not to say, that at first, he fully understood their meaning.

The first of his sonnets—the first 18—are altogether unlike those of any of the Petrarchists. In none of the sonnets of the time is there anything of a similar nature, that can be said to have suggested to Shakespeare the ideas with which he begun. It will be recalled that his introductory sonnets are his pleadings in his efforts to persuade himself that he would be justified in partaking of wine, that he might be stimulated to the achievement of his poetical aspirations. In this respect his sonnets are altogether his own. He expressly declares that he is not under the influence of wine, but that it is the absence of its inspiration that has rendered his talents inactive. It has been seen, after this stage had been passed, and he had converted himself to the use of wine, how for a long while he struggles with his subject, finding it difficult to master expression, and provide substance with which to feed his poetry. Neither, at first, could he give to wine a name nor define its character. In the 20th sonnet he calls it the "Master-Mistress of his passion." Thereafter he continues to exalt it higher and higher, and to increase its dominion until it becomes an ally, and then his alter ego, and then his soul—his supreme genius.

None of the Petrarchists go through such stages of development. We only know them in their thralldom. After Shakespeare had reached a like stage in his evolution, then he perceives the hidden meaning of the sonnets that had preceded his, and then he lapsed into their train of thought and treatment, borrowing largely from them, as they had borrowed from others. Thus in the end he became a true Petrarchist.

Prior to Shakespeare each sonneteer, Italian, French or English, sought to dissemble his subject under the guise of a woman, and succeeded so well that subsequent research has, in some cases, gone so far as to discover the identity of her who had so perturbed the spirit of the particular poet. In Shakespeare's case, the first 126 sonnets have been persistently read as addressed, not to a woman, but to some man whose identity a most tireless search has failed utterly to divulge. This impression, as has been seen, comes solely from these first, or introductory, sonnets, whose very nature precludes the possibility of a woman being their subject.

To account for these radical variances between Shakespeare and the others, it must be assumed, either that he was not actuated by the spirit that guided and directed them, or if he was he was possessed of an originality that could not be confined to a set method, but venturously sought, as he ever did, new ways to achieve his end.